V&R

Leibniz Institute for Jewish History and Culture – Simon Dubnow

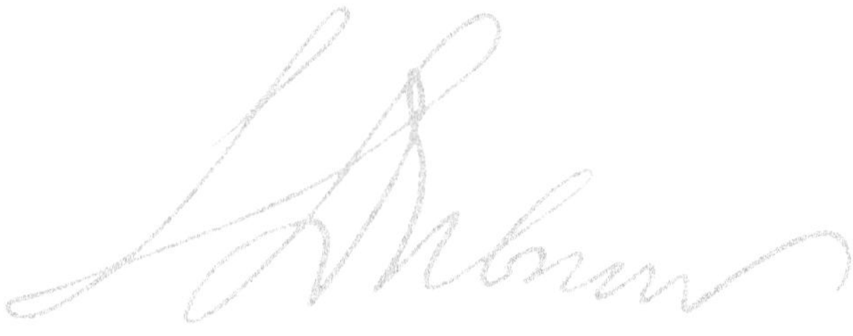

ELISABETH GALLAS, ANNA HOLZER-KAWALKO,
CAROLINE JESSEN, YFAAT WEISS (EDS.)

Contested Heritage

Jewish Cultural Property after 1945

Vandenhoeck & Ruprecht

This publication is financed by the Saxon State government out of the State budget approved by the Saxon State Parliament.

STAATSMINISTERIUM FÜR WISSENSCHAFT UND KUNST | Freistaat SACHSEN

The funding of this publication was generously supported by the Franz Rosenzweig Minerva Research Center at the Hebrew University of Jerusalem (Rosenzweig Center) and the German Literature Archive (DLA) in Marbach.

The Franz Rosenzweig Minerva Research Center for German-Jewish Literature and Cultural History

deutsches literatur archiv marbach

Language editing: Avner Greenberg
Layout and typesetting: textformart, Göttingen | www.text-form-art.de
Printed and bound: Books on Demand, Norderstedt
Printed in the EU

Vandenhoeck & Ruprecht Verlage | www.vandenhoeck-ruprecht-verlage.com

ISBN 978-3-525-31083-0

Contents

ELISABETH GALLAS, ANNA HOLZER-KAWALKO,
CAROLINE JESSEN, YFAAT WEISS

Preface

The essays collected in this volume explore the history and fate of Jewish European cultural property in the aftermath of World War II. This history of Jewish heritage on the old continent has a peculiar trajectory. It unfolded over centuries of Jewish presence in Europe, which has ever been accompanied by multiple expressions—both religious and secular—of a vivid and diversified cultural life, to be found in synagogues, yeshivas, rabbinical seminaries, as well as in museums, communal archives, libraries, and art collections. Their historical development testifies not only to the variety of intellectual and spiritual traditions of European Jews but also to their unique entanglement with European culture. While Jewish culture in Europe grew and developed over centuries, the Nazi regime took only a few years to obliterate it. During twelve years of Nazis, first in Germany and later on in wide parts of occupied Europe, Jewish cultural property was plundered, dispersed, and largely destroyed. Only a small part of the material manifestation of Jewish culture survived past 1945. Some materials had been transferred outside Europe already in the interwar period, when their owners decided to migrate voluntarily. Some collections came to Palestine, the United States or, to lesser extent, other centers of Jewish exile in the 1930s, along with those who were forced into a hasty flight from their increasingly hostile homelands. Finally, a significant number of artifacts were discovered in Germany and the formerly German-occupied territories by the Allied armies and local populations at the end of the war. Ironically, these objects most often survived as a result of the vast and systematic looting processes that the Nazi administration had orchestrated. Yet the majority of them was heirless—their legal owners perished in the Holocaust and their former institutional homes had been destroyed. The future of these remains was settled by the postwar restitution organizations, such as the Hebrew University's Committee for the Salvaging of Diaspora Treasures *(Oẓrot ha-Golah)* and Jewish Cultural Reconstruction, Inc., in the late 1940s. As a consequence of their work, the bulk of these cultural remains was not returned to their places of origin, now emptied of most traces of prewar Jewish life.

The salvaging of cultural remnants was perceived as a reversal of the powerlessness experienced by European Jewry in the face of annihilation. It was undertaken with the utmost devotion and passion. A broad circle of eminent Jewish scholars—not least of all Hannah Arendt, Salo W. Baron, Hugo Bergman, Cecil Roth, and Gershom Scholem—exerted enormous efforts to rescue books and archival collections for the reconstruction of Jewish life in the wake of the Holocaust. However, the restitution of Jewish cultural property simultaneously instigated many controversies and fights over successorship between the new centers of Jewish existence and the reestablished Jewish communities in Europe. The restitution negotiations entailed some fundamental and highly contested questions on the status and future of Jewish people, for which different Jewish leaders offered opposite answers.

Eventually, the displaced Jewish cultural property was slowly disconnected from its original owners and homelands. Some of the salvaged treasures were moved to new locations in Palestine (later the State of Israel) and the United States, where their accommodation generated multiple difficulties with regard to their placement and distribution as well as their status and function. Different, but equally challenging problems arose when objects were returned to the reconstructed Jewish communities in Europe. Repatriation in the proper sense of the word could not take place since most of the appertaining communities, institutions, libraries, and organizations had been dismantled, their members murdered. In light of this unprecedented ruination, the relations between the prewar and postwar Jewish communities may be described rather in terms of rupture than continuity. Thus, in many stories presented in this volume, restitution reveals the difficulties in placing and framing the cultural heritage under political and social conditions that made the attempts at finding fruitful contexts for the objects impossible. Last but not least, the different layers of meaning attached to Jewish cultural property and the endeavor of postwar cultural restitution resonate to this day, provoking continued public debates and legal uncertainties.

This volume examines cases of migration, displacement, and restitution of Jewish archives, art, and book collections and illuminates the complicate paths these materials took from their prewar to the postwar locations. Not only had their geographical location changed: Many Jewish archival collections and cultural objects are vested with layers of meaning. As witnesses of wartime pillage and destruction, these objects constitute a symbolic restitution for the loss of life. Against this background, they form part of the profane fields of everyday life, research, and scholarship as well as the sacred fields of belief, tradition, and ritual. Their value and meaning may have changed in different social contexts, in the course of time, for different persons or groups; but on a fundamental level, only the interplay of profane and sacred qualities seems to constitute the genuine cultural, political, and hermeneutical status of those materials that have become (personal) mementos of a specific time, of places and people—that is, of a past now off limits—as well as objects of public value, debate, and ownership conflicts in Israel, Germany, and beyond. While the smooth-tongued rhetoric of digital accessibility tends to downplay persistent features such as uniqueness, authenticity, originality, and materiality, museums and archives have adopted the functions of sacred sites. The architecture of these institutions, their usage restrictions, and modes of display all allude to this fact. Beyond ownership conflicts, this tension underlines the contested status of rare tangible objects and documents in the history of Jewish migration—and Jewish reconstruction.

In recent years, increasing attention has been drawn to the provenance of Jewish objects in private as well as public collections and museums in Europe, Israel, and the United States. Moreover, a large body of literature dealing with plundering and restitution has emerged in various languages. The whereabouts and the distribution of looted Jewish artworks, archives, and libraries has always been a major focus of this research. The present volume adds to this discussion by presenting new case studies based on a range of unknown materials detected recently in American, European, and Israeli archives. All of them explore, on different levels and from various perspectives, the wider significance of a material culture approach to postwar history and memory. This is also the reason why the setup of this book does not quite resemble the usual format of collected volumes: The objects themselves, their biographies and paths, their resonances and impact take center stage here. In order to achieve this goal, we decided to adopt shorter, rather essayistic text formats, enriched with a broad array of visuals.

The papers of this volume present the results of a Minerva-Gentner Symposium held at the Hebrew University of Jerusalem in 2016, generously funded by the Minerva Foundation of the Max Planck Society. This symposium was a collaborative project of the Franz Rosenzweig Minerva Research Center at the Hebrew University of Jerusalem (Rosenzweig Center), the German Literature Archive (DLA) in Marbach, and the Dubnow Institute in Leipzig, which for many years have been involved in the scholarly study of Jewish cultural property. The Rosenzweig Center and DLA conducted multiple cataloguing projects in Israeli and German archives unearthing—and making accessible to a broad public—relevant documents connected to the history of actors involved in salvaging as well as to broader questions of migration, flight, and transfers of knowledge and property. We have been fortunate to have their continuous support while preparing this volume. We would also like to acknowledge the invaluable assistance of Avner Greenberg in the language edition and of Tim Corbett, Margarita Lerman, and Jana Duman in the last steps of finalizing the manuscript. Moreover, we want to thank Petra Klara Gamke-Breitschopf who advised us through the entire process of creating this book and navigated its final phase before publication with great commitment.

Many of the collected essays refer to the materials that have been made accessible through the above-mentioned archival endeavors, not least of all in order to draw attention to the rich sources for researchers in areas of Jewish migration that are still waiting to be explored. Beyond that, the papers—and the images that accompany them—point to the central hermeneutical relevance of tangible objects for research into the history of Jewish migration, even if only historical photographs of objects may attest to their very existence at a specific point of time and at a specific place. In such cases, photos of burning books, looted collections, and historical libraries may sometimes mark a blank position in the present. This collection of essays draws heavily on historical images, thereby underlining the fact that photographs have become witnesses to objects that have been destroyed, decayed, or lost as a consequence of National Socialism.

We hope that this volume will contribute to a more nuanced understanding of both the contested history of Jewish heritage and the ongoing questions of cultural ownership and belonging.

Jerusalem/Leipzig/Marbach — Summer 2019

1. Shifting Meanings: Objects, Emotions, Memory

ELISABETH GALLAS

Capsules of Time, Tradition, and Memory: Salvaging Jewish Books after 1945

The history of European Jewish cultural property in the twentieth century is a history of destruction, displacement, loss, and reconfiguration, and is deeply intertwined with the history of Jewish persecution and flight, migration and resettlement. World War II and the Holocaust ended with an unprecedented devastation of the Jewish cultural sphere and the dispersion of its material treasures. Millions of books, artworks, ritual objects, and documents were looted, destroyed, or abandoned, or disappeared in German and other European institutions. This process of willful destruction of the Jewish cultural landscape of Europe was keenly felt by Jewish individuals and organizations. Already during the war it created a deep sense of injustice and of profound loss described by witnesses, but also by Jewish contemporaries outside Europe who received notice of the systematic plundering, book-burning, and looting. Many transformed this feeling into a herculean effort aimed at salvage and restitution: individuals transferred collections abroad or risked their lives just to conceal and rescue treasures in imminent danger, while major Jewish institutions and organizations of the time, such as the American Jewish Joint Distribution Committee, the British Committee on Restoration of Jewish Libraries, Archives and Museums, Jewish Cultural Reconstruction, Inc., the *Oẓrot ha-Golah* Committee of the Hebrew University, the World Jewish Congress, and YIVO, planned and later conducted restitution initiatives. It was to a large extent due to their endeavors that Jewish collections—preserved for generations in thousands of different cultural and private facilities all over Europe—were then distributed around the globe. We find treasures from Vilnius in Buenos Aires, from Paris in Melbourne, from Odessa in Cape Town, and from Berlin in Jerusalem. The postwar topography of Jewish cultural property in many ways reflects general Jewish migration patterns and the rise of new cultural centers outside Europe after 1945.

The question as to why these treasures, and especially books, attracted such extraordinary attention, and what made Jewish actors believe that they should do their utmost to preserve them reveals intriguing insights into postwar strategies of rebuilding and survival per se. One way to

Contested Heritage, 15–25 | doi.org/10.13109/9783666310836.15

approach this story is via the manifold ways in which the aforementioned organizations sought to negotiate over and set about the restoration of the myriads of Jewish cultural items scattered around Germany and found by the Allied armies. Another is to take the objects themselves into account. What was it that made their survival so crucial for contemporaries?

Philip Friedman, an eminent historian from Lvov (then Lemberg) who survived the Holocaust in hiding and subsequently devoted his life to the documentation and historical understanding of the cataclysm, provides some answers to this question in a largely forgotten piece about the history of the Jewish book collections during the Nazi Era, which he wrote in the 1950s. This is ample testament to the significance and impact Jews attributed to the "greatest book pogrom in Jewish history." Friedman's concise review of the agents and processes of the Nazi looting and destruction policy begins with the following assumption:

> "Jewish books often share the persecutions inflicted upon Jews, the 'people of the book.' The first recorded persecution of the Jewish book probably occurred 2,100 years ago. [...] None of the recorded confiscations and destructions, however, attained the gigantic dimensions of the Nazi crusade against the Jewish book."[1]

Besides his precise account of the meticulous efforts made by the Germans to destroy and steal the treasures as part of their genocidal practice, the specific terminology of this short introductory passage indicates how Friedman grasped these events. The terms he uses remind us of the world of the living rather than the world of inanimate objects. By speaking of a "book pogrom," "the crusade against the book," "the diabolical form of destruction," and "warfare against the book," he equates the fate of the books with that of the human beings (fig. 1).

A practice that might seem somewhat disturbing today was commonplace in descriptions by Jewish contemporaries in the early postwar period. Leora Auslander has argued that it is precisely the "close relation to the human body that gives material culture its particular meaning- and memory-bearing capacities" and has pointed to the fact that "things, in their three-dimensionality, touchability, and mortality mirror human embodiedness."[2] In the post-catastrophe situation following the Holocaust, as people began to deal with material remains from the lost world, this relatedness of object and human body assumed even more existential dimen-

1 Philip Friedman, The Fate of the Jewish Book during the Nazi Era, in: Jewish Book Annual 15 (1957), 3–13, here 3.

2 Leora Auslander, Jews and Material Culture, in: Mitchell B. Hart/Tony Michaels (eds.), The Cambridge History of Judaism, 8 vols., Cambridge et al. 2008–2017, here vol. 8: The Modern World, 1815–2000, Cambridge et al. 2017, 831–857, here 832.

sions. Given the loss of millions of lives, these material remains were the only tangible and visible traces left, and began to function as material insignia of the ultimate genocide.[3] This, I argue, was especially true of the perception of salvaged books—to which the Jewish collectivity has traditionally ascribed a special significance.

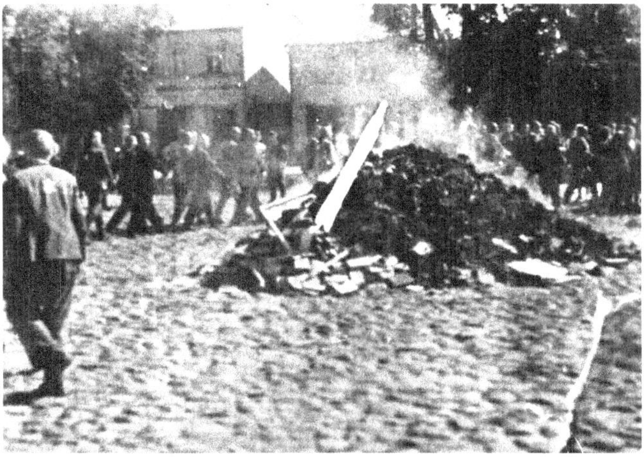

Fig. 1: Book burnings in Riga, not dated.

This particular meaning is obviously linked to the fact that in the Jewish diaspora books, most prominently the sacred text of the Torah, preserved the law and served as a common point of reference for the scattered community. The description of the Jews as "text-centered"—people of the book—points to this influential function of the sacred book in the constitution of Jewish collective self-awareness. Numerous scholars have analyzed this Jewish attitude toward scripture. Moshe Halbertal, for example, in his seminal study *The People of the Book*, stressed that "major developments in Jewish tradition can be understood through the community's notions of its relation to text, of what text is, and how text functions in its midst" and considered text to be "one of the Jewish tradition's central operative concepts."[4] With the onset of Jewish modernization and the evolution of pluralist and often more secular forms of self-awareness, manifested in increasing degrees of assimilation and emancipation, not only the Torah and the sacred texts but also various other genres of books served as a means for Jewish self-fashioning and expression of belonging. Moreover, it was precisely these spheres of belonging that were beginning to fan out with the increasing integration of the Jews into their surrounding societies. The relation to text could indicate both a Jewish identity and a national consciousness. By the time of World War II, the Jews' diverse textual territory extended far beyond religious exegesis and laws to include a broad literary canon. Thus, the book was approached both as a vessel of the collectivity's history and remembrance, a substitute for the missing geographical territory

3 This quality of the material remains of the murdered is highlighted by Dan Diner, Eigentum restituieren, in: idem, Zeitenschwelle. Gegenwartsfragen an die Geschichte, Munich 2010, 207–221, here 209.

4 Moshe Halbertal, People of the Book. Canon, Meaning, and Authority, Cambridge, Mass./London 1997, 2.

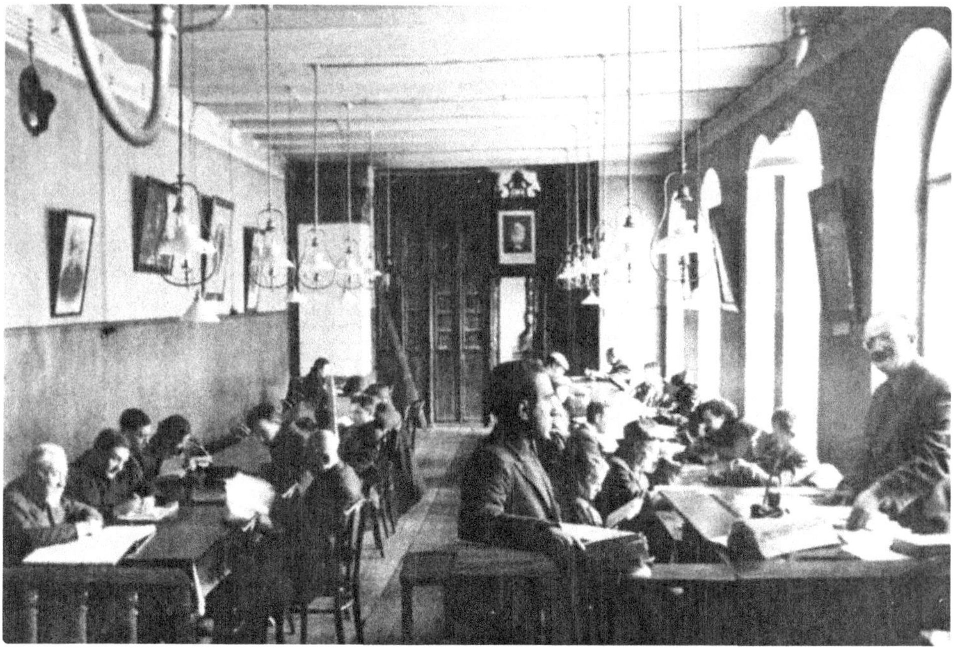

Fig. 2: One outstanding example of modern Jewish reading culture: the reading room of Vilna Strashun Library, the first Jewish public library in Eastern Europe.

or homeland, and as an expression of belonging to the wider European cultural realm (fig. 2).

This is the background that should be reconsidered as we examine the different and interrelated layers of meaning attached to the books stemming from all over Europe that Jewish actors began to salvage in the wake of the Holocaust. In the following I focus on certain aspects that highlight how books were considered as capsules of time, tradition, and memory, and how their restoration was perceived as nothing less than an opportunity for the Jews to "reclaim their past, revive their memories, and renew their sense of belonging" in a post-Holocaust world, as Leora Auslander aptly put it in reference to French Jews claiming their former property.[5] If we acknowledge these dimensions of the restitution operation it becomes evident that it meant far more than the return of stolen items—the rescued books functioned as a form of embodiment and legacy of the murdered collective.

5 Auslander, Jews and Material Culture, 852.

Reentering History

As reports, newspaper articles, and letters indicate, the processes of spoliation of Jewish cultural property by the Nazis were perceived as far more than yet another element of wartime destruction. Rather, Jews worldwide considered it a fundamental attack upon the Jewish collective self. This assessment echoes in Alon Confino's recent study *A World without Jews*, in which he discusses the centrality of the Nazi vision to erase Jewish historical and traditional traces from European culture and create a new German Aryan civilization based on what he calls a "purified origin." Confino sketches here various measures taken by the Nazis to exclude the Jews from the shared spiritual and religious realm of thought; one of these was to burn, destroy, or misuse Jewish texts and ritual objects.[6] The librarian of the American Jewish Historical Society, Isidore S. Meyer, alluded to precisely this dimension of the looting process already in 1944 in his article *The Enemies of the Book*, observing the following:

> "The modern Goliath rashly and discriminatingly seeks to destroy the records of the conquered. He realizes that the cultural treasures of a people's spirit are the greatest guarantee of their will to live. Destroy the spirit and your conquest is assured. [Thus] those who have sought to destroy Israel have sought to destroy Israel's books."[7]

In more abstract terms, another contemporary witness of the events—the sociologist of the Frankfurt School Leo Löwenthal—portrayed the Nazis' book burnings in the same vein, as "the expunging of memory, the expunging of the specific; the declaration of war on the individual; the relapse from the continuity of meaningful history into nothingness, chaos; and finally the transformation of historical space into brute nature."[8]

Accordingly, the Jews who experienced these processes of devastation and displacement of their book collections expressed the feeling of having been erased from the collective space, namely the history and the realm of thought which constituted the shared immaterial territory of the dispersed collective. Above all, the memories and reports from ghettos and camps reveal these modes of perception, a most striking example being Avraham Sutzkever's accounts from the Vilna Ghetto (fig. 3). They show how the destruction and plunder were perceived as inherent to the annihilation procedure, and these material losses were mourned accordingly.

6 Alon Confino, A World without Jews. The Nazi Imagination from Persecution to Genocide, New Haven, Conn. / London 2014, 5.

7 Isidore S. Meyer, The Enemies of the Books, in: Jewish Book Annual 2 (1943–44), 42.

8 Leo Löwenthal, Caliban's Legacy, in: Cultural Critique 8 (Winter 1987–1988), 5–17, here 13.

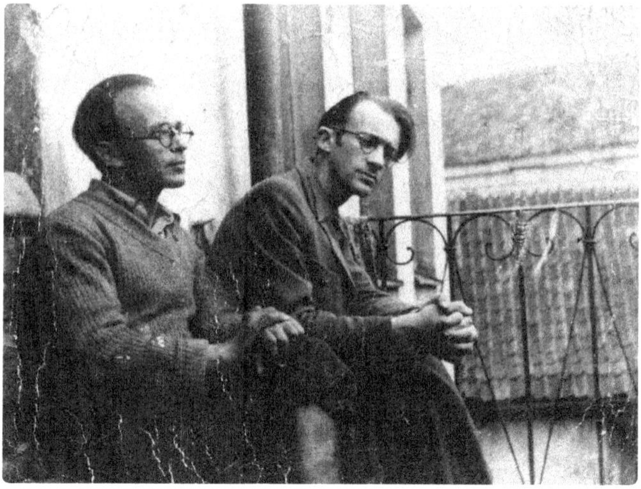

Fig. 3: Avraham Sutzkever and Shmerke Kaczerginski, underground fighters in the Vilna Ghetto, 1943.

The re-appropriation of rescued books after the war was therefore conceived as nothing less than a reentry into history—from which the Nazis had forcefully tried to erase the Jews. Making use of the books and restoring them to Jewish communities helped to recreate the link between past, present, and future, a continuum destroyed by the Nazi extermination policy. This vision was reflected in the discussion about the rightful distribution of books found by Allied soldiers in the various Nazi caches. Broadly speaking, the issue of the allocation of this material gave rise to two opposing conceptions regarding Jewish life after 1945: the vision of an ever-growing Jewish diaspora in the New World of the United States, and the vision of a prosperous Jewish nation-state in *Eretz Israel*. Most of the emissaries involved in the activities of Jewish cultural restitution after the war agreed upon the goal of shipping as many collections as possible out of Germany. But the American organizations unsurprisingly lobbied for the transfer of a fair share of property to the United States. The Israeli, and to a lesser degree many of the British delegates, adamantly insisted that the bulk of the salvaged treasures be conveyed to Israel. Beyond their squabbling over the appropriate location, all parties agreed about the importance of the treasures for a general Jewish reconstruction process (which, in its broadest sense, meant the survival of the collective). The capacity of these books and documents to preserve and maintain a shared Jewish past was seen to be essential to the recreation of future cultures of knowledge at the new Jewish centers. Their further usage appeared to promote the resurrection of an (admittedly ambivalent) sense of continuity following the experience of fundamental rupture. Or to borrow Löwenthal's terms, the intention was to retransform brute nature into civilization by recreating suitable spaces for the books to be used by Jewish readers and thereby to reenter a continuous time structure. The possibility to make use once again of the collective past (preserved in the texts) constituted a decisive element in the production of meaning around the salvage of books.

Preserving Tradition and Knowledge

Inherent to this perception of the books was the notion that they should be read as vessels of tradition and knowledge—the ideas, laws, rituals, articulations, and experiences of former generations. In the wake of the ultimate assault on the collective, a key task was to recreate a sense of collective belonging. It was felt that the rescued books from centuries old yeshivot, places of learning, communities, and institutions offered an ideal tool for this endeavor.

The example of the *Oẓrot ha-Golah* committee's engagement in salvaging German-Jewish collections illuminates how this quality generally ascribed to books gained a different and more existential value at the time. The committee's great interest in the allocation of books of German-Jewish provenance was by no means shared by the majority of the Yishuv. Many people in fact viewed German-Jewish culture somewhat unfavorably. It was considered to be rather elitist and alienated from its Jewish origins. More problematic was this culture's strong ties to the German realm of thought and tradition, now obviously associated with the Nazis' crimes and therefore generally detested. Like many German Jews in the pre-state Yishuv, the scholars of the *Oẓrot ha-Golah* committee took a different approach to their own cultural and spiritual tradition. While they adopted the new national culture of Israel, they equally sought general recognition of the historical significance of German Jewry and its spiritual achievements. Their strong urge to find, claim, and distribute all the books and documents they could lay their hands on in Germany attested to their attachment to the lost world of German Jewry.

To ground their mission on a consensual foundation, the committee members sought to fit the program of salvaging cultural property into the Yishuv's overall self-perception as safe haven for Jewish survivors. In a 1946 programmatic paper the Hebrew University's president Judah Magnes stated:

> "We are to be the chief country for the absorption of the living human beings who have escaped from Nazi persecution […]. By the same token we should be the trustee of these spiritual goods which destroyed German Jewry has left behind. […] [W]e are […] anxious that the Jews of the world should recognize that it is our duty to establish our spiritual and moral claim to be in the direct line of succession to the Jewish culture and scholarship of European Jewry."[9]

9 National Library of Israel, Archives Department (henceforth NLI), ARC. 4 793/212/I 1946, Judah L. Magnes to Koppel S. Pinson, 3 May 1946.

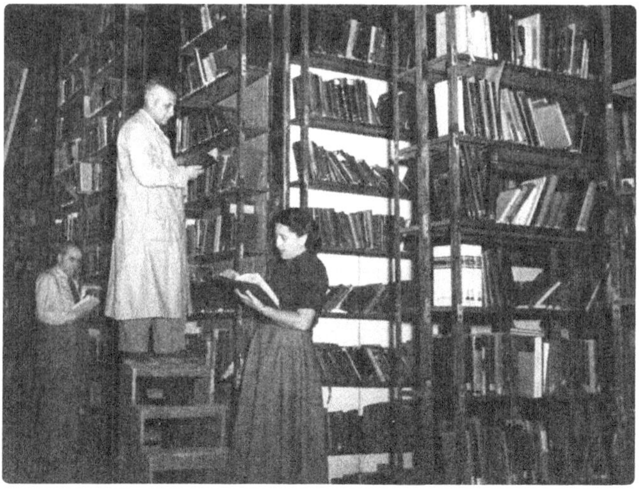

Fig. 4: Books in the interim storage of the Jewish National and University Library in the Terra Santa Building, 1949, Jerusalem.

This "direct line of succession" was, however, a contested vision within the Yishuv. While many felt that the objects from Europe and Germany should be saved, they ascribed to them primarily a commemorative function, regarding them as relics fit for a museum. These objects appeared to belong to a past that the dominant sections of society sought to consign to history with the founding of the new Jewish state. The *Oẓrot ha-Golah* committee represented the opposite perspective: The Jewish National Library's head librarian Curt Wormann retrospectively summed up its unequivocal position by observing that the preservation and dissemination of German-Jewish culture was important "not for the sake of creating a memorial, but so as to make sure that even after the end of the history of the Jews in Germany its legacy and heritage should be fruitful for later generations."[10] While the Yishuv's non-German-Jewish majority perceived the books and objects to be mere monuments of the past, the committee members infused them with a role for the future. On the one hand the scholars felt that the intellectual and religious tradition preserved in these books from Germany was essential to the overall project of Jewish renaissance in Israel. On the other hand most of them were founding members of the Hebrew University. To transfer the books to Israel for them meant to preserve the material basis of their tradition of *Wissenschaft* and thereby to enrich the university with important tools for research, methodology, and teaching. Their mission was to ensure that Israel should be established as a spiritual and cultural center *incorporating* the historical legacy of the diaspora into a new national culture. The salvaged books from Europe were to serve as tools to facilitate the continuation of specific traditions of learning and thought in Israel and were therefore considered precious (fig. 4).

10 Curt D. Wormann, German Jews in Israel. Their Cultural Situation since 1933, in: The Leo Baeck Institute Year Book 15 (1970), 73–103, here 103.

Commemorating the Dead

Perceived from a different angle, the books from Europe were obviously infused with commemorative functions. In many cases they represented the last material fragments and traces of their anonymously murdered owners or ultimately destroyed collections. Seen from that perspective the books became relics or symbolic tombstones, as Jonathan Boyarin and Jack Kugelmass described them, and served the memory of the dead. The later Holocaust historian Lucy S. Dawidowicz, who played a major role in the salvaging and restitution of the sections of the YIVO library looted by the Einsatzstab Reichsleiter Rosenberg and stored in Frankfurt, underscored this function in her memoir. Confronted with the hundreds of thousands of Nazi confiscated books that the American Forces had found and assembled in Offenbach to prepare for restitution, she concluded:

> "Since the Jewish culture which had flourished in Eastern Europe had been wiped out and since it was unlikely that Hebrew and Yiddish books would ever again be published there, every surviving book from that world had become a historical document, a cultural artifact, specimen, and testament of a murdered civilization."[11]

And she went even further in finding parallels between the fate of human beings and the fate of books, just as Philip Friedman did. As mentioned above, we can detect in the testimonies of contemporaries a form of humanization of the objects: Friedman talks of the "book pogroms"; Isidore Meyer refers to the imprisonment of books and their placement in library-shelf ghettos by the Nazis; Rabbi Severin Rochman, who helped the Americans to identify and sort the books, tells a story of the "persecution" that books had to "endure"; and Lucy Dawidowicz denotes the salvaged YIVO books as "mute survivors." This very particular, time-bound perspective on the books and documents is characteristic of this specific period. In the wake of the horrors, during which it had been virtually impossible to rescue people from their fate at the hand of the Nazis, to salvage these tangible embodiments of their former owners became an existential task. Not only because the objects enabled people to remember the dead, constituting precious traces of vanished people and spaces, but because they were likewise infused with hopes and visions of the rescue and survival of the collective. It was also Meyer who emphatically proclaimed: "The Book has been Israel's badge of immortality." Or, in similar vein, US Chaplain Herbert Friedman, who worked on the book identification and salvage with

11 Lucy S. Dawidowicz, From that Place and Time. A Memoir, 1938–1947, introduced and ed. by Nancy Sinkoff, New Brunswick, N.J., 2008, 316.

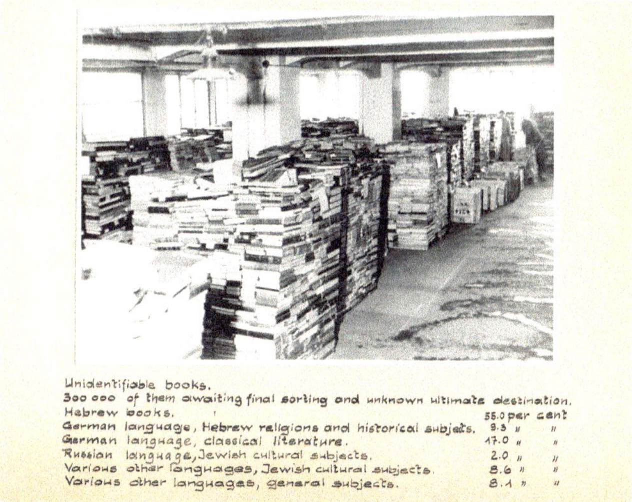

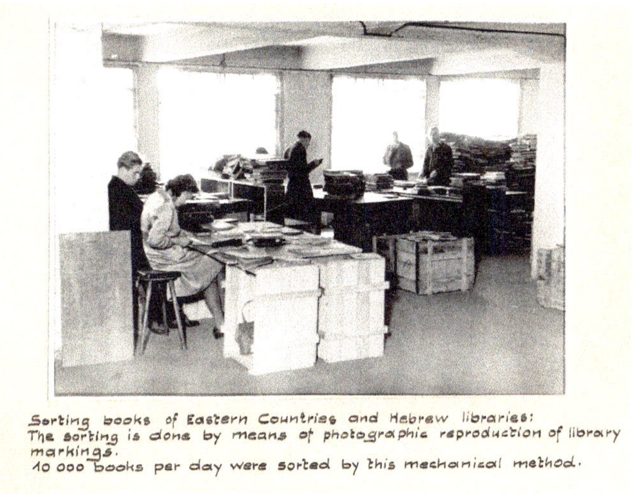

Figs. 5 and 6: Nazi looted books collected and preserved by the Office of Military Government for Germany in the Offenbach Archival Depot, and prepared for restitution to Jewish institutions worldwide, 1946.

Gershom Scholem in Germany in 1946, declared in his memoir: "saving those books amounts to saving the people of the book, for the intellectual and spiritual messages they contain are the best guarantee of the people's continued physical existence."[12] (figs. 5 and 6)

Only if we consider these layers of meaning and expectation attached to the books can we fully grasp what their restitution and the implied reconstruction of Jewish cultural life after 1945 meant for contemporaries and why it was of such essential importance. The books performed many tasks: They built a bridge to the lost past, the lost people, the world of yesterday; they stood as memorials for the dead; they preserved knowledge, tradition, and thought that was envisioned to help lay the spiritual and cultural foundation for the Jewish collective anew, facilitating a shared religious and historical consciousness. And even if this was but a fleeting reflection on these objects, which shed some of their functions over time, it helps us understand the motives and ideas that underpinned the grand initiatives for the rescue and restitution of books as well as the heated debates over the rightful places in which to store and collect them. These books were precisely not "only books" as Heinrich Blücher, Hannah Arendt's husband, is reputed to have remarked laconically upon observing his wife become immersed in the restitution campaign of

12 Herbert A. Friedman, Roots of the Future, Jerusalem / New York 1999, 112.

Jewish Cultural Reconstruction—in light of the annihilation of European Jewry they were far more, offering a (however fragile) prospect for collective continuity and survival.

Literature

Leora Auslander, Beyond Words, in: American Historical Review 110 (2005), 1015–1045.

James Jordan/Lisa Moses Leff/Joachim Schlör, Jewish Migration and the Archive. Introduction, in: Jewish History and Culture 15 (2014), nos. 1–2, 1–5.

Jack Kugelmass/Jonathan Boyarin (eds. and translators), From a Ruined Garden. The Memorial Books of Polish Jewry, second and expanded edition, Bloomington, Ind., 1998.

Dov Schidorsky, Books as Mute Witnesses to Mass Murder. The Archival Depot in Offenbach as an Agent of Memory and a Testimony to Persecution, Migration, and Genocide, in: Moreshet. Journal for the Study of the Holocaust and Antisemitism 13 (2016), 44–83.

Natan Sznaider, Culture and Memory. The Role of Jewish Cultural Property, in: Kwartalnik Historii Żydów. Jewish History Quarterly 246 (2013), no. 2, 227–235.

Author

Elisabeth Gallas is chief research associate at the Leibniz Institute for Jewish History and Culture – Simon Dubnow. She received her PhD from Leipzig University in 2011, where she conducted a historical study on the restitution of Jewish cultural property after 1945. From 2012 to 2015, she was a research fellow at the Vienna Wiesenthal Institute for Holocaust Studies, and held a Minerva Research Fellowship at the Hebrew University of Jerusalem. She rejoined the Dubnow-Institute in 2015, where she currently heads the research unit Law. *Selected Publications*: A Mortuary of Books. The Rescue of Jewish Culture after the Holocaust, New York 2019 (Germ.: "Das Leichenhaus der Bücher." Kulturrestitution und jüdisches Geschichtsdenken nach 1945, Göttingen / Bristol, Conn., 2013); Spiritual Sources for Zion. Gershom Scholem and the Salvage of Looted Books and Manuscripts after the Holocaust, in: Mirjam Zadoff / Noam Zadoff (eds.), Scholar and Kabbalist. The Life and Work of Gershom Scholem, Leiden / Boston, Mass., 2019, 272–291.

CAROLINE JESSEN

Affirming Ownership, Obscuring Provenance? Émigré Collections in Israel and Germany after 1945

The Israeli businessman Gabi Goldwein collects German books from discarded stocks of public libraries and old-age homes throughout Israel. Besides picking up abandoned books from dissolved collections or trash containers, he has posted ads in Israeli German-language magazines asking readers to send books and printed materials to his storage space in Haifa. Motivated by a strong desire to render these books useful again, he planned to ship the entire collection to Germany one day and envisioned the setting up of a central repository, a supply-depot for German libraries. In a different scenario, Goldwein projected the repository as a special collection: a memorial to émigré German-Jewish reading cultures. Goldwein wrote to German archives, libraries, and museums. The outcome can be summed up quickly and briefly: Library usage is hardly a realistic option for these collections. Thus, the boxes of books that Goldwein collected have been piling up in the unused rooms of a small synagogue in Haifa.

Old German books in Israel are memory fetishes, and yet they are also complex symbolic artifacts. They have come to stand for something rescued, in whose shadow all that has been destroyed becomes more clearly visible. Once they were portable things, even research tools—now they appear to be mementos and tangible markers of sustained loss. This is one perspective from which to grasp their strange status: untouchables, leftovers, and junk. Few of Goldwein's books are rare items, and few are of interest as textual media. Most of them mark a dead end in the lifecycle of printed sources: no-one reads them anymore. Today, their value seems to lie in episodes of their history and references to their former readers.

They are valuable as individual objects, but have often been torn from the physical and historical context to which they once belonged. If they bear information about their readers, this has become cryptic. They are fragments of narratives and yet seem to tell stories of life before and after the Nazis' rise to power; stories of migration or salvage, or of individual reading practices. Yet these stories are blurred, and indicate that the history of migration from Nazi Germany to Israel cannot possibly be arranged into

Contested Heritage, 27–41 | doi.org/10.13109/9783666310836.27

a coherent and tidy narrative. In this sense they are a persistent irritation, and as such they bear epistemic relevance.

Gabi Goldwein has merely been collecting the last venerable remnants of a world of books that was once a heterotopia. The sight of the cardboard boxes piled up in the courtyard of his storage facility was depressing. Other collections and catalogues seem to reflect more "fully" the scope and contents of a perished German-Jewish subculture rooted in texts. These are mainly German texts, but often also Hebrew, French, and English texts. To name only the most prominent instance, the historical holdings of the National Library of Israel appear, even without proper provenance records, to represent the wide spectrum of what readers "actually" read. Many private, scholarly book collections, such as those of Martin Buber, Käte Hamburger, Karl Mannheim, Martin Plessner, Felix Weltsch and those of countless unnamed donors, have been partly or fully merged into its stocks over time. Previously, during the periods of the Wilhelminian Empire and the Weimar Republic, German-language collections made their way to Jerusalem. Zionists such as Heinrich Loewe (1869–1951), a research librarian at the Royal University Library of Berlin until the Nazis' rise to power, initiated campaigns intended to foster library development in Mandate Palestine's Yishuv. Then, after 1933, the Berlin-based collecting point of the Gesellschaft der Freunde der Hebräischen Universität und Bibliothek Jerusalem (Society of Friends of the Hebrew University and Library Jerusalem) received books from collections dissolved prior to their owners' emigration or escape from Germany. Donations to the Jewish National and University Library turned into ambivalent gifts, since they were all too often linked to National Socialist persecution and restrictive emigration laws. Nevertheless, they also represented a meaningful act of resistance to these very actions. Thus, donated German-language collections form complex historical clusters within the general holdings of the National Library of Israel, existing "beneath" the standardized cataloguing system applied to them. They have turned the library into an enormous archive, defining the exceptional status of its holdings.

The iconic qualities of German books in Israel—books as memory, as portable homeland, as metonymy of *Bildung*—have become more powerful over time, and have impressed researchers and visitors from Germany in particular. Eminent scholars such as Wilfried Barner, an expert on Lessing and Goethe and one of the first visiting professors in the German department of the Hebrew University of Jerusalem in 1982/1983, have repeatedly referred to German-language collections in Jerusalem and stressed their symbolical status. As Barner once asserted, old editions of Goethe's works and scholarly monographs "from the stacks of the Jewish National and

University Library, from its rich collections of donations and estates of German Jews" prompted his study *Von Rahel Varnhagen bis Friedrich Gundolf. Juden als deutsche Goethe-Verehrer.* Barner was apparently deeply touched by the discovery that

> "more than the average bourgeois possessions of the 1920s and 1930s had been salvaged and brought to the Land of the Fathers: an impressive abundance of valuable first printings and luxury editions of the 19th century, of critical and popular editions, monographs on poets, graphic-art portfolios, introductions and special studies."[1]

The books Barner mentions held a twofold significance for him. On the one hand they were agents of cultural memory; on the other hand they marked a transfer. An early version of Barner's study was published together with Albrecht Schöne's essay on Walter Benjamin's *Deutsche Menschen* titled *Diese nach jüdischem Vorbild erbaute Arche*. Translating Barner's language into a strong image, the metaphor *Arche* (or Noah's Ark) points to the core of the issue at stake, namely salvage and transfer. The title of Schöne's essay derives from a dedication Walter Benjamin wrote in Gershom Scholem's copy of *Deutsche Menschen* in 1937.[2] Schöne addressed the salvage of a textual culture, but by referring to a unique, handwritten dedication attached to a concrete object owned by Gershom Scholem, he alluded to the fact that this *Arche* contained not only texts but also actual books, salvaged materials. The works of German-Jewish scholars, writers, and intellectuals such as Gershom Scholem, Ernst Simon, Kitty Steinschneider, and Curt Wormann may be regarded as components of a transfer of knowledge that cannot be conceived without books and manuscripts. As a cultural and scholarly resource, the printed material shipped to Palestine formed an active repository, which people could access and read afresh. In fact, already by the late 1930s scholarly and scientific German-language books in particular had become much sought-after commodities in Mandate Palestine. During World War II, when it became impossible to import books from Nazi Germany, booksellers in Haifa, Jerusalem, and Tel Aviv started to fill the void with used books from private collections. Ideological differences were of no consequence here:

> "We are searching urgently: [...] Festschriften, Genealogy, National Economy, Flavius Josephus [in] old editions, Philosophy: Friedell,

1 Cit. in Wilfried Barner, Von Rahel Varnhagen bis Friedrich Gundolf. Juden als deutsche Goethe-Verehrer, Göttingen 1992, 6f.

2 Albrecht Schöne, "Diese nach jüdischem Vorbild erbaute Arche." Walter Benjamins "Deutsche Menschen," in: Stéphane Mosès/Albrecht Schöne (eds.), Juden in der deutschen Literatur. Ein deutsch-israelisches Symposion, Frankfurt a. M. 1986, 350–365.

> Husserl, Dilthey, Bergson, Fischer, Vorländer, Deussen, Spinoza, Kant, Nietzsche, Schopenhauer etc., everything about the Orient, new and old literature, Archeology, History, Decorative Arts, Judaica."[3]

Such advertisements, which mushroomed in makeshift German-language periodicals published in Tel Aviv and Jerusalem, are a marvel of clear, efficient communication: German-language books were rare goods, notwithstanding the overt objections to German as a lingua franca in the Yishuv/Israel. Catering to academic institutions, students, and scholars, bookshops such as the Ludwig Mayer Bookshop in Jerusalem sought to meet the needs of a scholarly and scientific community that relied heavily on German scholarship. They established lending libraries, but also imported books from Germany up until 1938, and continued to do so after the founding of the State of Israel. The history of these transfers and shifting trade constellations may constitute a vital source of information for the study of complex continuities and of a covert pre-history of German-Israeli research collaboration—and on shifting ways of attaching meaning to cultural goods.

In the following I focus on one aspect of such *material politics*, since the bare pragmatics of trade point us toward a facet of German-Israeli relations and cultural memory that has yet to be adequately explored, despite the fact that some contemporary disputes on Jewish cultural property after 1945 find their prequel and a significant context there. As I hope to show, the discourse on the "rightful" place of Jewish libraries and archives—of irreplaceable books, objects, and texts—has a long, multi-layered history.

For several years, melancholic attention and archival preservation efforts have been directed at a German-Jewish "heritage" and the "materiality of emigration" in order to gain a new perspective on German, German-Jewish, and Israeli history, and perhaps deeper insight into them. These efforts find a less ostentatious counterpart in the businesslike sobriety and pragmatism with which salvaged possessions from Germany in private collections in Israel have been integrated into old-new contexts in Germany since the late 1950s. Most of these transfers are difficult to trace today, but we find numerous subtle indications of their significance.

Some years ago, Eberhard Köstler, head of the *Verband deutscher Antiquare*, provided readers with his version of the history of the emigration of Jewish colleagues after 1933. After pointing to what the German antiquarian book trade had "irreversibly" lost, Köstler stressed the extent to which

3 [Lehmann, Tel Aviv] Buecher-Suchliste Nr. 1, in: Mitteilungsblatt des Irgun Olej Merkaz Europa (MB), no. 17 (1946), 6.

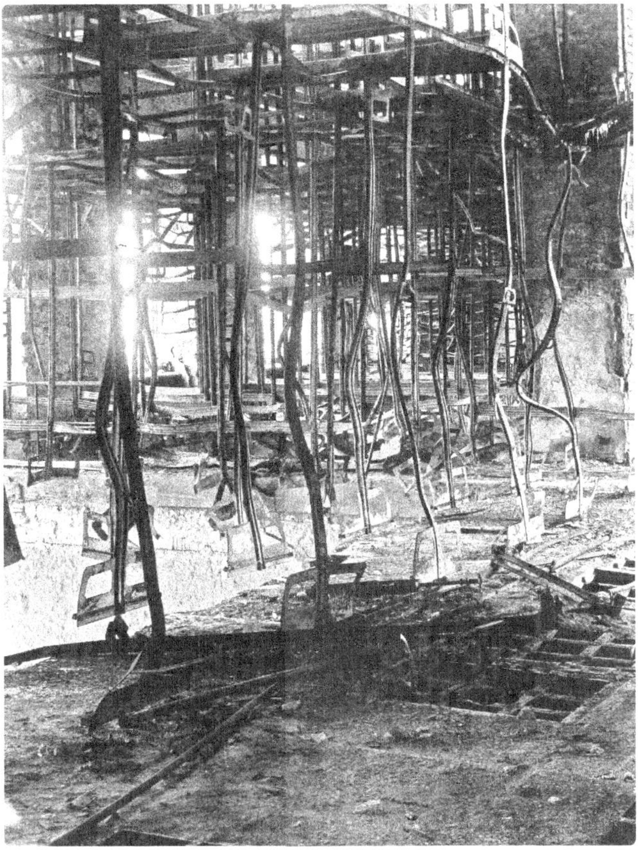

Fig. 1: Bombed stacks of the Hessische Landesbibliothek Darmstadt after 11 September 1944.

countries of migration had benefited culturally, politically, and economically from the influx of excellent bibliophile personnel, knowledge, and experience. Our loss—their gain, so his story of a transfer of knowledge goes. Yet the German rare books trade quickly recovered from its losses. The German Association of Antiquarian Booksellers, autograph and graphic art dealers joined the International League of Antiquarian Booksellers (ILAB) in 1951, and managed to rehabilitate its members easily, although some dealers had been involved in forced sales and tacitly profited therefrom. Köstler states: "Antiquarian booksellers, dealers, and publishers are pragmatic as far as business is concerned, and especially the antiquarian market is a sphere of business that lives off international trade."[4] At times aware of history, at others forgetful of it, trade has always affirmed circulation (figs. 1 and 2).

Utilizing its contacts with colleagues and collectors abroad, the antiquarian book trade started to cater to German research libraries that had lost significant parts of their collections, buildings, and catalogues during World War II. From the end of the 1940s onward, many German libraries were able to invest in the reconstruction of their collections, not least by virtue of the funding allocated by the re-established Notgemeinschaft der deutschen Wissenschaft (Emergency Association of German Science), later to become the Deutsche Forschungsgemeinschaft (DFG), or the Volkswagenstiftung. During this period of "restoration," library

4 Eberhard Köstler, Vorwort, in: Ernst Fischer, Verleger, Buchhändler und Antiquare aus Deutschland und Österreich in der Emigration nach 1933. Ein biographisches Handbuch, Elbingen 2011, 5f., here 6.

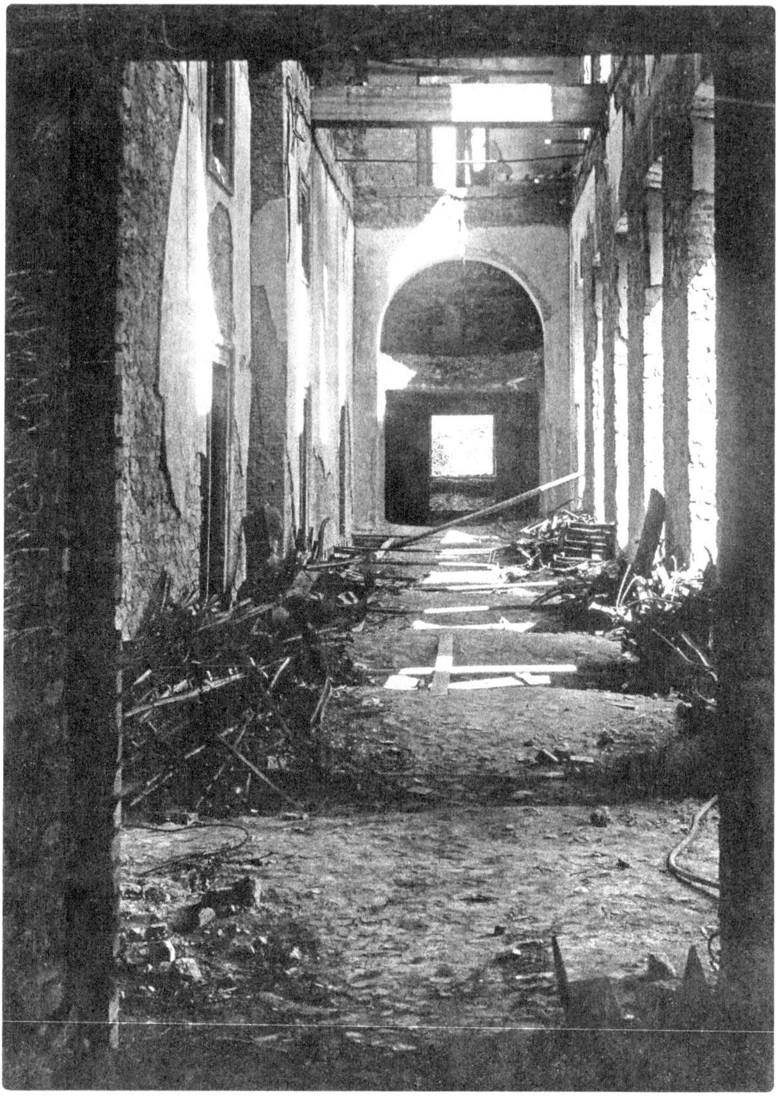

Fig. 2: Floor of the main entrance of the Hessische Landesbibliothek after 11 September 1944.

acquisitions depended on private collections, but also, to a considerable extent, on materials offered on the rare book and autograph market. The history of the antiquarian book trade in Germany since 1945 has yet to be written, and while individual recollections abound, as the market for autographs and rare books is discreet and as the archives of active companies are rarely accessible, it is difficult to trace the routes taken by books and manuscripts after 1945. Therefore, I limit myself here to a discussion of concrete instances of a German-Israeli "trade" in books and archival materials that has made a distinct impact on the material basis of philological research in Germany.

Legends pertaining to the origins of *Exilliteratur* collections in Germany abound. What they have in common is the importance they ascribe to collaboration with émigré intellectuals and antiquarian booksellers abroad. One early survey was the catalogue *Deutsche Literatur im Exil 1933–1945*, issued by the second-hand bookshop Amelang in 1961. As a bibliographic resource, the dealer-catalogue still stands on reference shelves in libraries. Ten years after its publication, the bookseller Walter Zadek, who had fled from Berlin to Tel Aviv in 1933, revealed his substantial contribution. His article *Der Antiquar und die Exilliteratur oder: Der noch unentdeckte Anteil des Buchhandels am Aufbau der seltenen Sammlungen*[5] points to routes of migration and modes of circulation after 1945 that are largely forgotten today. Zadek supplied Amelang with émigré publications from Israel and other European countries that were not available in Germany. Institutions were among his clients, but in the small apartment he rented in Frankfurt the Berlin-born resident of Tel Aviv also sold rare books, graphic art, and maps from émigré collections in Israel to private collectors. In 1964, Zadek analyzed this situation and concluded that his German colleagues were able to pay prices that Israeli readers and collectors could not afford.[6] Moreover, there was only a small and shrinking market in Israel for old and rare German-language books. Struggling to make a living, Zadek was pragmatic in his approach. And his example might help to put the idea of a Noah's Ark of German-language books in Israel today into perspective, as many salvaged books were shipped back to Germany a long time ago. Labels of defunct stores in Tel Aviv and Jerusalem or marks of ownership inside books in German research libraries indicate their complex paths of circulation and transmission. However, apart from illustrious names and Nazi looted property, public research libraries rarely volunteer information on the provenance of their holdings, although it would be fairly simple to digitize and to make accessible accession logs, prior to systematic provenance checks.

Against the backdrop of these transfers from Israel to Germany, Gabi Goldwein's remnants of collections are provocative. They raise the question of what it means to treat "leftovers" of libraries as relics or museum artifacts, in face of the long-standing practice of *nonchalant* trading,

5 Uri Benjamin (Walter Zadek), Der Antiquar und die Exilliteratur oder: Der noch unentdeckte Anteil des Buchhandels am Aufbau der seltenen Sammlungen, in: Börsenblatt für den deutschen Buchhandel, Frankfurter Ausgabe, no. 49 (1970), A82–A84, here A82.
6 Uri Benjamin (Walter Zadek), Sumus de vagantium ordine laudando, in: Börsenblatt für den deutschen Buchhandel, Frankfurter Ausgabe, no. 33 (1964), 705–719, here 718.

circulating, and incorporating books from libraries of emigrants into existing research collections in Germany. A further example might help to demonstrate that the dynamics outlined here impact the material politics of research as well.

The exceptional businessman, publisher, and intellectual Salman Schocken was an ardent collector of art, Hebraica, Judaica, German books, and autographs. During the economically turbulent years of the Weimar Republic, when literary estates of poets such as Bettine von Arnim, Clemens Brentano, Theodor Fontane, Friedrich von Hardenberg (Novalis), and many private libraries were dissolved, Schocken purchased books and manuscripts on a large scale. He continued to do so after 1933, as if he were building a paper-world German-Jewish heterotopia. While in 1938 Schocken's publishing house was liquidated and his department stores were sold to a German syndicate of banks for a sum far below their actual value, Schocken managed to transfer his book and art collections to Jerusalem. This transfer and its circumstances are topics worthy of study in their own right. I shall focus here on what became of the collection after Schocken's death in 1959, and in particular on one of the auction houses (Dr. Ernst Hauswedell, later Hauswedell & Nolte) that helped to sell his enormous collections. Ernst Hauswedell, one of the most remarkable German antiquarian booksellers, was not only an auctioneer but also a publisher, a representative of the FDP at the senate's office for culture in Hamburg, and a high-level functionary in the Association of German Booksellers. After 1945, he was one of the first booksellers to re-establish contact with colleagues abroad. "The road to Canossa is rewarding,"[7] a journalist observed once in the *Frankfurter Allgemeine Zeitung*.

In the early days of postwar Germany, Hauswedell (re-)established connections with booksellers who had managed to escape from Nazi Germany and had continued to ply their trade abroad. During the 1960s and 1970s, these contacts turned him into Germany's internationally most renowned antiquarian bookseller.[8] With his support, German trade profited from collections that had been salvaged from Nazi Germany and appeared on a market that transcended national boundaries and operated independently of diplomatic relations. Hauswedell's sale of Salman Schocken's collection—a rich resource of books and manuscripts of the highest quality that contributed substantially to the company's success—is probably the most striking instance of this phenomenon. One year after Schocken's death

7 Susanne Klingenstein, Qualität ist das Anständige, in: Frankfurter Allgemeine Zeitung, 7 January 2006, 40 (translation by the author).

8 Gunnar A. Kaldewey, Der Antiquar, in: idem (ed.), Ernst Hauswedell 1901–1983, Hamburg 1987, 57–65, here 60.

Hauswedell was authorized to offer for sale manuscripts by Novalis that Schocken had bought in 1930. These manuscripts constituted practically all of Novalis' philosophical writings, taking up 29 pages in the auction catalogue. They were bought on behalf of the Freies Deutsches Hochstift by Ernst Beutler, an eminent Goethe scholar and a founding father of the Goethe Museum in Frankfurt, and edited some years later (1965/68) as volumes 2 and 3 of Novalis' *Schriften*. In a preface to the edition the editor Richard Samuel revealed the link between the complex history of the estate and his edition, thereby pointing to the dynamics of research and resources during times of economic crisis and war. When Novalis' heirs had been forced to sell the estate in 1930, the poet's papers were scattered. As Samuel explains, this had

> "tragic, but also fortunate effects. At the end of the war, the estate was widely dispersed, but had, with a few exceptions, escaped the fate of destruction during the war. The Berlin State Library had bought important parts [...] of the estate and stored these materials [in remote stacks]. The originals have now shown up in Krakow/Poland, but I could not access them until the date of this preface. With few exceptions, the entire philosophical-theoretical estate, i.e., the bulk of our volumes 2 and 3, were bought by the department store owner and publisher Salman Schocken (1877–1959) and transferred to his archive in Jerusalem after his emigration [...]."[9]

Only after these manuscripts were transferred back to Germany and acquired by the Freies Deutsches Hochstift, did work on their critical editing begin. In 1963 Hauswedell sold more than 750 letters by Theodor Fontane from Schocken's collection to the State Library Berlin. This rich resource enabled Kurt Schreinert and Charlotte Jolles to edit and publish Fontane's *Briefe* in four volumes (Berlin 1968–1971). The collection was all the more valuable, since in 1963 countless other Fontane letters were still "missing" as a result of World War II.

The sense of loss and of a break in tradition in Germany's world of letters was palpable and pervasive. Many early German publications on the post-war situation of archives and libraries express such alarm and obsession with their "own" losses that the historical context—the persecution and murder of Jewish colleagues, Nazi lootings, and the destruction of Jewish books—fades out of sight.

9 Richard Samuel, Vorbemerkung zur dritten Auflage, in: idem (ed. in cooperation with Hans-Joachim Mähl and Gerhard Schulz), Novalis. Schriften, 6 vols., Stuttgart 1977–2006, here vol. 3: Das philosophische Werk, 3rd revised edition, Stuttgart et al. 1983, ix–xv, here ix–x.

In 1964, the Hamburg-based auction house of Dr. Ernst Hauswedell sold autographs and manuscripts by Stifter, Schopenhauer, Beethoven, and Schubert from Schocken's collection—among them the manuscripts of *Bunte Steine* and *Nachsommer* as well as Schopenhauer's own copies of the first, second, and third editions of *Die Welt als Wille und Vorstellung* with his own corrections, and sixteen works from Schopenhauer's library. Most of the Stifter manuscripts were bought by the Bavarian State Library, an institution that had declined Schocken's offer to exchange his collection of Novalis and Stifter for Hebrew manuscripts from their holdings.[10] The Stifter papers acquired in 1964 served as the material basis for a critical edition of the poet's works.

The year 1966 marked a disruption: Schocken's heirs were prepared to sell a substantial collection of Heinrich Heine autographs, but Hauswedell was unable to raise the sum required to purchase the stock, although he had been given a 14 day preemption right, after which the Bibliothèque Nationale de France took its chance. Once in Paris, the edition of manuscripts from the collection, a German-French collaboration, promoted the idea of *critique génetique*. Hauswedell's shortfall was counterbalanced by his sale of Schocken's works by Käthe Kollwitz in 1967, the most important private collection of her works at that time. The Stuttgart State Gallery purchased several items. In 1968, other parts of Schocken's graphic art collection, including works by Nolde, Kokoschka, and Klee were sold. In 1970, Schocken's heirs sold several Goethe autographs. And then, in 1975 and 1976, Hauswedell auctioned Salman Schocken's extraordinary library of German literature. Two catalogues were devoted to this library alone, while (in some cases rather precious) odds and ends appeared in later catalogues (fig. 3).[11]

Hauswedell described this sale as "a final climax of the longstanding connection to the Schocken family, a connection that should be remembered with the utmost gratitude."[12] Various research libraries and collectors purchased books such as Tycho Brahe's own copy of his *Astronomiae*

10 Sigrid von Moisy, Die Adalbert-Stifter-Manuskripte der "Schocken-Bibliothek," in: Antje Borrmann/Doreen Mölders/Sabine Wolfram (eds.), Konsum und Gestalt. Leben und Werk von Salman Schocken und Erich Mendelsohn vor 1933 und im Exil, Berlin 2016, 235–248.

11 Dr. Ernst Hauswedell & Ernst Nolte, Auktion 208. Die Bibliotheken Salman Schocken, Karl Wolfskehl. Teil I, Auktion vom 26. bis 28. November 1975, Hamburg 1975; Dr. Ernst Hauswedell & Ernst Nolte, Auktion 211. Die Bibliotheken Salman Schocken, Karl Wolfskehl. Teil II, Auktion am 28. u. 29. April 1976, Hamburg 1976; Dr. Ernst Hauswedell & Ernst Nolte, Auktion 218. Auktion vom 24.–26. November 1976. Wertvolle Bücher des 15.–20. Jahrhunderts, Handschriften, Autographen, Hamburg 1976.

12 Ernst L. Hauswedell, Ein Arbeitsbericht 1927–1981, in: Gunnar A. Kaldewey (ed.), Ernst Hauswedell 1901–1983, Hamburg 1987, 199–293, here 290.

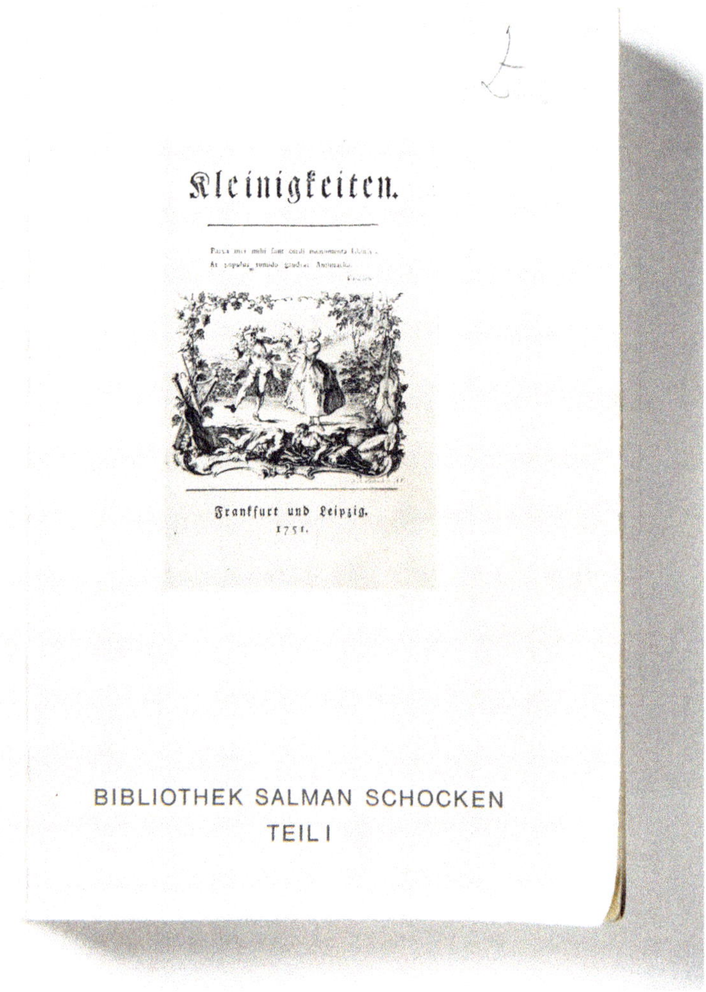

Fig. 3: Dr. Ernst Hauswedell & Ernst Nolte, Auktion 208. Die Bibliotheken Salman Schocken und Karl Wolfskehl. Teil I, Auktion vom 26. bis 28. November 1975, Hamburg 1975.

Mechanica (1598), rare sixteenth- and seventeenth-century books by Jakob Böhme, Martin Opitz, Andreas Gryphius, Grimmelshausen, and others; the complete *Wandsbecker Bothe* (1773–1775), and numerous first editions of Goethe, Hölderlin, Lessing, Kleist, George, Hofmannsthal, Rilke, and others. Many of these objects were rare or even unique, as they contained autographed dedications and corrections or featured binding peculiar to their time. Hauswedell also offered for sale one of the earliest known *Eulenspiegel* printings from 1510/1511, the first edition of the *Manifest der kommunistischen Partei* (London 1848), and thirty further editions of that text as well as various manuscripts by Wilhelm Grimm, Stefan George, Friedrich Gundolf, Ricarda Huch, Lavater, and others. The German Literature Archive bought books to supplement its collections of Cotta and Eduard Mörike, as well as manuscripts by Ricarda Huch, Karl Wolfskehl, Friedrich Gundolf, and others. The Bavarian State Library supplemented its holdings of regional *Überlieferung* with medieval and early modern Bavarian manuscripts. Many of these materials had once formed part of Karl Wolfskehl's library, which Schocken bought in 1937, salvaged from Nazi Germany, and made accessible to scholars in Jerusalem. Just one year prior to the auction, a small German-language bulletin in Israel had explicitly commended this collection and stressed its value for a future German department at the Hebrew University of Jerusalem. Expressing at once melancholy and expectation, the article was titled *Vom Sterben der Antiquariate, vom Fortleben der Archive und der Zukunft der deutschen Literaturforschung in Israel.* It noted that:

> "The Nibelungenlied alone has been collected in forty editions: one can well imagine the practical relevance this special library will have, once the Judeo-German literature of the Middle Ages becomes a major research focus at the Hebrew University. The recent decision to establish a department of German language and literature should render possible the examination of Wolfskehl's Nibelungen collection in Jerusalem."[13]

This, of course, was not to be. Most of Wolfskehl's books and manuscripts were shipped to Germany, where most were bought by research libraries seeking to fill gaps in their collections and to cater to the needs of Nibelungen researchers in German libraries.

If archives and rare books can be deemed "cultural property" or even "cultural heritage," then the re-integration of these materials into German public institutions has major implications on two levels: 1.) The Deutsche Forschungsgemeinschaft and other German foundations have supported research libraries in Israel in their acquisition of scholarly German-language literature, while, at the same time, unique material resources were returned to Germany and purchased by archives, museums, research institutes, and German libraries funded by these very foundations. Thus, the products of German research were sent to Israel to acknowledge a symbolically relevant *Auslandsgermanistik*, while sources for genuine research

13 Erich Gottgetreu, Vom Sterben der Antiquariate, vom Fortleben der Archive und der Zukunft der deutschen Literaturforschung in Israel, in: Mitteilungsblatt des Irgun Olej Merkaz Europa (MB), 1 November 1974, 4.

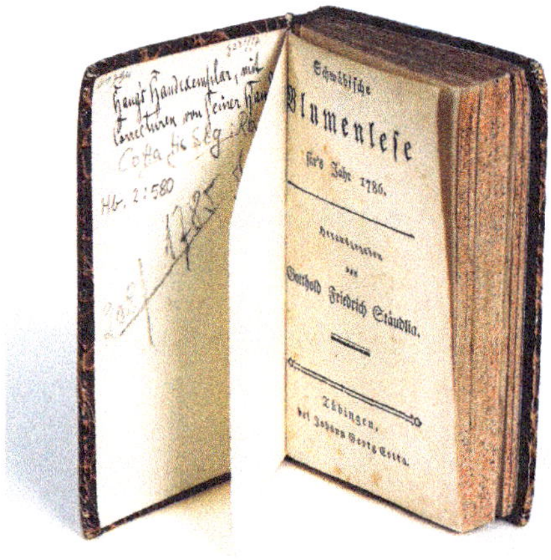

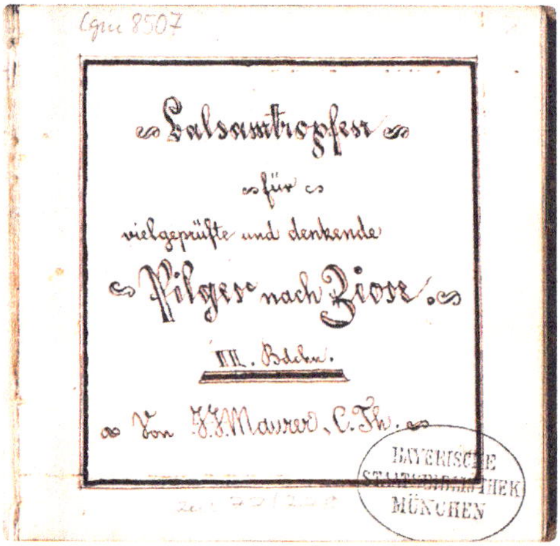

Fig. 4 (left): Gotthold Friedrich Stäudlin (ed.), Schwäbische Blumenlese für's Jahr 1786, Tübingen 1786. With handwritten annotations by Johann Christoph Friedrich Haug and others.

Fig. 5 (right): W. Maurer, Balsamtropfen für vielgeprüfte und denkende Pilger nach Zion, um 1851–1854, 52 pages.

were returned to what seems to have been regarded as their "natural" or "national" habitat. These materials generated critical editions and research, enhanced German scholarship, and affirmed the right of German scholars and universities to read, to interpret, and to exhibit these materials. 2.) On a more abstract and yet critical level, this migration of cultural goods had implications for a prominent idea of historical continuity. Archives and libraries can be thought of as guardians of a literary tradition. They are not mere repositories and do not represent a passive memory. Their collection-building and material politics are driven by value judgments and power; their holdings represent the idea of a trans-historical community of texts that exceeds the sum of its parts. The integration of *Exilliteratur* into archives and libraries was an important step and laid the foundation for a revision of the postwar literary canon and cultural memory in Germany. At the same time, the covert "re-migration" of icons of German cultural heritage from émigré collections has made it possible to elide a most radical break in tradition (figs. 4 and 5).

In his striking study *Die deutschen Bibliotheken von der Aufklärung bis zur Gegenwart* (1956), Georg Leyh—still under the impression of what he refers to as the "the catastrophe that struck the German research libraries in World War II"—repeatedly refers to the "filling of war gaps" (*Auffüllung der Kriegslücken*).[14] The image he uses captures the essence of the striking efforts of libraries and research foundations to reconstruct a tradition that had, of course, been shattered long before German libraries were bombed. Libraries concealed signs of repair and restoration, while at the same time

14 Georg Leyh, Die deutschen Bibliotheken von der Aufklärung bis zur Gegenwart, in: Handbuch der Bibliothekswissenschaft, vol. 3, ed. by Aloys Börner, 2nd, revised edition, Wiesbaden 1957, 478 and 481.

publicizing their losses. The Bavarian State Library, the Prussian State Library, and the German Literature Archive Marbach—to name but three major institutions fostering research and cultural memory—have yet to add adequate provenance information to their catalogues and have yet to reveal the history of irreplaceable autographs and manuscripts that might owe their preservation to Jewish collectors who took them to locations outside Nazi Germany.

Who is now able to discern that Fontane's letters were stored in Jerusalem for some three decades, or that Bavarian religious songs did not always have a safe haven in Munich? Their tacit "return" fosters a conception of historical and cultural continuity that most archives still strive to represent. Moreover, the re-migration of "German" books and autographs from émigré collections in Israel, the United States, Great Britain, the Netherlands, and other countries to Germany marked the end of the idea of a so-called German-Jewish "symbiosis" that might have existed only in these very collections.

Literature

Volker Dahm, Das jüdische Buch im Dritten Reich, 2nd revised ed., Munich 1993.

Ernst Fischer, Verleger, Buchhändler und Antiquare aus Deutschland und Österreich in der Emigration nach 1933. Ein biographisches Handbuch, Elbingen 2011.

Caroline Jessen, Überlebsel. Karl Wolfskehls Bibliothek und ihre Zerstreuung, in: Zeitschrift für Ideengeschichte 11 (2017), no. 2, 93–110.

Gunnar A. Kaldewey (ed.), Ernst Hauswedell 1901–1983, Hamburg 1987.

Frank Kermode, Pleasure and Change. The Aesthetics of Canon, ed. by Robert Alter, New York 2004.

Georg Leyh, Die deutschen Bibliotheken von der Aufklärung bis zur Gegenwart, Handbuch der Bibliothekswissenschaft, vol. 3, ed. by Aloys Börner, 2nd, revised edition, Wiesbaden 1957.

Author

Since 2012 Caroline Jessen has been research associate at the German Literature Archive Marbach (DLA), from 2015 as a member of the "Writers' Libraries" research group at the Marbach Weimar Wolfenbüttel Research Association. She completed her PhD at Bonn University in 2015 with a thesis titled "Canon in Exile" and coordinated "Traces of German-Jewish History" (2012–2015), a project conducted jointly by the Rosenzweig Minerva Research Center and the DLA. She is interested in the relationship between archives and philology and in the hermeneutic aspects of "provenance." *Selected Publications*: Kanon im Exil. Lektüren deutsch-jüdischer Emigranten in Palästina / Israel, Göttingen 2019; Der Sammler Karl Wolfskehl, Berlin 2018; Bücher als Dinge. Funktionen emigrierter Bücher und Büchersammlungen für deutsch-jüdische Einwanderer in Palästina / Israel nach 1933 aus Perspektive der Kanonforschung, in: Bibliotheken und Sammlungen im Exil, ed. on behalf of the Society for Exile Studies by Claus-Dieter Krohn and Lutz Winckler, Munich 2011, 12–27; Der Kanon im Archiv. Deutsch-jüdische Geschichte an der Schnittstelle von Archiv, Erinnerung und Forschung, in: Naharaim. Zeitschrift für deutsch-jüdische Literatur und Kulturgeschichte / Journal of German-Jewish Literature and Cultural History 7 (2013), no. 1–2, 202–216.

YONATAN SHILOH-DAYAN

Bücherfreunde: German-Jewish Émigrés as Unintentional Guardians of German Books

How did it come about that German-Jewish émigrés who resided in Palestine after fleeing from Nazi-occupied territories became the unwitting guardians of German cultural property? The traffic of cultural property during World War II and its immediate aftermath was just as vast, arbitrary and subject to timing and chance as the massive movements and deportations of individuals, families, and entire communities. Jewish libraries throughout those territories were plundered, precious artworks seized, religious artifacts with deep communal meaning looted, and personal possessions confiscated and often lost for good. In the early 1930s, members of communities subjected to Nazi persecution for reasons of ethnicity or political affiliation who managed to flee in time were still able to transfer some of their personal belongings, including their libraries, to their adopted countries. The contents of these libraries frequently included volumes whose authors, Jewish and gentile alike, appeared on the list of banned literature in Nazi Germany. Hence, during that period privately owned transferred libraries and literary collections provided access to cultural assets that were otherwise unattainable. For the sake of our discussion, these assets—along with literary works written by German and German-Jewish authors in exile—are considered to be German cultural goods, since they were cultural creations written in German that engaged in a dialogue with the German literary tradition. It is an irony of history that exiled German Jews formed one of the distinct dispossessed groups that maintained access to banned German literature. Perhaps we need not confine our discussion to the strictly concrete aspect of "accessibility," but rather direct our attention to the volitional dimension implied by the term "access" in this context—that is, the émigrés' desire to retain an affinity with German culture and its manifestations in practice. As "stakeholders," German-Jewish authors and intellectuals attempted to utilize their unique position in the cause of cultural preservation, recreation, and transmission, thereby turning themselves into unintentional guardians of German culture.

Contested Heritage, 43–53 | doi.org/10.13109/9783666310836.43

This article examines three typical cases that demonstrate how émigré German Jews served as custodians, promoters, and transmitters of German literary culture. These case studies reflect the émigrés' vital role in a process of cultural preservation, as they maintained an impetus of cultural creation that was German in character and in form. Paradoxical as it may seem, having been part of German culture's widely celebrated burst of creativity during the Weimar period, the accumulated experience of German-Jewish artists, thinkers, and writers rendered them especially suited to the task of cultural salvation and transmission. Like a gatekeeper to his garden, members of the German-Jewish educated elite shared an intimate knowledge of a cultural legacy embodied in their characters and spiritual achievements. This attribute, along with an inferred ability to master the core of German literary culture, was contested even before the Weimar period and within the German-Jewish communities themselves, as exemplified by the well-known article by Moritz Goldstein that sparked the *Kunstwart* debate. In the cases discussed here, the content of this debate acquires a striking materialist dimension that took shape during the war years. That German-speaking Jews should actively engage in preserving the legacy of a Central European and specifically German culture during the years of Nazi rule constitutes a further expression of the unique phenomenon of German Jewry, compared to other instances of assimilation. The more extreme critical observers who identified with the Zionist narrative would have considered this a late manifestation of an illusionary and distorted "assimilatory" project. However, committed to a particular cultural heritage bound up with the concept of *Bildung*, the émigrés' sought to transcend their conventional definition as members of a national minority; they adhered to a liberal sentiment, manifested in its most refined form as a variation of *Deutschtum*. These forced emigrants, whose arrival to Palestine was not considered to be ideologically motivated, appear to have almost naturally clung to "Germanness" as an idea, a subtle virtue which they vehemently defended on occasion, even after being so brutally deprived of their former national affiliation. Indeed, they were impelled to defend something that they still thought of as their own. Clinging to a German literary canon—reformed and reinterpreted in exile—was an important means through which to preserve a cultural memory within which exiled German literature could evolve and engage in a dialogue with previous German literary legacies.

Antiquarians: Preservation and Circulation

As mentioned in the introductory passage, private libraries were essential in maintaining access to the German literary canon. In retrospect, a significant function that this canon performed was to facilitate, as a point of reference, the flowering of new literary voices that echoed the experience of exile. These voices were intent on engaging in dialogue with the German literary legacy as it resonated in exile. Besides their sentimental and social value as cultural capital, the role of private libraries and book collections became more prominent in view of the tension that existed between the private domain and the outside world, given the widespread public antipathy toward German culture and everything German that reached its peak during the war years. Yet despite this widely discussed cultural dismissal, which on occasion resulted in acts of violence, the German-Jewish migrants retained their attachment to the German language and culture. One indication of this was that private libraries and collections were not allowed to stagnate and become a dusty remnant of a glorious past. Rather, such libraries were rehabilitated or completed, rebuilt from scratch, or simply maintained and added to, reflecting the state of transition in which their owners found themselves. To a large extent, this was facilitated by a flourishing trade in antiquarian books in Palestine.

Already a respected literary figure upon his arrival in Palestine, Arnold Zweig recalls in an essay that appeared in a Parisian daily in 1938 how, having been deprived of his own books, he had little trouble obtaining eighteenth- and nineteenth-century German classics, which formed the basis for his new collection. He relates how one could find most of the *Horen* edition of Friedrich Schiller's works and letters in an antiquarian bookstore in Jerusalem, and the *Propyläen* edition of Goethe's works in a store in Tel Aviv. In Haifa, he laid hands on three volumes of a Heine edition bound in leather, Voss' Homer, Grimm's fairy tales, and many other works.[1] Zweig is possibly referring here to an antiquarian bookshop owned by his friend and an active member of the circle of left-wing German-speaking émigrés, the author Friedrich Sally Grosshut. In his store, which operated for ten years, German-speaking residents of Haifa could attend literary evenings with lectures delivered by Max Brod, Josef Kastein, Else Lasker-Schüler, Josef Karl Friedjung, Arnold Zweig, and others (figs. 1, 2, and 3). In a timeworn essay kept among his files, Grosshut recalls a reading with Lasker-Schüler as an "unforgettable experience": In a packed

1 Arnold Zweig, Alte Bücher, in: Pariser Tageszeitung 3 (1938), no. 732, 4, cit. in Caroline Jessen, "Vergangenheiten haben ihr eigenes Beharrungsvermögen ..." Josef Kastein and the Troublesome Persistence of a Canon of German Literature in Palestine/Israel, in: Leo Baeck Institute Year Book 57 (2012), 35–51, here 35.

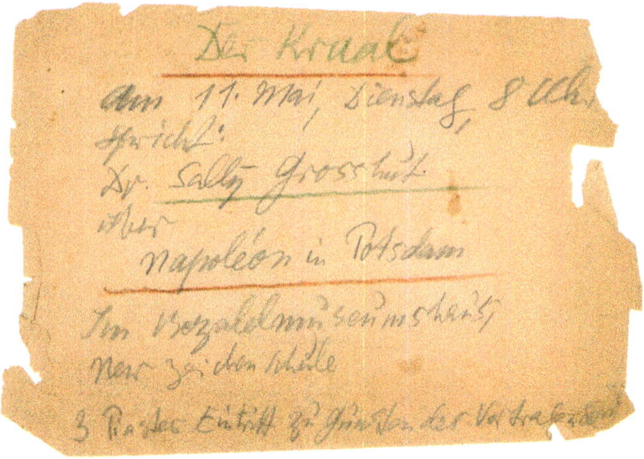

Fig. 1: Invitation to a lecture by Dr. Friedrich Sally Grosshut.

hall, darkened due to the "raging war outside," two lit candles were placed before the poet, without which she had stoutly refused to read.[2] Indeed, antiquarians were instrumental in a rapid process by which cultural capital was transformed into a financial asset. Given the circumstances in which emigrants from Central Europe brought with them book collections that took up far more space than they could now afford, a lively trade in German books sprang up in the three major cities, fueled by these surplus volumes. Book dealers and antiquarians snapped up this influx of private cultural property, which included rare editions whose value was not always appreciated in Palestine.

The relative accessibility of German classics contrasted with the growing difficulty of obtaining contemporary German literature in Palestine owing to restrictions that resulted from local anti-German sentiment and the desire to cultivate a common Hebrew language cultural identity in the Yishuv. This was something that Zweig experienced in person when, much to his chagrin, his anti-Nazi novel *Das Beil von Wandsbek*, written in Haifa, could not find a publisher in its original form and appeared in Palestine in Hebrew translation only. In general, local literary works that did not directly address Jewish topics could only be printed abroad. Among those were Max Brod's *Diesseits und Jenseits* (published by Mondial-Verlag, Winterthur, 1947), Louis Fürnberg's cycle of poems *Hölle, Hass und Liebe* (Die Einheit, London, 1943), and Friedrich Sally Grosshut's novels published by *Die Tribüne Verlag* (Fanara, Egypt, 1946). Given these circumstances, journals and periodicals, such as *Orient*, *Heute und Morgen. Antifaschistische Revue*, and *Tribüne*, took it upon themselves to publish verses, poems, literary sketches, and excerpts from novels written by established and lesser known German language authors living in Palestine, which were otherwise unattainable in the language in which they had been written. Thus, faced with the unwillingness on the part of local publishers to deal with these works, the editors in chief of the *Orient*, Wolfgang Yourgrau and Arnold

2 Archives of the Leo Baeck Institute, New York (henceforth LBINY), Friedrich Sally Grosshut Collection, AR 1559, MF 574, Begegnung mit Else Lasker-Schüler.

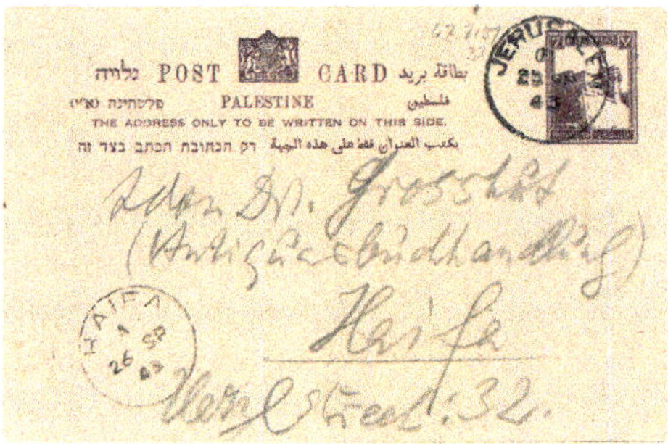

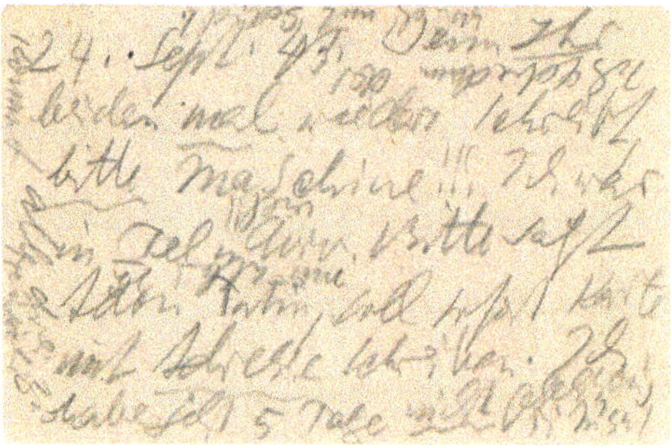

Fig. 2 and 3: Postcard (front side and back side) sent by Else Lasker-Schüler to Friedrich Sally Grosshut, 24. September 1944.

Zweig, offered Max Jungmann and Hermann Vallentin an outlet for their satirical verses; subscribers to *Heute und Morgen* could read excerpts from Zweig's *Das Beil*, the German edition of which first appeared in Stockholm; and Ernst Loewy, the managing editor, encouraged local German-speaking writers such as Hans Rosenthal, Willy Verkauf, and Hermann Rabinowitz to publish their works in the journal.

German-Language Journals: Nurture and Print

Let us move on to the role played by local German-language journals and periodicals and their approach toward the German cultural legacy in Palestine. Members of the community of left-wing German-speaking émigrés in Palestine conceived of themselves as a distinctive cohort belonging to a broader community of German exiles (Jews and non-Jews alike, dispersed between Moscow, London, New York, New Mexico, and other loci of exile), or at least as sharing common objectives and modes of operation with its members and intellectual leadership. The establishment and more or less continuous operation of independent publishing initiatives in Palestine by members of the cohort did not only serve the immediate needs of the local German readership, but also sought to win this circle recognition by their counterparts abroad as a legitimate, functioning organ in the body of exiled communities. One of these projects was the independent monthly *Heute und Morgen. Antifaschistische Revue* (fig. 4), which appeared in Mandate Palestine from 1943 to 1945, edited by Arnold Czempin, Ludwig Biro, and Ernst Loewy, who subsequently became a distinguished scholar of exile literature in West Germany. The journal was originally titled *Chug. Kreis der Bücherfreunde* (fig. 5), before the editors decided to change its title in order to broadcast their desire to promote the antifascist cause, as leading exile journals often did. The first stencil issue of the journal was distributed in April 1943, only two months after its predecessor, the *Orient*—a critical left-wing independent weekly—ceased to appear after a

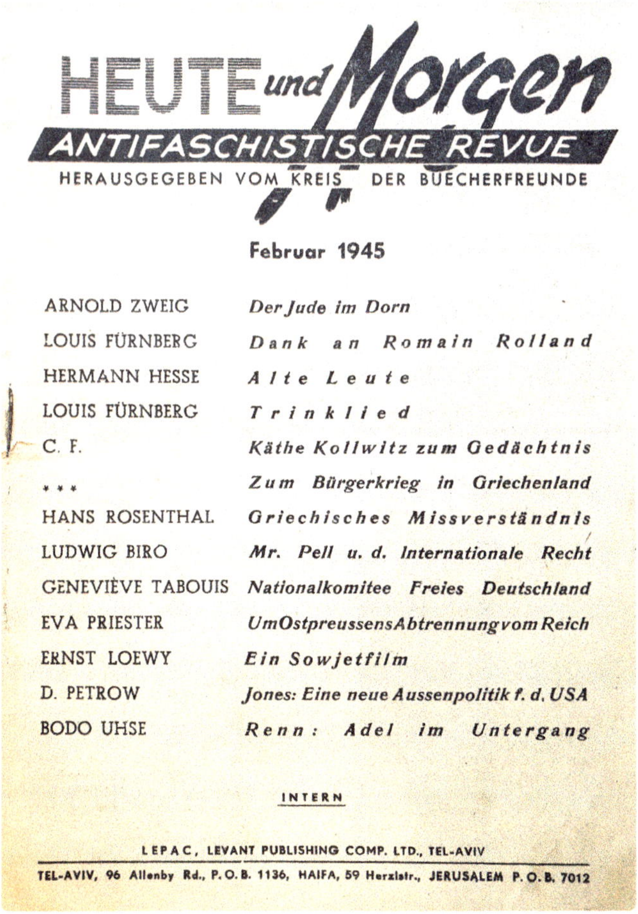
HEUTE und Morgen
ANTIFASCHISTISCHE REVUE
HERAUSGEGEBEN VOM KREIS DER BUECHERFREUNDE

Februar 1945

ARNOLD ZWEIG	Der Jude im Dorn
LOUIS FÜRNBERG	Dank an Romain Rolland
HERMANN HESSE	Alte Leute
LOUIS FÜRNBERG	Trinklied
C. F.	Käthe Kollwitz zum Gedächtnis
* * *	Zum Bürgerkrieg in Griechenland
HANS ROSENTHAL	Griechisches Missverständnis
LUDWIG BIRO	Mr. Pell u. d. Internationale Recht
GENEVIÈVE TABOUIS	Nationalkomitee Freies Deutschland
EVA PRIESTER	Um Ostpreussens Abtrennung vom Reich
ERNST LOEWY	Ein Sowjetfilm
D. PETROW	Jones: Eine neue Aussenpolitik f. d. USA
BODO UHSE	Renn: Adel im Untergang

INTERN

LEPAC, LEVANT PUBLISHING COMP. LTD., TEL-AVIV
TEL-AVIV, 96 Allenby Rd., P. O. B. 1136, HAIFA, 59 Herzlstr., JERUSALEM P. O. B. 7012

Fig. 4: Front cover of the February 1945 issue of *Heute und Morgen. Antifaschistische Revue.*

bomb exploded in the Jerusalem printing press where its issues were printed. The establishment of a new journal was facilitated through collaboration between the Kreis der Bücherfreunde—an independent organization founded by a group of engaged German speakers from Tel Aviv and Haifa—and a cooperative organization named Lepac (Levant Publishing Co.).

The declared goals of the journal were to provide the German-speaking inhabitants of Palestine access to contemporary literary sources and the international press, to acquaint them with "the problems of their time," and to draw them toward the antifascist groups operating worldwide. The journal was committed above all to "strengthening the bonds with Anglo-American and Soviet-Russian cultural centers as a means of contributing to the antifascist battle."[3] These goals were reflected in the issues' composition, the mix of articles on local and international politics, excerpts from Western classical and contemporary literary works, cultural and literary reviews, and pro-Soviet inclined polemical pieces. Broadly speaking, *Heute und Morgen* followed existing journalistic models shaped by exiled communities abroad. In its community of readers and writers, its tone, and its objectives, the journal had much in common with the *Orient*. The latter set great store by defending highly valued German cultural assets, both Jewish and non-Jewish, as a means whereby to argue in favor of "the other Germany." Quotes and excerpts from works by Goethe and

3 Kreis der Bücherfreunde, in: Chug. Kreis der Bücherfreunde 1 (April 1943), 24 (quotations from the German source were translated by the author).

Börne, Arthur Schnitzler and Karl Kraus, Richard Dehmel, Hermann Hesse, and many others appeared in every issue. *Heute und Morgen* followed a similar path, offering excerpts from works by writers such as Bertolt Brecht, Anna Seghers, Thomas Mann, Louis Fürnberg, Arnold Zweig, and Ferdinand Bruckner. The latter two—a Jew and a non-Jew—had both featured on the list of banned authors issued by the Nazi authorities. Thus, by reprinting literary works that were unattainable within the sphere of Nazi influence, both periodicals defied the distinction between German and German-Jewish cultural goods. In the editors' eyes, all these works were parts of a disjointed legacy that German-Jewish émigrés in Palestine were seeking to preserve with the means at their disposal. Those who believed in the existence of "the other Germany" regarded the German literary legacy as a tangible manifestation of a world view and an inner essence that were facing the prospect of total eradication. The juxtaposition of literary works written in exile and those of writers identified with the German classical canon indicated the émigrés' perception of the German language's extra-historical capacity to withstand a momentous collapse of German culture in its totality; and to serve as a means whereby to reclaim a German essence through the spirit of a liberal culture. For obvious reasons, such an attempt could only be carried out in exile, by émigrés.

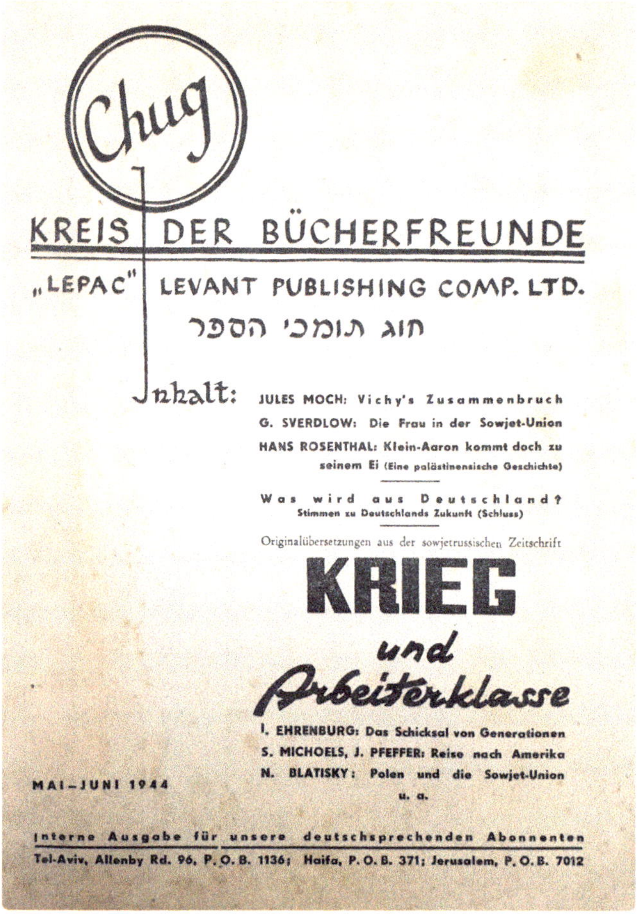

Fig. 5: Front cover of the May/June 1944 issue of *Chug. Kreis der Bücherfreunde.*

Emissaries: Transmission and Mediation

Between the spring and summer of 1946, a large stock of German books was collected and offered to a group of several thousand German POWs held in British captivity in Eastern North Africa. Divided into reading groups, soldiers belonging to the former *Afrikakorps*, some of whom had been held captive for more than three years, could spend their time in group readings of literary works that were frowned upon in the Third Reich, such as Heinrich Mann's *Professor Unrath*, Arnold Zweig's *Erziehung von Verdun*, and Stefan Zweig's *Ungeduld des Herzens*, alongside works by Georg Büchner, Ludwig Renn, Jakob Wassermann, Franz Werfel, and others. The majority of these books were selected, assembled, and delivered by German Jews from Palestine. The establishment of an inmates' library was part of a rehabilitative program directed by a German-Jewish physician by the name of Adolf Sindler, who migrated from Düsseldorf to Haifa in 1937 and served with the British forces, first as an army doctor and later as a "training adviser." During the immediate postwar era, the British Army carried out the largest POW re-education operation among the Allied forces, and the programs provided in camps located in North Africa were the most extensive. As part of his duty, Sindler transformed army tents into lecture halls where educational activities became part of the captives' daily routine.

At the core of Sindler's program was a publishing house, *Tribüne Verlag*, run by the captives themselves, which issued numerous journals, magazines, educational materials, and first editions of books. These were circulated by the thousands, both within the camp and in other British incarceration facilities. The monthly *Tribüne* frequently included contributions by German-speaking émigrés in Palestine, many of them by Friedrich Sally Grosshut and Arnold Zweig (who were both personally acquainted with Sindler), as well as by Martin Buber, Otto Zarek, Ernst Simon, and Ernst Loewy. Aside from writing these texts and authorizing the use of his texts originally published elsewhere, Zweig was personally engaged in providing German inmates access to literary materials. Together with a group of German-speaking socialist émigrés (which comprised mostly former members of the German Communist Party and the Socialist Workers' Party of Germany), these writers would gather on a weekly basis in an apartment in Tel Aviv to discuss, among other matters, the content of literary stocks that were to be dispatched to the desert camps through an intermediary. Most of the selected materials were obtained and purchased in antiquarian bookshops and bookstores in Tel Aviv, Haifa, and Jerusalem. Since these consignments included contemporary German-Jewish works alongside banned and exile literature, the cultural goods that these émigrés sent out to the desert were unique, in the sense that they could hardly be found elsewhere, and certainly not in the Middle East.

In an article titled *Literatur in der Wüste*, which appeared in the *Argentinisches Tagesblatt* on 27 November 1949, in which he addressed Sindler's endeavors in the prisoner-of-war (POW) camp and the vital support he received from his comrades in Palestine, Friedrich Sally Grosshut commented: "Goebels hatte am 10. Mai 1933 die freie Literatur verbrennen lassen, den Geist in die ›Wüste‹ geschickt [...]. Der Geist, in die ›Wüste‹ geschickt, ging buchstäblich in die Wüste!" This witticism, which Grosshut apparently took great delight in as it also appeared in his correspondences, alludes to the rationale that led the émigrés to engage in this unusual act of transmission. They did not view the POW camps located in North Africa as the final destinations of the ideas and values conveyed by the books and journals that arrived there. Rather, the camps were to function as temporary transitory sites (which they indeed were), in which young Germans, some of whom were ardent Nazis, would absorb the foundations of an erstwhile German culture and transmit them back to their homeland upon their return. It was not merely the camp inmates to whom members of the cohort of German-speaking émigrés in Palestine were trying to reach out, but German society in its entirety.

Closing Remarks

The function and significance of the German literary canon underwent considerable transformations among the communities of German-speaking émigrés in Palestine and elsewhere. From the point at which the canon functioned not only as a medium of cultural memory or a reference system, but also as a monument for "absent people and absent places," for a culture that existed in the German-speaking world before the Nazis' accession to power,[4] books and other literary artifacts kept in private libraries and collections transformed into tangible manifestations of a negative legacy. However, the function of a monument is far removed from the idea of a canon, which is a stable yet lively and condensed body of work that represents the value judgments of a collective and constitutes a repository of its cultural achievements. Conventionally, a monument bears witness to a certain individual, community, event, or cultural phenomenon that belongs to the past—such as the German-Jewish culture in the social

4 See Caroline Jessen, Bücher als Dinge. Funktionen emigrierter Bücher und Büchersammlungen für deutsch-jüdische Einwanderer in Palästina/Israel nach 1933 aus Perspektive der Kanonforschung, in: Jahrbuch für Exilforschung 29 (2011), 12–27.

and geographical sphere of its origins. Commemorating someone or something of the past, a monument does not change, whereas a canon does. Thus, the German-speaking émigrés did not set out to preserve, cherish, and pass on a literary culture overshadowed by a very dark chapter of cultural history. Negativity was imposed upon it from the outside. One should therefore distinguish between the meanings inferred by the three actions represented in the cases discussed above: preserving, nurturing, and transmitting. While the impetus underlying the first two actions may be considered a manifestation of a desire to commemorate a lost people and a lost culture, the motivation underlying the third was apparently different. The drive to transmit these works of literature implied a belief that a German literary canon, in its revised form, was something that could outlive the catastrophe and reclaim a respectable place within a postwar German society on the mend. In Palestine, German-speaking Jews found themselves in a peculiar position by serving as guardians and transmitters of cultural assets that the National Socialists regime had sought to do away with. They did so virtually unintentionally, as they grappled with a negative legacy while seeking to revive a literary tradition that was surely also their own.

Literature

Steven E. Aschheim, Beyond the Border. The German-Jewish Legacy Abroad, Princeton, N.J., 2007.

Walter A. Berendsohn, Die humanistische Front. Einführung in die deutsche Emigranten-Literatur, 2 vols., Worms 1976–1978, here vol. 2: Vom Kriegsausbruch 1939 bis Ende 1946, Worms 1976.

Adi Gordon, "In Palestine. In a Foreign Land." The Orient: A German-Language Weekly Between German Exile and Aliyah, Jerusalem 2004 (Heb.).

Caroline Jessen, Das problematische Bild der geretteten Kultur. Büchersammlungen deutsch-jüdischer Einwanderer in Israel, in: Tel Aviver Jahrbuch für deutsche Geschichte 41 (2013), 179–194.

Yonatan Shiloh-Dayan, Re-education of German POWs as a German-Jewish Task. The Case of Adolf Sindler, in: Naharaim. Zeitschrift für deutsch-jüdische Literatur und Kulturgeschichte/Journal of German-Jewish Literature and Cultural History 10 (2016), no. 2, 247–272.

Author

Yonatan Shiloh-Dayan is a PhD candidate in the Department of History of the Jewish People and Contemporary Jewry at the Hebrew University of Jerusalem. His dissertation project addresses the lives and works of German-speaking émigré historians in Israel and their approach to modern German history and German historiography. Yonatan's primary research interests include migration history and its intersections with Central European intellectual history, German-Israeli collaborations in the field of humanities, and the origins of left-oriented political criticism in Palestine and the young State of Israel. *Selected Publications*: Observant Ventures. Early German-Israeli Conferences on German History, in: Jahrbuch des Simon-Dubnow-Instituts / Simon Dubnow Institute Yearbook 15 (2016), 315–339 (with Irene Aue-Ben-David); On the Point of Return. "Heute und Morgen" and the German-speaking Left-Wing Émigrés in Palestine, in: Bettina Bannasch / Michael Rupp (eds.), Rückkehrerzählungen. Über die (Un-)Möglichkeit nach 1945 als Jude in Deutschland zu leben, Göttingen 2017, 35–56.

YECHIEL WEIZMAN

Eliminating the Traces: The Postwar Fate of the Synagogue in Olkusz, Poland

Crossing the market square in Olkusz, heading north and proceeding a few meters up Floriańska Street, one catches sight of a grassy rectangular patch of land. Its startling and symmetrical emptiness breaks the line of buildings and leaves an unexpected, striking void, that emphasizes the presence of something that seems to be absent, and inevitably evokes reflections on the origins of this vacant spot. Only the current name of the street, *ulica Bóżnicza* (Synagogue Street), and a recently installed memorial plaque on a nearby wall, recall the not so distant history of the place as the site of the town's synagogue (fig. 1).

This essay addresses the postwar fate of the Olkusz synagogue and the debates concerning its future. The concrete and symbolic transformation of the synagogue since the end of World War II up until its final demolition in the late 1950s embodies the ambivalent status of Jewish heritage sites in Poland after the Holocaust. As the story of the synagogue demonstrates, the contentious debates over the fate of abandoned Jewish sites in postwar Poland reflected contradicting political, economic, and moral considerations on the part of Jewish organizations, the regime, and local authorities. For many Poles, abandoned Jewish sites evoked a unique sense of dissonance. They were generally perceived as desirable and ownerless property; but also, as this essay argues, as a disturbing presence that ultimately had to be removed.

The synagogue in Olkusz was built in 1584 and served as the main religious and communal Jewish institution in the town up until the liquidation of the Jewish community during the Holocaust. On the eve of World War II, Jews constituted around 40 percent of the 10,000 inhabitants of Olkusz. Shortly after the outbreak of the war, the town was annexed to Nazi Germany. A ghetto was established in Olkusz, and in the summer of 1942 almost all of the town's Jews were sent to their death in Auschwitz. Only a few dozen, mostly young men and women who survived the concentration camps, returned to Olkusz after the war, hoping to find relatives and reclaim their property. As in many other Polish towns, they

Contested Heritage, 55–64 | doi.org/10.13109/9783666310836.55

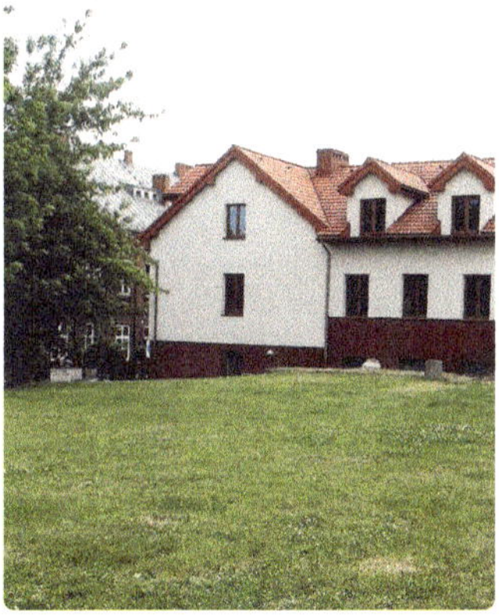

Fig. 1: The site of the former synagogue in Olkusz, 2014.

encountered hostile and violent behavior on the part of their neighbors, who had generally been quick to occupy the empty apartments and appropriate objects left behind after the Jews' deportation. In early 1947, only a handful of Jews remained in Olkusz. The Jews left behind not only private houses and objects, but also communal property, among which were two cemeteries, a synagogue, and various religious objects.

Under a series of decrees and regulations issued by the provisional communist-led government, all Jewish property, both private and communal, was categorized as "abandoned property" *(mienie opuszczone)*. Houses and other private property were generally allocated to Polish citizens by the local authorities, which contended with a severe shortage of housing as a result of the war. Communal property such as cemeteries, synagogues, and other buildings that belonged to the Jewish communities were for the most part nationalized and handed over to local authorities. While private Jewish property could be restituted, albeit only after negotiating numerous legal and practical issues, no such option was available with regard to communal property. No Jewish body in Communist Poland was entitled to lay claim to properties belonging to the prewar Jewish communities and associations, since the regime defined the postwar Jewish organizations as totally new legal entities, which thus possessed no inheritance rights relating to the property of the former communities, which had formally ceased to exist. Thus, apart from a small number of buildings and sites made available to the existing Jewish congregations, thousands of Jewish cemeteries, synagogues, and other communal properties were now regarded and treated as "heirless" and "ownerless."

This new juridical state of affairs was in many ways already in force on the ground. Immediately after the town's liberation, the two Jewish cemeteries in Olkusz, which had been extensively damaged during the war by the Germans, fell victim to acts of plunder by members of the local population, who frequently removed *matẓevot* (Jewish headstones) for their own use. The situation in Olkusz was no different from that which pertained in other nearby towns. In June 1948, the regional authorities issued an urgent circular to all mayors to take immediate action to protect abandoned Jewish cemeteries from widespread plunder by the local population.

Most municipalities were initially very reluctant to do so. The mayor of Olkusz maintained that the town lacked the necessary budget for this purpose. In fact, he ordered the few Jewish survivors still resident in

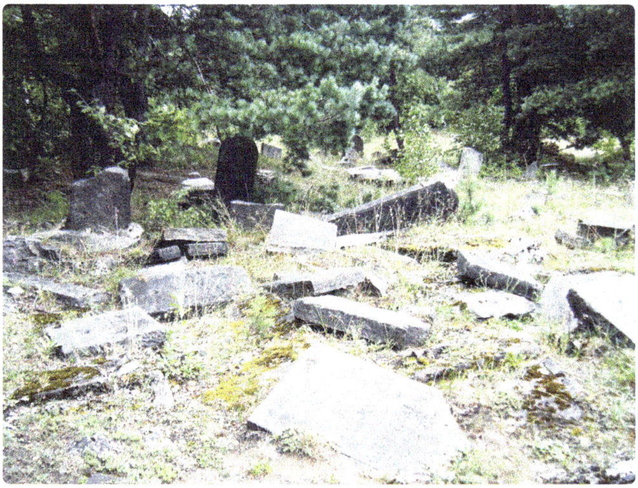

Fig. 2: The new Jewish cemetery in Olkusz, 2014.

the town to take care of the cemeteries, arguing that "it is your relatives who are buried there."[1] He furthermore proposed to erase the sixteenth-century Jewish cemetery altogether and in its stead to build a park or a square, since "the cemetery has no monuments of historical or artistic value."[2] Following strong protests from Jewish leaders, the mayor was brought into line by state officials, who rejected his plan to erase the old cemetery and informed him that he was now responsible for the protection of both Jewish cemeteries. However, as in most Polish towns, this did not prevent the further decay of the cemeteries owing to the ravages of time, nature, and man. While the old cemetery was recently symbolically reconstructed, the condition of the new one in many ways still resembles its postwar state (fig. 2).

Cases such as this, in which the central authorities forbade municipalities to use Jewish sites for public purposes and compelled local authorities to protect them, were common in the early postwar years in Poland. While on the one hand, the Communist regime implemented a strict policy of nationalization and confiscation of Jewish property, on the other hand, at least until the end of the 1940s, they were relatively attentive to Jewish concerns and protests at the profanation and misuse of religious sites. Whereas the government's policy was largely motivated by strategic-political considerations—and in particular the desire to appease Western governments, which showed some interest in the fate of the Jewish survivors—local leaders, especially in the provinces, appeared to have different concerns. In the wake of the material damage caused by the war, utilizing the town's budget to preserve abandoned Jewish sites was generally not a top priority. A deserted cemetery or synagogue was not regarded as worthy of preservation and local officials tended to perceive such sites as a perfect space for construction or for other purposes.

1 Archiwum Państwowe w Katowicach [State Archive in Katowice] (henceforth APK), Zarząd Miejski i MRN w Olkuszu [Municipality and National Council in Olkusz], File 74, 1 July 1948.

2 APK, Zarząd Miejski i MRN w Olkuszu, File 74, 10 November 1948.

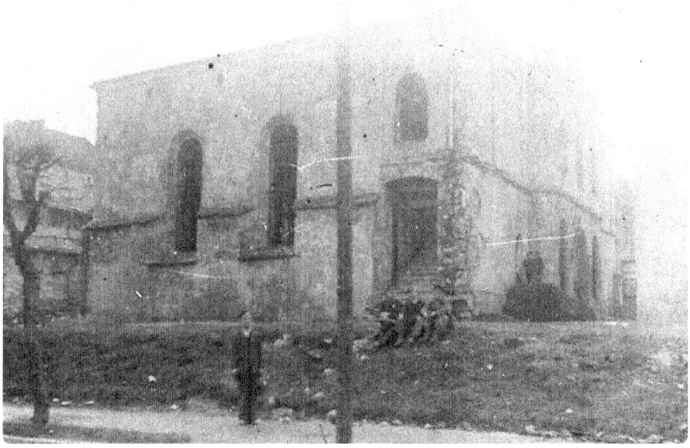

Fig. 3: The synagogue in Olkusz immediately after World War II.

While a cemetery had little value in terms of real estate, and clearing it for construction was regarded as highly problematic and sensitive, converting a synagogue for a different use was in many respects—religiously, morally, and politically—far simpler. Moreover, an empty synagogue—generally a large and imposing building lying at the very heart of town—was a valuable piece of real estate, and could meet various public needs, for instance a cinema, a cultural center, a warehouse, a factory, a school, or a police station. Thus, throughout Poland, local officials and organizations were eager to lay their hands on synagogues. In the chaotic period immediately after the war, local bodies that still enjoyed some degree of independence were able to undertake such initiatives. With the growing consolidation of central rule from 1947 onward, however, local bodies were losing their autonomy to the government in Warsaw, which was tightening its regulation of the usage of religious sites.

Such was the case of the synagogue in Olkusz. It was partly destroyed by the German forces and turned into a warehouse during the war. After the liberation it was used for various purposes and not cared for. Its condition steadily deteriorated, while several local organizations competed with one another to gain possession of it (fig. 3).

In May 1947, the local firefighters petitioned the provisional government in Warsaw to be allowed to use the synagogue and the adjoining Talmudic house *(beit midrash)* as their new station:

> "We kindly request to transfer to our possession the properties that belonged to the former Jewish community, that is: the building of the former synagogue and the Jewish school. [...] [T]hese buildings have no historical value, they are completely ruined and remain without proper care. [...] [O]ur current station is located in a small and old building that does not meet our needs. [...] [T]he requested buildings, after appropriate and necessary renovations, could serve as a modern fire station."

The firefighters attached to their appeal a letter of consent from the mayor, who wrote:

> "[T]he municipal board in Olkusz fully concurs with the above request, and confirms that the former Jewish object in its current state is a ruin. [...] [T]his object was built only forty years ago without [adhering to] architectural principles, and it therefore has no historical value [...]."[3]

Beyond the stated goal of these letters, a careful reading of the petition reveals certain crucial assumptions and linguistic patterns underlying the officials' perception of the Jewish space, which are deliberately employed to reinforce their request. First, the applicants consistently refer to the synagogue and the Jewish community in the past tense, for example: "the former Jewish community" *(była gmina wyznaniowa żydowska)*, "the building of the former synagogue" *(budynek po synagodze)*, and the "the former Jewish object" *(obiekt pożydowski).*

This constant use of the past tense was a common linguistic norm in similar requests. While the abandoned Jewish spaces were indeed no longer Jewish, neither formally nor practically, it appears that rather than a mere description of reality, this repetitive lingual pattern served to reaffirm the transformation that such Jewish properties had undergone. This local discourse, which sprouted rapidly after the war throughout the country, not only reflected a new normative order but helped instill it in the postwar Polish consciousness. The trend of entrenching through language the notion that the "Jewishness" of space was a thing of the past was likewise manifested in the newly coined and popular phrase *mienie pożydowskie*. Literally translated as "formerly Jewish" or "leftover Jewish" property, this rendering fails to capture the significance of the term. Polish words beginning with the prefix *po* denote something that no longer exists in the same place. The word *pożydowskie* thus both reflected and constructed the legitimation and moral justification for using Jewish property.

The assertion that the synagogue (which, contrary to the mayor's claim, was built in the sixteenth century) lacked any historical value, also appears to convey multiple meanings. Functionally, it serves to rule out any reason to preserve the place and to justify its designation for "mundane" purposes. This claim can moreover be viewed as part of a broader general performative discourse that seeks to establish the preconditions underlying the notion that Jewish sites were not worthy of preservation as Jewish, or at all. In other words, the repetitive arguments that Jewish sites possessed no

3 Archiwum Żydowskiego Instytutu Historycznego [Archive of the Jewish Historical Institute] (henceforth AŻIH), CKŻP, File 1/171, 2 June 1948. Cited also in Kazimierz Urban, Cmentarze żydowskie, synagogi i domy modlitwy w Polsce w latach 1944–1966 (wybór materiałów) [Jewish Cemeteries, Synagogues and Houses of Prayer in Poland in the Years 1944–1966 (Selected Sources)], Kraków 2006, 141f.

value and that they were "a thing of the past," reflect a widely held view on the place of Jewishness in postwar Polish culture and spatial consciousness, but also help to construct the concrete and mental process of "de-Judaizing" the postwar landscape.

The authorities in Warsaw consulted Jewish representatives from Olkusz and Kraków on the matter, who expressed their strong opposition to the firefighters' request. They argued that the building was in fact in fairly good condition and did not require a substantial outlay to preserve it. Refuting the erroneous claim made by the mayor, according to whom the synagogue was only forty years old, they insisted that it was indeed a historical monument, and questioned the real motives underlying the firefighters' request:

> "They are not competent to decide whether the synagogue is a historical monument. If the firefighters have a need for a station, then there are plenty of other abandoned buildings. [...] [T]he attempt to take over the synagogue and *beit ha-midrash* [study house] is only a pretext on the part of some members of the firefighters—who are determined not to leave any Jewish trace in Olkusz."[4]

The objections voiced by the Jewish representatives apparently had the desired effect, since the attempt to transform the synagogue into a firefighting station eventually came to nothing. State officials expressed their reservations and argued that any future use of a synagogue "should not stand in contradiction to its original nature." Over the following years the synagogue stood empty as its condition continued to deteriorate owing to neglect and unauthorized use by local firms and individuals. From time to time different elements attempted to take control of the building. In 1952, local officials requested the government to allow them to use the synagogue as a permanent grain storage for a regional bakery. They argued that the lack of an appropriate grain storage meant that the people of the area were denied the supply of fresh bread, and that the synagogue was "the only suitable space for this purpose." A year later, other officials sought to promote a project to convert the synagogue into a gymnastics hall for the town's high school. Although by now the increasingly rigid Stalinist regime was far less committed to the inviolability of Jewish sites, these initiatives too were unfruitful, due not so much to political sensitivity as to bureaucratic and technical obstacles.

4 AŻIH, CKŻP, File 1/171, 2 June 1948. Cited also in Urban, Cmentarze żydowskie synagogi i domy modlitwy w Polsce w latach 1944–1966 (wybór materiałów) [Jewish Cementaries, Synagogues and Houses of Prayers in Poland in the Years 1944–1966 (Selected Sources)], 144.

From the early 1950s onward, the state's increasingly hostile policy regarding the Jewish minority and Jewish issues in general began to trickle down to the periphery and was manifested in the radicalization of the local discourse concerning the remaining material traces of a Jewish presence in the town. In 1954, a further request concerning the allocation of the Olkusz synagogue was submitted to Warsaw, this time by a local cooperative for the employment of the handicapped, which proposed that the building be converted into a productive facility for rehabilitation purposes. What is particularly interesting here is not the substance of the letter, but rather the language employed to portray the synagogue:

> "[T]he ruined building of the former synagogue is a hotbed for everything which is filthy [*siedliskiem wszelkich nieczystości*]. [...] Local residents and passersby use the place as public toilets and as a dump [...]. Rats, mice and flies swarm there and turn this place into a breeding ground for infectious diseases [*rozsadniki zakaźnych chorób*]. [...] It is not considered a historical monument. [...] The building of the former synagogue is suitable for our needs. [...] The town's board fully supports our request as it is the only rational solution to the problem [...]."[5]

The synagogue, as described in the letter, is perceived as a health and hygienic hazard and as an unsanitary place. This abrasive language brings to mind the ideas of the anthropologist Mary Douglas. In her seminal work *Purity and Danger* she argues that what is perceived as filthy and polluting is not necessarily so; it is rather the manifestation of a taboo that is constructed as something filthy—since it threatens and endangers the integrity and boundaries of the community. Whether or not the above portrayal of the synagogue was an accurate description of the site's condition or an exaggeration, it may also be interpreted as a calculated attempt to construct the synagogue as an abject space, thereby creating the conditions for its cleansing. At the same time, this discourse reflects the extent to which the very existence of the synagogue was regarded as a problem that needed to be resolved. Almost ten years after the end of the war, the empty and dilapidated synagogue was increasingly perceived as a nuisance. It occupied a valuable construction site in the heart of the town and left a vivid scar that obstructed attempts at rebuilding and aestheticizing the public space. It may furthermore have threatened to evoke memories of one of the strongest taboos and silenced subjects in postwar Poland—the Holocaust and its implications for Polish society.

5 Archiwum Akt Nowych [Central Archives of Modern Records] (henceforth AAN), Urząd ds. Wyznań [Office for Religious Affairs], File 22/446, 8 September 1954.

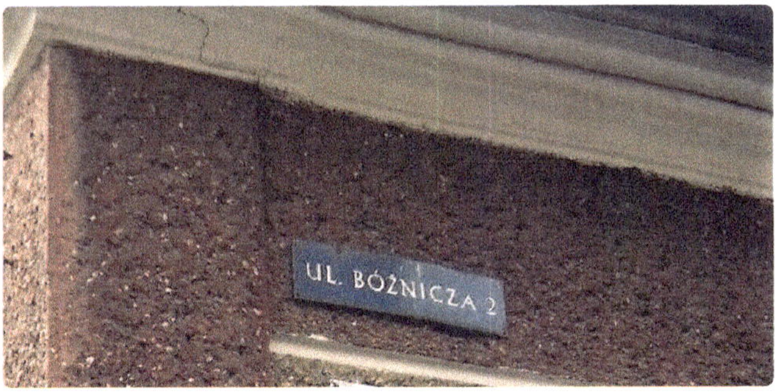

Fig. 4: Synagogue Street, Olkusz 2014.

Eventually, this last request was rejected as well, yet it reflected the growing impatience in Olkusz regarding the unresolved issue of the synagogue's future. Town officials now appeared to be concerned not merely with the material and economic aspects of the problem, but also with the very presence of the building, which was becoming too perturbing. No wonder then that in 1955—at the request of the local council—the provincial authorities decided to demolish the synagogue, acting under a law regulating the demolition of war-damaged structures passed only a few months previously by the government. According to a report submitted by the provincial official, the building was now three quarters destroyed and was "regularly being disassembled by unknown perpetrators." The demolition was to proceed immediately, but was delayed by administrative and bureaucratic red tape. Eager to remove the ruins, in the summer of 1957 the town's leaders and local inhabitants took matters into their own hands, subsequently claiming that "the demolition needed to be performed as quickly as possible because of sanitary and aesthetic reasons." Since the appropriate mechanical equipment was not at hand, the demolition was conducted by local residents who used the bricks for their own purposes. As an official report stated, "the town council had found volunteers among the locals who pulled down the building in exchange for the remaining building materials, which they then used for their private purposes."[6]

Thereafter, the last traces of the synagogue building were removed, in a symbolic and final act of erasure. Two years after the demolition, the local council decided to change the name of the street on which the synagogue had stood in the recent past. As the minutes of the council's meeting on 6 June 1959 indicate, its original name, Synagogue Street *(ulica Bóżnicza)*, was changed to "Corporal Kamienka," in honor of a local Polish policeman who was murdered after the war. However, as is often the case, this deliberate act of reshaping the space did not become part of the local spatial consciousness. From the interviews I conducted, I learned that for many years after the synagogue's demolition people continued to refer to the street as Synagogue Street. Some were apparently unaware that the

6 AAN, Urząd ds. Wyznań, File 26/478, 31 March 1958.

name had been changed. Just a few years ago, the street officially acquired its original name once again (fig. 4).

A further indication that, despite the physical removal of the synagogue from the local landscape, the townspeople of Olkusz may have found it difficult to come to terms with its absence, is the fact that the site has remained vacant to this day. Although it has been at the town's disposal since 1957, nothing has been built on it—even though there was no legal or material impediment to allocating the site for construction.

How come, then, that the site has remained vacant? Why has nothing been built on it? The documentation fails to provide a clear answer to this mystery. Was this merely a case of technical or bureaucratic hindrances, or of something more substantive? Perhaps the erasure of the synagogue generated a degree of uneasiness that was manifested in a sense of apprehension about using a former religious space for mundane purposes? Or perhaps the void left after the demolition of the synagogue evoked doubts regarding the juridical, conceptual, or even moral question—to whom does this empty site actually belong? During one of my visits to Olkusz I met a local man in his nineties who had been active in the town's public life during the Communist era. I asked him: "Why did the town never build anything there?" The man looked at me with a puzzled expression and replied: "You must understand, they couldn't build anything there—it simply did not belong to them."

Literature

Krzysztof Kocjan, Zagłada olkuskich Żydów [The Destruction of the Olkusz Jews], Olkusz 2002.

Michael Meng, Shattered Spaces. Encountering Jewish Ruins in Postwar Germany and Poland, Cambridge, Mass., 2011.

Kazimierz Urban, Cmentarze żydowskie, synagogi i domy modlitwy w Polsce w latach 1944–1966 (wybór materiałów) [Jewish Cemeteries, Synagogues and Houses of Prayer in Poland in the Years 1944–1966 (Selected Sources)], Kraków 2006.

Michael C. Steinlauf, Bondage to the Dead. Poland and the Memory of the Holocaust, Syracuse, N.Y., 1997.

Mary Douglas, Purity and Danger. An Analysis of Concepts of Pollution and Taboo, London 1966.

Author

Yechiel Weizman is a Minerva Foundation postdoctoral fellow at the Leibniz Institute for Jewish History and Culture – Simon Dubnow in Leipzig. He received his PhD from the Department of Jewish History at Haifa University in 2018 and he holds degrees in cultural studies and philosophy from the Hebrew University in Jerusalem. His research focuses on the function, status, and perception of Jewish sites and objects in Poland after the Holocaust. *Selected Publications*: Abandoned Property? The Status and Future of Jewish Communal Property in Poland after the Holocaust, in: Moreshet. Journal for the Study of the Holocaust and Antisemitism 14 (2017), 260–290 (Heb.); Unsettled Possession. The Question of Ownership of Jewish Sites in Poland after the Holocaust from a Local Perspective, in: Jewish Culture and History 18 (2017), no. 1, 34–53; The Sacralization and Secularization of the Jewish Cemeteries in Poland, in: Lucyna Aleksandrowicz-Pędich / Jacek Partyka (eds.), Jews and Non-Jews. Memories and Interactions from the Perspective of Cultural Studies, Frankfurt a. M. 2014, 205–220.

2. Salvage and Loss: Dealing with the Fragments

IRIS LAUTERBACH

Art Restitution in the Aftermath of World War II: The Central Collecting Point in Munich

The dynamics of the seizure, storage, and restitution of looted art after World War II were conditioned by international and German postwar politics, which defined the institutional framework of the first postwar restitutions of looted property, as demonstrated by the history of the Central Collecting Point (CCP) in Munich. The CCP in Munich was established in early June 1945 and functioned until autumn 1949. Its operation was impacted by common and conflicting political and juridical interests; its history highlights the fragility of the translocated works of art, the existence and integrity of which was jeopardized by looting, transportation, and inadequate storage. Last but not least, the history of the CCP is also the history of a singular type of extra-territorial international community: Different people and personalities were required to cooperate with one another and to contend with an often fraught political situation. While a judicial framework approved by all the Great Powers had yet to be put into place—and in fact never was—the initial restitution of art works took place. High politics and everyday "fieldwork" had to advance hand in hand, but in fact were often conducted in different geographical areas and "time zones." The present essay focuses on the praxis of restitution in the Munich CCP during the early postwar years. The history of the Munich CCP impresses upon the historian, once again, that political decisions are made by prominent and ordinary people, whose personal efficacy and conviction may set in motion shifts and create margins of tolerance.

General Political Outlines

At the end of World War II, most of the German public art collections had been evacuated from the cities, and were found, side by side with looted art, at remote locations—in castles, monasteries, mines, and tunnels. Most of these art depositories were located in Central and Southern Germany, in areas that were part of the British and the American occupied zones. This

Contested Heritage, 67–77 | doi.org/10.13109/9783666310836.67

was where the major art collecting points were established: Offenbach specialized in archives and cultural items of Jewish origin; Wiesbaden was the destination to which the majority of Berlin's art collections had been sent. And approximately 80 percent of the looted art objects from all over Europe was discovered at that time at the Munich Collecting Point.

In the early 1940s, in the United States as well as in several European countries, governmental and private cultural initiatives were set up to protect threatened art works and monuments in the European war theatre. From 1943 onward, the American Commission for the Protection and Salvage of Artistic and Historic Monuments in War Areas (the Roberts Commission) worked together with the military and other bodies of the US and Allied governments. The central Allied information center, the Art Looting Investigation Unit (ALIU), was located in London, which was also the seat of several exiled European governments. It was in London, for example, that, from 1940 onward, the Polish art historian Karol Estreicher gathered information on art works looted from Poland. In 1944, the US administration established the Monuments, Fine Arts, and Archives Section (MFA&A), a military body set up to protect monuments and art works in the European war theatre and to prepare for and organize the restitution of these works. The large number of depositories of looted art works discovered in the spring and summer of 1945 revealed the hitherto unknown dimension of the looting. The Report of the Roberts Commission (1946) and the records of the Nuremberg trials published in 1945 and 1946 informed the international public of the activities of the most prominent National Socialist art robbers. In Nuremberg, for the first time in history, an international tribunal addressed the issue of politically motivated looting of art.

Despite a number of Allied initiatives on the matter, after the war the United States, its European allies, and the Soviet Union failed to adopt a common restitution policy to be followed by all the four occupying powers. Each occupation zone applied its own restitution policy. Since most of the looted art works were found in the US zone and therefore had to be restituted by the United States, the American standards served as a guideline, at least for the Western occupied zones. However, at Potsdam in July 1945, the three Great Powers agreed on a program of so-called restitution "ad interim," which applied primarily to prominent art works. The first restitution "ad interim" took place in August 1945 when the panels of the Ghent altarpiece were returned to Belgium. The so-called external restitutions to foreign countries were regulated in September 1945 by the Allied Control Council. The so-called internal restitutions to German, and mostly Jewish owners, constituted a smaller proportion of the activities of the Collecting Point.

The Central Collecting Point in Munich

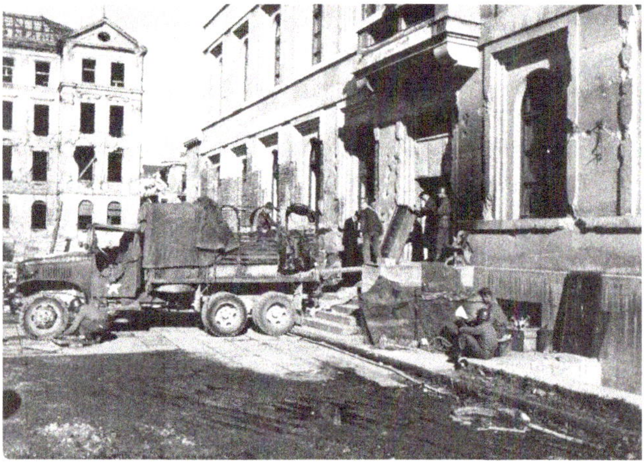

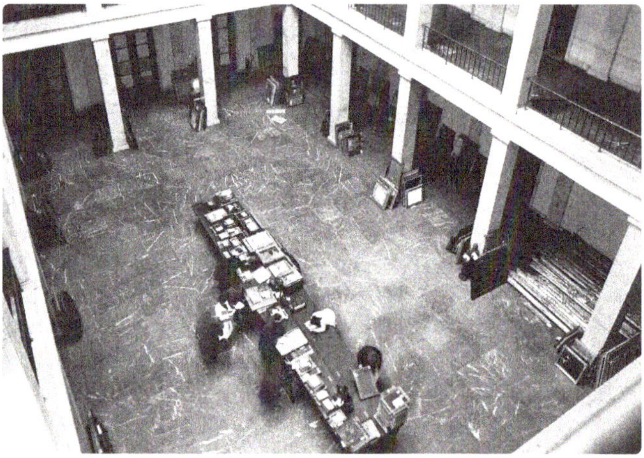

Fig. 1 and 2: The Central Collecting Point in Munich, 1945/46; the southern entrance (top) and the registration of art works (bottom).

On 30 April 1945, the US Seventh Army advanced into the Munich city center and occupied the buildings that housed the headquarters of the Nazi party (the NSDAP), the most prominent of which were those located on the Königsplatz: the *Führerbau*, and its architectural equivalent, the "administration building," housing the offices of the party treasurer. In June, the US Military Government set up the Collecting Point in the former "administration building." Working under the supervision of the members of the MFA&A, the so-called monuments men, the German staff comprised art historians, registrars, librarians, photographers, restorers, and technicians. In early June, the young art historian Craig Hugh Smyth (1915–2006) was appointed the first American director of the Collecting Point. Further American experts subsequently joined the team up until 1949. They included the ethnologist Frederick R. Pleasants (1906–1978), and the art historians Edwin C. Rae (1911–2002) and Herbert S. Leonard (1908–1952).

The monuments men tracked down and inspected the numerous art depositories in the US occupation zones on German and Austrian territory. Most of the objects that had been confiscated by the Einsatzstab Reichsleiter Rosenberg (Reichsleiter Rosenberg Taskforce, ERR) were found in the Upper Bavarian castles Neuschwanstein and Herrenchiemsee, and in the Carthusian monastery of Buxheim in Swabia. Art objects of different origins, mostly intended to become part of the Linz museum, were stored in the salt mines of Altaussee and Bad Ischl, near Salzburg.

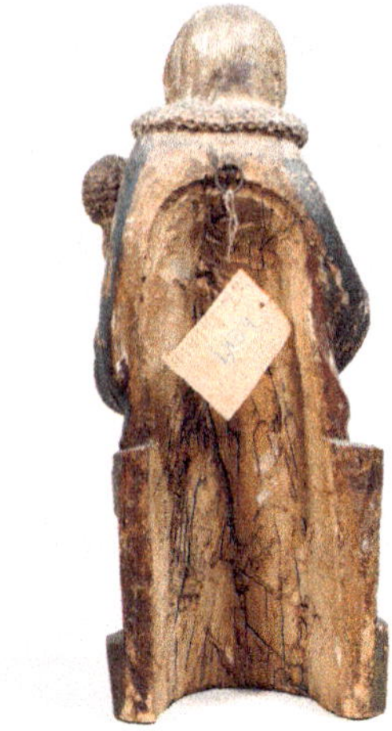

Fig. 3: Sitting Madonna with Child, Munich no. 6069; today Bayerisches Nationalmuseum, Munich.

Packed and wrapped rather shoddily, thousands of art objects were transferred to the CCP Munich, where the wooden crates and their contents were registered and identified, as far as possible (figs. 1 and 2). A blue registration number, known as the "Munich number," was marked on the back of the paintings or on a label attached to the statues or art objects (fig. 3). Several files kept by the looting organizations, such as the ERR, proved helpful in the process of identification. German art dealers and collectors were interrogated about the provenance of art works. Dealers such as Adolf Weinmüller, who had been among the principal suppliers of Hitler, Göring, and other high-ranking National Socialist art lovers, however, successfully concealed their former actions and generally got off rather lightly.

The personnel of the Munich Collecting Point was mostly occupied with the external restitution. Following a decision of the Allied Control Council, the restituted objects were to be handed over not to individuals, but to governmental organizations. The respective European governments prepared the "claims" and submitted them to the CCP Munich. On the invitation of the US authorities, from August 1945 onward representatives of the European missions came to Munich and set up their offices there. Upon their arrival, the art objects were stored in general depositories to which the foreign representatives were denied access. They thus had to prepare their claims on the basis of lists of objects they had drawn up or received from museum curators and private art collectors in their country. On the one hand, the US monuments men wished to prevent the depositories turning into a sort of "self-service" store. On the other hand, this denial of access generated ongoing friction between the foreign missions and the Collecting Point personnel.

External Restitution

External restitutions began in August 1945. At this point, trucks were still constantly ferrying in growing amounts of cultural items and art works of all dimensions, from Madame Rothschild's thimble to a copy of Rodin's sculpture The Burghers of Calais. Rodin's work had been acquired on the Paris art market by Hildebrand Gurlitt for the Wallraf-Richartz-Museum in Cologne. Evacuated to the Castle of Unterdießen in Swabia, the heavy bronze group was brought to Munich in October 1946 on the way of being restituted to Paris (fig. 4).

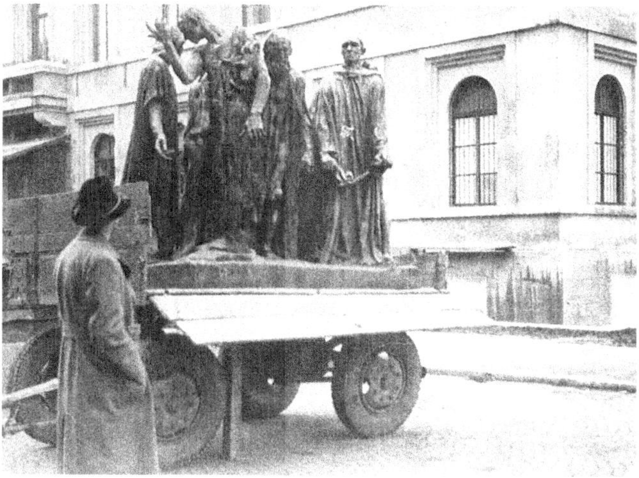

Fig. 4: Transport of Auguste Rodin's The Burghers of Calais to Munich in October 1946.

Statistics provided by the US authorities show the distribution of the restitutions to the various nations (fig. 5): Up until August 1947, two thirds of the restitutions went to France, and the remaining third went to the Soviet Union, the Netherlands, Poland, Hungary, Belgium, Czechoslovakia, and other countries. The USA sought to benefit politically from the restitutions by creating a positive image for itself, which it could exploit in its dealings with European countries at the beginning of the Cold War. In both the opposing blocs, in the East as well as in the West, the restitutions were exploited for political purposes.

An overview of the external restitutions processed by the CCP Munich should therefore begin with France. Unlike an occupying power such as the United States, France had suffered heavily from National Socialist looting. This had a strong impact on French restitution policy and claims, which included so-called restitutions in kind. These involved claims by the French authorities to art works from public collections in compensation for looted or lost art, but they were never processed. In fact, after World War II restitutions in kind were undertaken only by the Soviet Union.

The majority of art works from French collections were found not in the French zone, but in the US occupation zone. The search for looted art was carried out by several governmental institutions, chief among them the Office des biens et intérêts privés (OBIP) and, from 1944, the Commission de récupération artistique (CRA). From May 1945, the French representative, Rose Valland (1898–1980), went to Germany in order to inspect the depositories. From June 1946, a selection of returned masterpieces from French private collections, mostly that of the Rothschild family, was exhibited in the Orangery in the Tuileries Garden in Paris. Up until December 1948, thirty-three shipments containing some 15,000 objects were dispatched from Munich to France, where some were restituted. Others were chosen by a French museum commission and are still to be found in French national museums classified under the label "Musées nationaux récupération" (MNR).

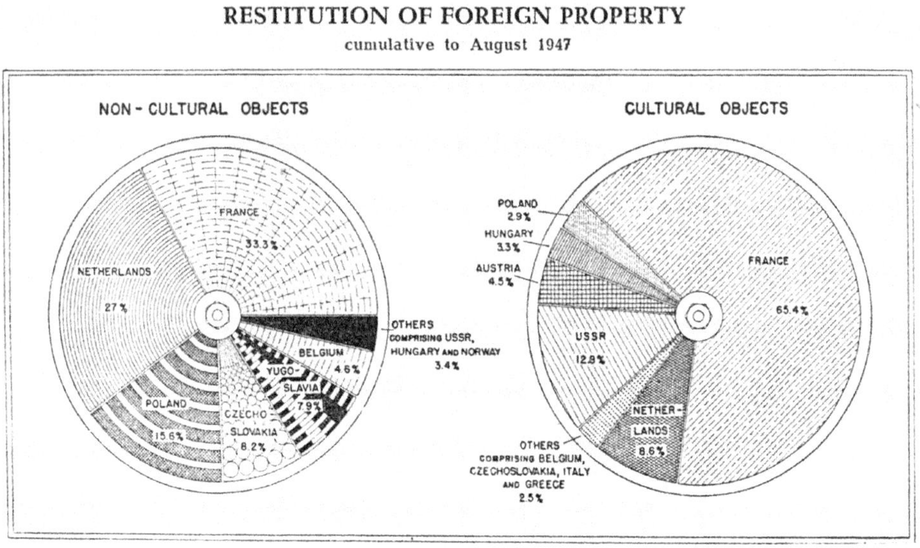

Fig. 5: Restitution of Foreign Property cumulative to August 1947.

In the Netherlands, from June 1945, a foundation for Dutch art collections (Stichting Nederlands Kunstbezit) was authorized to claim and restitute looted art works. Since 1940, the office of Kajetan Mühlmann (Dienststelle Mühlmann) had coordinated the National Socialist looting of art in the country, mostly of large private collections owned by Jews such as Fritz Mannheimer, Otto Lanz, and Nathan Katz.

Among the Belgian restitutions were famous art works such as the Ghent Altar Piece and Michelangelo's Bruge Madonna. The restitutions to the Soviet Union were particularly plentiful, comprising cultural and archaeological items looted from museums in Ukraine, Belarus, and Russia. The restitutions to Hungary, Poland, and Czechoslovakia involved primarily important art works with public and private provenance. In the countries under Soviet rule, most of the art works restituted to the state were not returned to their private owners but nationalized. Their final restitution was effected only after the fall of the Iron Curtain.

A problematic case was that of erroneous restitutions to Yugoslavia, in 1949, during the final months of the operation of the CCP Munich, at a time when the American authorities were intent on accelerating the restitution process before handing over responsibility to the young German Federal Republic. The Yugoslav claims were submitted to the Collecting Point by Ante Topić Mimara (1898–1987), who played the leading role in an affair that has all the ingredients of a thriller. He submitted false claims that were discovered to be fraudulent only belatedly, with the result that a number of art works were mistakenly transferred to Yugoslavia, where they can probably still be found.

Restitutions to "Ex-Enemy States": Italy and Austria

The restitutions to the "ex-enemy states" Italy and Austria were politically and juridically complicated, and were considered, how Otto Demus put it, "political dynamite."[1] Following an Allied directive issued in 1943 (the London Declaration), these two countries were treated differently from the member states of the United Nations. Art objects which had been acquired or confiscated and taken to Germany between September 1943 and May 1945 (from Italy) and between March 1938 and May 1945 (from Austria) were subject to restitution only after new US directives were issued in 1946 and 1947.

The restitution of famous paintings from the Museo Nazionale di Capodimonte and the no less famous statues from the Museo Nazionale Archeologico in Naples was uncontested, and was conducted in 1946. The Italian representative Rodolfo Siviero (1911–1983) was granted the restitution of other art works that had left Italy with the permission of the fascist government. The return of Myron's *Discobolus* to Italy in 1948, for example, unconnected to any financial compensation, provoked a heated controversy in Germany over the legitimacy of the restitutions to Italy.

The relations between the Austrian representatives and the German personnel of the Collecting Point were particularly inimical, with each party accusing the other of having been Nazis. The Austrian representatives accused the CCP of withholding art works from the *Sonderauftrag Linz* stock, which had been brought to Munich from the Altaussee depository, among others.

In 1952, the Munich CCP consigned some 1,000 art objects, mostly paintings, to the Austrian authorities. After some restitutions were effected, certain unidentified works were brought to the Carthusian monastery in Mauerbach. In 1995, the remaining unidentified objects were handed over to the Bundesverband der Israelitischen Kultusgemeinde Österreich (Federal Association of Jewish Communities of Austria) for its use. In 1996, these objects were sold in the so-called Mauerbach auction. This was not the only case of capitulation in the face of the challenge of provenance research.

1 See Iris Lauterbach, Der Central Collecting Point in München. Kunstschutz, Restitution, Neubeginn, Berlin/Munich 2015, fn. 380.

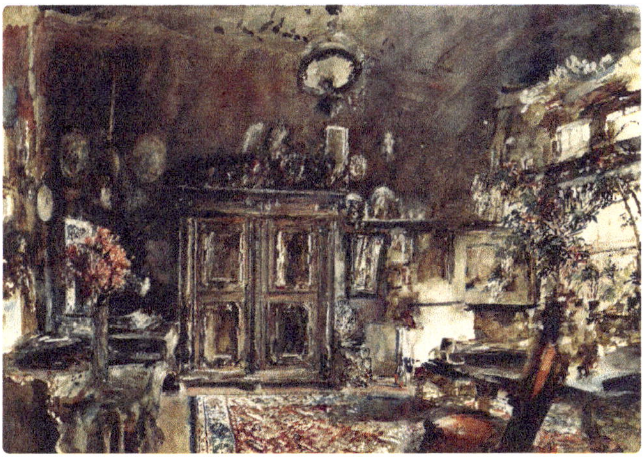

Fig. 6: Rudolf von Alt, The Artist's Studio.

Only recently, a group of 617 drawings by the Austrian artists Jakob and Rudolf von Alt kept in the Staatliche Graphische Sammlung München was subject to intense provenance research. Many of them having been owned by—mostly still unidentified—Jewish collectors in Vienna, the drawings were acquired by Martin Bormann after the "Anschluss" of Austria in 1938. Part of the "non-identified remainder" of the CCP stock, they were transferred to the Staatliche Graphische Sammlung München by the CCP's successor organization, the Treuhandverwaltung von Kulturgut (Trustee Administration for Cultural Property), in the late 1950s. One of these notable drawings exemplifies the complex nature of provenance research. Rudolf von Alt's last, uncompleted work created in 1905, portrays the artist's studio (fig. 6).[2] It was part of the collection of the Jewish Viennese industrialist Stephan Mautner, who was forced to sell it. *The Artist's Studio* was bought for Bormann, removed to Altaussee, and from there brought to the CCP in October 1945. In 1947, Mautner's son Karl who, unlike his parents, had escaped Nazi persecution, claimed four of the drawings, but the CCP was unable to identify them in the stock, and for unknown reasons did not even find Alt's last work. Following a further inquiry by Mautner in 1980/81, after discovering the drawing in the Staatliche Graphische Sammlung München, it was restituted to the heirs only in September 2016 and acquired from them by the Ernst von Siemens Kunststiftung.[3]

2 See Meike Hopp, "Weiß gar nicht, wo sie alle hingerathen sind." Der Münchner Bestand der Werke Rudolf von Alts und die "Sammlung Bormann." Eine Herausforderung für die Provenienzforschung, in: Andreas Strobl (ed.), Rudolf von Alt, … genial, lebhaft, natürlich und wahr. Der Münchner Bestand und seine Provenienz, Berlin/Munich 2015 (exhibition catalogue), 147–190.

3 See Andreas Strobl, Letzter Blick. Die Ernst von Siemens Kunststiftung erwirbt das letzte Bild von Rudolf von Alt, in: Arsprototo. Das Magazin der Kulturstiftung der Länder (2017), no. 1, 46f.; idem, Rudolf von Alt, Das Arbeitszimmer des Künstlers, 1905, in: Jahresbericht der Ernst von Siemens Kunststiftung 2015/2016, Munich 2017, 42.

Internal Restitutions

The so-called internal restitutions involved predominantly Jewish individuals who used to live or were still living in Germany. Law no. 59 enacted by the US Military Government in November 1947 governed "restitution [...] to persons who were wrongfully deprived of [their] property from 30 January 1933 to 8 May 1945 for reasons of race, religion, nationality, ideology or political opposition to National Socialism." Restitutions processed under this law involved not only German nationals, but also—if the looting had taken place in Germany—German-Jewish owners who had emigrated and were living abroad.

The case of the CCP Munich demonstrates that, among the many other beneficiaries, museums profited from the looting perpetrated by the National Socialist authorities. In 1938/39 the Gestapo confiscated art objects from numerous private collections. Some were auctioned abroad, such as Alfred Pringsheim's majolica collection, in London, in 1939, or donated to Bavarian museums. One may assume that the curators of the Bavarian National Museum, for example, had few qualms about accepting works of art belonging to the Jewish collectors and dealers Pringsheim, Siegfried Lämmle or Ludwig Gerngroß in order to enrich their collections. The Gestapo's confiscation of art works in 1938 was subsequently explained as a measure taken "to protect these objects from displacement, disappearance, or looting. Works of gold and silver thus were saved from the melting-pot."[4] From the Bavarian National Museum via the CCP, Alfred Pringsheim's entire silver collection was restituted to his heirs, who had emigrated to the United States. A list compiled before the war, however, marked several of the Pringsheim art objects as "cultural items of national importance" that could not be taken out of Germany. This presented an obstacle to their legitimate restitution, which understandably upset the Pringsheim heirs. They had to wait until 1953 to have their property returned.

Unclaimed looted art objects that had belonged to Jewish owners and institutions were handed over to the Jewish Cultural Reconstruction organization (JCR), founded in the USA and acting from 1947 under the roof of the Jewish Restitution Successor Organization (JRSO), the predecessor of the Jewish Claims Conference.

4 See Lauterbach, Der Central Collecting Point in München, fn. 404: Theodor Müller, 7 January 1948.

Conclusion

In November 1949, the US Government transferred the art works of doubtful provenance that were still in the custody of the CCP to the German authorities, subject to their commitment to conduct further provenance research with a view to the works' subsequent restitution. From 1952 to 1963, the successor organization Treuhandverwaltung von Kulturgut was responsible for this "unidentified remainder" of both the Wiesbaden and Munich Collecting Points. Currently, the Bundesverwaltungsamt still keeps around 3,000 items, the provenance of which has been examined and appears to be uncontentious according to the current state of knowledge.[5]

It is difficult to draw up an accurate accounting of the restitutions processed by the CCP Munich. The institution issued approximately 50,000 registration numbers, which correspond to a total of some 80,000 items. Not all of these, however, were looted art works. The CCP Munich also registered and numbered art objects from legitimate public German collections. Between 1945 and 1952 more than 33,000 items were returned to foreign countries, as well as 58 running meters of archival material, and 900 objects returned to Austria. More than 23,000 items were restituted to German and to Jewish owners under Law no. 59.

5 See Bundesverwaltungsamt, Provenienzforschung des Bundes, <http://www.bva.bund.de/DE/Themen/Kunstverwaltung/Provenienzforschung_Kunstbesitz/start.html> (1 August 2019).

Literature

Meike Hopp, Kunsthandel im Nationalsozialismus. Adolf Weinmüller in München und Wien, Cologne/Weimar/Vienna 2012.

Iris Lauterbach, The Central Collecting Point in Munich. A New Beginning for the Restitution and Protection of Art, transl. by Fiona Elliot, Los Angeles, Calif., 2018.

Lorenz Seelig, Die Münchner Sammlung Alfred Pringsheim. Versteigerung, Beschlagnahmung, Restitution, in: Andrea Baresel-Brand (ed.), Entehrt. Ausgeplündert. Arisiert. Entrechtung und Enteignung der Juden, Magdeburg 2005, 265–290.

Lorenz Seelig, Die Silbersammlung Alfred Pringsheim, Riggisberg 2013.

Andreas Strobl (ed.), Rudolf von Alt ... genial, lebhaft, natürlich und wahr. Der Münchner Bestand und seine Provenienz, Berlin/Munich 2015 (exhibition catalogue).

Matthias Weniger, Die Sammlungen Siegfried Lämmle und Ludwig Gerngroß im Bayerischen Nationalmuseum 1938–1953, in: Andrea Baresel-Brand (ed.), Entehrt. Ausgeplündert. Arisiert. Entrechtung und Enteignung der Juden, Magdeburg 2005, 291–307.

Author

Iris Lauterbach studied art history and French and Italian philology at the universities of Mainz, Pavia (Collegio Ghislieri), and Paris (Paris IV). She received her PhD from the Johannes Gutenberg-Universität Mainz in 1985. Since 1991 she has been a member of the research department of the Zentralinstitut für Kunstgeschichte in Munich. Since 2001 she has taught garden history at the Munich Technical University, where she was appointed honorary professor in 2012. Her fields of research are the history of gardens, architecture and the visual arts under National Socialism, and cultural policy in postwar Germany (1945–1949). *Selected Publications*: The NSDAP Centre in Munich, transl. by Julia Schmidt-Pirro, Munich/Berlin 2015 (with Ulrike Grammbitter); Antoine Watteau 1684–1721, transl. by Karen Williams, Hong Kong/Cologne 2008; Bürokratie und Kult. Das Parteizentrum der NSDAP am Königsplatz in München. Geschichte und Rezeption, Munich/Berlin 1995 (ed. with Julian Rosefeldt and Piero Steinle).

BILHA SHILO

When YIVO was Defined by Territory: Two Perspectives on the Restitution of YIVO's Collections

In March 1951, the *Yedies fun YIVO*'s (News from YIVO) main headline announced: "YIVO library is back home."[1] This concise and unassuming title concealed a unique story; a momentous drama that accompanied the wartime history of one of the most important Jewish scientific institutions in Eastern Europe—the Yiddish Scientific Institute, or YIVO (Yidisher Visnshaftlekher Institute), in Vilna (today Vilnius). As were most of European Jewish cultural assets, YIVO's collections were confiscated by the Nazis and transferred to the Third Reich. During and especially after the war, the members of YIVO's branch in New York endeavored to restitute those collections to the United States. In June 1947 their efforts bore fruit when YIVO's collections were transported from Offenbach in Germany to New York. Why, then, was the return of the collections made public only three and a half years later? The answer is that alongside the successful restitution of YIVO's collection from Offenbach, the institute had failed to retrieve another part of its collections from Czechoslovakia. As long as YIVO's heads believed there was a chance of recovering this additional collection, they preferred not to reveal the great achievement. This essay seeks to present both sides of the affair—the resounding success and the failure. They not only shed light on each other, but also highlight some of the political, cultural, and national circumstances that impacted Jewish cultural property restitution after the war, and reveal some of the tensions between the new Jewish centers that evolved after the extermination of European Jewry.

1 Newsletter of the YIVO 40, March 1951, 1*–2*.

Contested Heritage, 79–90 | doi.org/10.13109/9783666310836.79

Early Restitution Efforts

The vast majority of Jewish cultural property stolen by the Nazis and found after World War II was located in the American occupation zone; four million books from Frankfurt and its surroundings were collected by the Offenbach Archival Depot (OAD), run by the US Military Government in Germany. According to the Territorial Principle that governed restitution processes in the wake of armed conflicts, the countries of origin claimed this property and most books were identified and returned, with the exception of the libraries originating in the prewar Baltic States, whose annexation to the Soviet Union was not recognized by the United States. Many of the collections in Offenbach were identified as heirless Jewish property, and difficulties arose with regard to their restitution. This formed the backdrop to the American Military Government's Law 59, which decreed that assets confiscated by the Nazis would be returned to their former owners, and those remaining heirless would be transferred over time to a successor organization.

Anxiety regarding the fate of Jewish cultural property had arisen already during the war. In the spring of 1944, the Commission on European Jewish Cultural Reconstruction was founded in New York, which in April 1947 became the Jewish Cultural Reconstruction, Inc. (JCR). In February 1949 JCR was legally recognized as the trustee of heirless Jewish cultural property, acting on behalf of a number of leading Jewish bodies, among them the Hebrew University of Jerusalem. Historian Salo W. Baron headed JCR, Hannah Arendt served as its executive secretary, and it was supported by many notable Jewish intellectuals. JCR strove to coordinate the endeavor to restitute heirless Jewish cultural property located in the American zone, and to distribute it equitably among Jewish centers worldwide. Even though Max Weinreich, who served as YIVO's head, was a member of JCR, he strongly objected to the idea that JCR would operate on behalf of YIVO for a simple reason: in his view, YIVO property was not heirless.

The Successful Episode: YIVO's Collections at the Offenbach Archival Depot

YIVO was founded in Vilna in 1925, and raised the banner of Yiddish and its culture (fig. 1). Its four departments were located in the main centers of Jewish life: Vilna, Berlin, Warsaw, and New York. YIVO was headed by Max Weinreich, Zalman Reizen, and Zelig Kalmanovich. The center in Vilna established a library and maintained archives, but also initiated research into Eastern European Jewry, conducted educational projects, and developed a standardized form of Yiddish. As an institute working "from the people, for the people, with the people,"[2] it enjoyed tremendous support from Yiddish speakers worldwide.

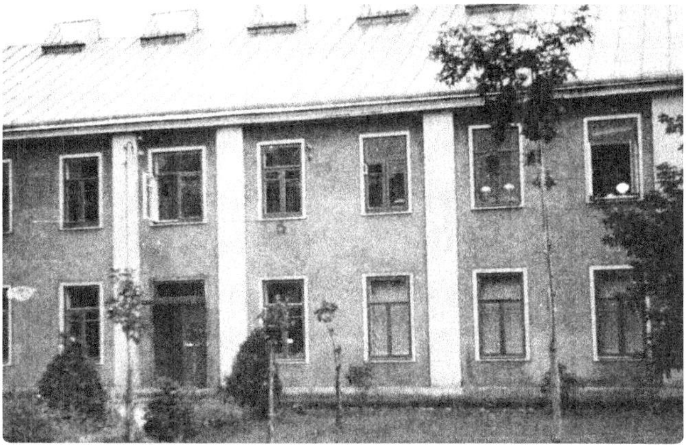

Fig. 1: YIVO building at 18 Wiwulskiego Street, Vilna, Poland, 1937.

When World War II broke out, Weinreich was visiting Copenhagen and remained there for six months until departing for New York in March 1940, from where he continued to lead the institution. In June 1941, a week after the German occupation of Vilna, the NS-Einsatzstab Reichsleiter Rosenberg (Reichsleiter Rosenberg Taskforce) arrived in the city. YIVO was dismantled, part of its collections destroyed, and other parts were transported to Germany. Forced laborers, known as the Papir-Brigade (Paper Brigade), some of them YIVO personnel, were coerced into taking part in YIVO's destruction. They risked their lives to rescue cultural treasures by hiding them in the building or in the Vilna ghetto. Some of these were subsequently rediscovered, smuggled to the West after the war, and then conveyed to YIVO-New York.

Weinreich appealed for help to the US State Department already in 1942. Laying the grounds for YIVO's claims, he argued that YIVO's collections were American property since YIVO-New York was funded in part by state budgets, but also because US bodies and citizens had supported YIVO-Vilna since the 1920s. On the strength of these claims Weinreich declared YIVO-New York to be a successor to YIVO-Vilna, pointing to the direct institutional, personal, and material continuity between them. Addressing the US Secretary of State, he stressed the rarity of the stolen European Jewish libraries:

> "These treasures should [...] be brought to the United States where is by far the largest single Jewish community in the world and where, under the protection of American democratic institutions, they would be accessible as tools of research and sources of inspiration to all concerned throughout the world."[3]

2 Y[udl] M[ark], "Funem folk, farn folk, mitn folk." Der veg tsu der Yiddisher visnshaft (Kaunas), 15 January 1926, cit. in Cecile Esther Kuznitz, YIVO and the Making of Modern Jewish Culture. Scholarship for the Yiddish Nation, New York 2014, 228, fn. 3.

3 YIVO Institute for Jewish Research, Office Archives (henceforth YIVO), Restitution 1945–49, Box 1, File 1945 and Earlier, Max Weinreich to Archibald MacLeish, 4 April 1945.

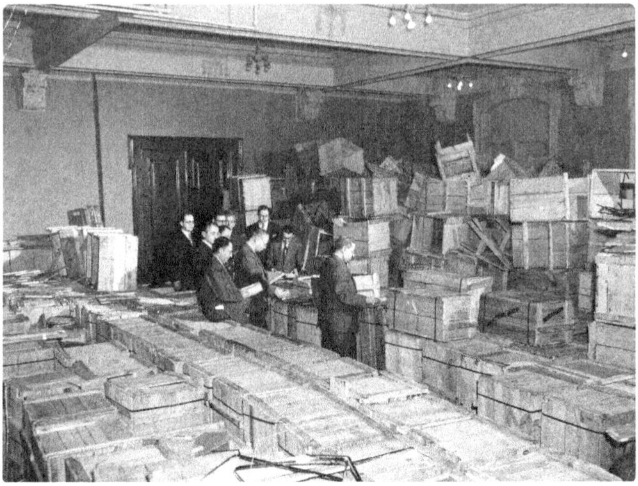

Fig. 2: Examination of books and documents from Vilna by the US government in New Jersey, 1947.

In June 1945, tens of thousands of YIVO's books and documents were found in a cave in Hungen and in the building of the former Institut zur Erforschung der Judenfrage (Institute for the Study of the Jewish Question) in Frankfurt. At first Weinreich believed that American Jewish soldiers, who had certain connections with YIVO, would deliver the collections to New York. However, it soon became apparent that official YIVO representation was required at the OAD, where a large collection of YIVO materials was identified and gathered (fig. 2). The first to undertake this task was YIVO member Koppel Pinson, director of the Educational Department of the American Jewish Joint Distribution Committee (AJDC). Despite his strenuous efforts, Pinson returned to America empty-handed. At the same time, Weinreich was busy lobbying in Washington in collaboration with the American Jewish Committee (AJC), and in May 1946 the State Department authorized in principle the transfer of YIVO's collection to the USA. The release of the collections was delayed owing to a disagreement between the State and War Departments regarding YIVO's status: Should YIVO's claim be considered under the general policy pertaining to Jewish property, or should it be treated as an individual unique case? Ultimately, Weinreich's position was accepted and YIVO's property was defined as American property. Hence, it was the Library of Congress that claimed the YIVO collections on behalf of the state, to the JCR's evident chagrin. In March 1947, following tough negotiations, the order was given to release the collections from Offenbach to the Library of Congress Mission (LCM), joined by YIVO representative Seymour Pomrenze. Additional sorting was necessary before the collection could be released. Lucy Schildkret (later Dawidowicz), the AJDC representative in Germany, volunteered to sort YIVO's volumes in Offenbach. In mid-June 1947, Pomrenze arrived with LCM, and within four days 420 crates containing almost 80,000 books were dispatched to Bremen and shipped to New York. By 1952, 12,000 more books had been sent to YIVO through JCR.

We have here a remarkable success story. YIVO's demand to return its collections was the first recognized claim by a Jewish organization's suc-

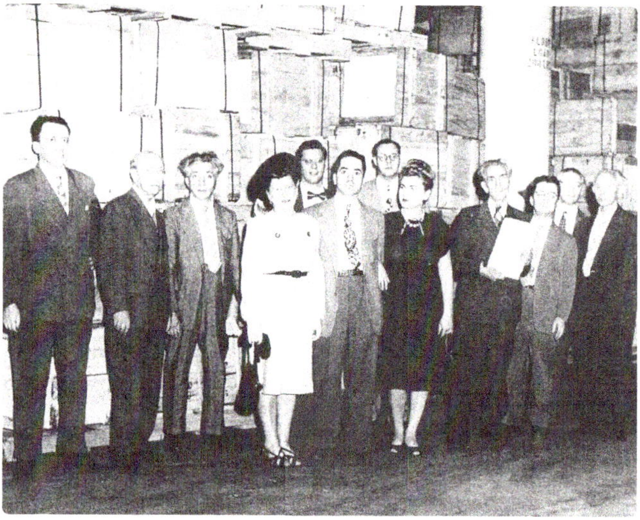

cessor, overriding the Territorial Principle. The interests of YIVO and of the US administration converged, and Weinreich's demands were accepted by the government in full. Thus, collections lacking any American affinity, including the famous Strashun Library, found their way to YIVO-New York. The restitution of YIVO's collection from Offenbach is a study in the evolution of the entire restitution process. YIVO progressed from taking independent and even underhand actions toward a diplomatic operation, coordinated with and recognized by government and military agencies. Furthermore, YIVO was held up as an example in the general debate over Jewish cultural property, and its achievement set a precedent with regard to the process of restituting heirless Jewish property to Jewish bodies worldwide. This accomplishment contributed to the recognition of JCR as a successor organization representing the Jewish people, and in fact to the recognition of the political-juridical status of the Jewish people (**fig. 3**).

Fig. 3: The heads of YIVO with the restituted collections in New Jersey, 1947.

The Story of the Failure: YIVO in Czechoslovakia

The other side of the affair is the failure of the restitution of YIVO's newspaper collection, which was confiscated from Vilna for the library of the *Reichssicherheitshauptamt* (Reich Main Security Office) in Berlin. As were many other collections, it was subsequently evacuated, for fear of bombing, to Mimoň (Niemes) Castle in Northern Bohemia (**fig. 4**).

The nationalization of property in general progressed rapidly in Czechoslovakia after the war. Under the pressure exerted by the Socialist and Communist parties, with backing from the USSR, all property belonging to anyone deemed German was expropriated, without distinguishing between Nazis and their victims. As American influence waned, representatives of *Ha-va'ada le-hazalat Ozrot ha-Golah* (Committee for the Salvaging of Diaspora Treasures) at the Hebrew University of Jerusalem operated in this legal/political, East/West thicket, in order to rescue, as they put it, "the cultural bequest of the shattered Jewish diaspora, for the national and spiritual center of the Jewish people in Jerusalem."[4] Hugo Bergman, the first rector of the Hebrew University, who was sent on a mission to persuade the Czech authorities to allow the transfer of the Jewish property to Jerusalem, discovered the YIVO newspaper collection at Mimoň, and in late 1946 notified YIVO of the existence of this site that awaited a new restitution endeavor. For YIVO, Bergman's letter was the last first-hand evidence of the newspaper collection's existence.

Upon receiving this news, YIVO authorized the Council of Jewish Communities in Bohemia and Moravia to represent it, and instructed the American embassy in Prague to assist it if necessary. In February 1947, Salo W. Baron and Weinreich discussed how to go about restoring the collection:

> "Prof. Baron rang [...], [he] had doubts if a separate appeal by YIVO was worthwhile, since the Commission on European Jewish Cultural Reconstruction had previously requested the State Department to hand over to the Hebrew University all Jewish treasures, taken by the Nazis to Czechoslovakia. According to their plan, the Hebrew University was supposed to serve as [...] the general trustee of all Jewish property looted by the Germans."[5]

During this conversation Baron linked Offenbach and Czechoslovakia, claiming that an independent operation mounted by YIVO might risk the entire restitution process and delay the retrieval of Jewish property. Weinreich disagreed:

> "I clarified to Prof. Baron that YIVO's case is an entirely specific one and if possible would best be separated from the larger, more general matters, which require considerable time and which involve legal intricacies. YIVO is not demanding anything but its own. The State Department has recognized YIVO in New York as the legal heir to YIVO Vilna. This justifies YIVO's ad-hoc decision, before all the general problems are dealt with."[6]

4 National Library of Israel (henceforth NLI), ARC. 4°793/288, March 1946, Tazkir ha-va'ada ha-mishpatit sheal yad ha-va'ada le-hazalat Ozrot ha-Golah [Abstract of the Legal Sub-Committee of the Committee for the Salvaging of Diaspora Treasures], cit. in Gish Amit, Ex-Libris. Chronicles of Theft, Preservation, and Appropriating at the Jewish National Library, Jerusalem 2014, 43–55 (Heb.).

5 American Jewish Historical Society, New York (henceforth AJHS), File P-675/52/4, Max Weinreich, Farẓeiyvenung vegen a telefonishn shmues mit Prof. Salo Baron, Freitik, 28stn Februar 1947 [Summary of a Telephone Conversation with Prof. Salo Baron, Friday, 28 February 1947].

6 AJHS, File P-675/52/4, Max Weinreich, Farẓeiyvenung vegen a telefonishn shmues mit Prof. Salo Baron, Freitik, 28stn Februar 1947 [Summary of a Telephone Conversation with Prof. Salo Baron, Friday, 28 February 1947].

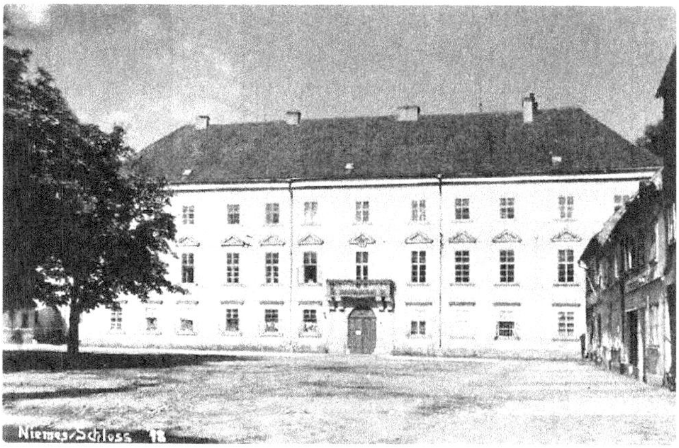

Fig. 4: Mimoň (Niemes) Castle, Northern Bohemia.

As Weinreich notes, the State Department supported YIVO in Czechoslovakia as well. Meanwhile, mutual suspicion between the parties rose to the point that Weinreich believed that JCR was attempting to sabotage the restitution of YIVO's collections from Offenbach.

Two YIVO representatives set off for Prague, but failed in their effort to effect the restitution of YIVO's newspaper collection. Lucy Dawidowicz spent a few days in the city in March 1947 to no avail, causing a minor commotion when members of *Ha-va'ada le-hazalat Oẓrot ha-Golah* discovered that someone was showing interest in YIVO's collections.[7] In July 1947, having completed his mission in Offenbach, Seymour Pomrenze arrived in Prague. Despite assurances by the Jewish Council and the Jewish Museum in Prague to include him in the party due to visit Mimoň Castle, he was reduced to chasing their people around Prague, only ultimately to be left behind. These local organizations were not acting alone; a representative of the Hebrew University, Arthur Bergman (Hugo's brother), was in Prague at the time, and Pomrenze ran into him as he was sorting books from Theresienstadt for the Hebrew University. Although he was aware of Pomrenze's mission, and could no doubt have exploited his good connections and assistance from the military, Bergman refrained from inviting Pomrenze to join him on his visit to Mimoň three days later. Pomrenze's mission ended in disappointment. Bergman, on the other hand, was not content with the books from Theresienstadt; in Mimoň he packed and delivered many collections to Prague, assisted by the Czechoslovak military, the Jewish Council, and the Jewish Museum. Bergman reported to Gershom Scholem that: "There may be manuscripts [in the YIVO collection], [but] this will be a matter for the University to sort out later with YIVO."[8]

In October 1947, on the order of the military, Mimoň Castle was cleared of its contents. Forced to find a speedy solution for the remaining collections, the Jewish Council hired a storehouse in Mimoň. Ze'ev Scheck, the Hebrew University's next envoy to Czechoslovakia, notified Scholem

7 The Archives of the Hebrew University (henceforth AHU), File 046/1947-I, Werner Senator to Salo W. Baron, 29 April 1947.
8 AHU, File 046/1947-I, Arthur Bergman to Gershom Scholem, 20 July 1947.

of this development, but unlike Hugo Bergman before him, he did not inform YIVO, leaving the task to the Jewish Council. In fact, YIVO failed to receive notification of the evacuation. Several days later, Scheck set off for Mimoň and packed up the remaining collections. Employing resourcefulness, manipulation, and bribery, he managed to complete the task that Arthur Bergman had begun, and dispatched tens of thousands of books, including numerous Yiddish collections, from Czechoslovakia on a circuitous route to Jerusalem. After returning home, in September 1948, Scheck submitted a report on the archives found in the castles, mentioning that:

> "One archive, YIVO America, [...] exists in a storehouse in the town of Niemes [Mimoň]. Prof. Bergman [...] had already made efforts to retrieve the archive to be sent to Palestine. YIVO demands it be returned, without practically caring for the materials themselves. [...] If in the future YIVO continues not to take care of this material, we can again try to retrieve it."[9]

At a meeting in November 1948, Werner Senator, Hebrew University's chief administrator, offered Weinreich the university's help. He asserted that there had been no progress in Prague, although by then the collections had already been sent out of Czechoslovakia. At that time Scheck was working for the East European department at the Israeli Foreign Office. He used this position to attempt to transfer the remaining collections to Jerusalem via the Israeli legation in Prague, reporting to Scholem as follows:

> "We have sent from Prague two letters to YIVO stating that transfer of the materials depends only on financial allocation, and a direct appeal to the government. [...] The institute has not replied, and apparently wants the Legation to take care of them. I have received the matter for processing, and here is my suggestion: the Legation will transfer—but to Israel."[10]

The letters, however, were not received by YIVO. Meanwhile, the only remaining way of transferring books to Jerusalem was in small packages containing valuable items sent through the diplomatic mail, in the hope that this would not raise suspicion. I assume, therefore, that the newspaper collection, which was moved from the storehouse in Mimoň to Houska Castle or to the Jewish Museum, was appropriated by the Prague National

9 AHU, File 046/1948, Ze'ev Scheck, Report Betr. Archive in den Schlössern Nordböhmens, 19 September 1948.
10 NLI, ARC. 4°793/288/2, Ze'ev Scheck to Gershom Scholem, 14 February 1949. (I thank Anna Holzer-Kawalko for this source.)

Library. Parts of it were perhaps transferred to Jerusalem or sold. But this is not the end of the affair.

At the time the Hebrew University considered inaugurating a Chair of Yiddish, and Weinreich was offered the position. In late 1948 he consulted Senator regarding the newspaper collection, and Senator spied a window of opportunity:

> "I told Dr. W. we were of course ready to help in any way possible but that our representative had already left Prague. [...] You may know that Dr. W. was mentioned here as a possible candidate for the Chair of Yiddish, [...] I should like you to get information discreetly. I had the impression [...] that the Institute would not be averse to transferring its quarters to Palestine, but this may be erroneous. Since the matter in connection with the Chair of Yiddish and its possible development into a department is of interest for us, I wonder whether you could get something definite for me."[11]

In October 1949 the two met again and Senator noted in his diary:

> "Met [...] Mr. Weinreich, who at one time had been proposed for the Chair of Yiddish. [...] Their books and archives in Czechoslovakia are still there. [...] Some parts of their library are valuable but surely professor Scholem will be able to judge the situation much better than I. I still believe that the time will come in the not too distant future when we consider the transfer of the Institute to the University."[12]

Final Remarks: Between Vilna, New York, and Jerusalem

It transpires that the new political configuration brought about by the Cold War was a major factor with regard to YIVO's successes and failures in restoring its property. In the West, YIVO achieved unprecedented success, masterfully establishing that Vilna was New York. Both the OAD and the authorities in Washington accepted that "everything the Germans

11 AHU, File 046/1948, Werner Senator to High Salpeter, 26 December 1948.

12 AHU, File 046/1949, Werner Senator, 25 October 1949 (diary entry). Weinreich considered the offer up until mid-1950, but ultimately turned it down. YIVO continued to enlist the help of the State Department to restitute the newspaper collection until late 1948, at least.

brought from Vilna apparently belongs to YIVO"[13]—to YIVO-New York that is. Undoubtedly, the fact that YIVO and its personnel had begun to make their way to the West before the war, and especially the rising status of YIVO-New York upon Weinreich's arrival, aided in establishing continuity between Vilna and New York. By contrast, the governments of Eastern Europe did not recognize the special status of Jewish property, and either treated it according to the Territorial Principle, which they applied ad absurdum, without taking account of its history, or nationalized it speedily in the spirit of communism. Thus, paradoxically, YIVO property originating in Eastern Europe was considered American property, and the chances to claim it were slim. Similarly, JCR found itself utterly paralyzed in communist-oriented countries, and therefore fully supported the Hebrew University in its efforts to lay its hands on the collections it sought from Czechoslovakia. Thus, the threat to YIVO lurked from the competing Jewish center in Palestine, which was able to act relatively freely in the Eastern space.

It appears that Weinreich believed that, while before the Holocaust American Jewry had been secondary to the communities in the former homeland of Eastern Europe, its time had come to serve as the world's primary Jewish center because it constituted the largest Jewish community worldwide. The story that played out off center stage was the latent rivalry between YIVO and the Hebrew University. Both institutes were founded in 1925 and sought to serve as Jewish national academies in two major spiritual centers of the interwar period: Jerusalem of *Eretz Israel* (Mandatory Palestine), and *Yerushalayim de-Lita* (the Jerusalem of Lithuania). They represented opposing worldviews: While YIVO considered itself an autonomist Yiddishist center representing the Jewish diaspora in the tradition of Dubnow and Zhitlowsky, the Hebrew University was perceived by its supporters as the exclusive intellectual center of the Jewish people, in the spirit of Ahad Ha'am. For them, the Jewish National and University Library served as the center for the ingathering of the cultural property of the Jewish people. Scholem and his colleagues sought to strengthen the Jewish Yishuv in Palestine, but also to attain for the university legal and historical validity by declaring it the main heir of European Jewry and its cultural property, including YIVO's collections. Their interest in YIVO and its collections was kindled even prior to WWII and grew thereafter. In 1937, following his service in Eastern Europe, the university's academic secretary, Ari Ibn-Sahav, reported on the situation in Vilna, and on YIVO and its collections:

13 YIVO, Restitution 1945–49, Box 1, File Operation Offenbach, Saul Kagan to Max Weinreich, 19 September 1945.

> "My impression is extremely poor. Situation in Vilna is dire; Yiddishists are finding friends for YIVO; [...] I visited YIVO as well. The director speaks perfect Hebrew and their people are working seriously. They have interesting collections, relating to the Enlightenment as well as Zionism."[14]

It appears that the Hebrew University's German legacy did not restrain it from seeking to appropriate the opposing Yiddishist heritage. On the contrary, its people tried all the harder to relocate YIVO, its collections, and its staff to Jerusalem despite the geographical and ideological distance between the two institutions. YIVO presented a formidable challenge to the Hebrew University, representing Eastern European Jewry and "Yiddishland," and holding the archives and collections of vast communities. By transferring YIVO to Jerusalem, the Hebrew University sought to fulfill the vision of the "Ingathering of the Exiles" and, as its personnel perceived it, breathe life into the institute's dry bones.

In conclusion, as we look back at both its success and failures in the Western and Eastern European spheres respectively, we may observe that if YIVO's phenomenal achievement in the Offenbach restitution reflected its glorious past as an international Yiddishist institute in Vilna, its failure in Czechoslovakia foreshadowed its future decline in America. In other words, YIVO was transformed from a scientific institute focused on the Yiddish heritage, its culture, and the Jewish diaspora, to a body defined by territory.

14 AHU, File 1937/106/660, A. Ibn-Sahav [Leo Goldstein], Report, 18 July 1937. (I thank Yael Levi for this source.)

Literature

David E. Fishman, The Book Smugglers. Partisans, Poets, and the Race to Save Jewish Treasures from the Nazis, Lebanon, N.H., 2017.

Dana Herman, Hashavat Avedah. A History of Jewish Cultural Reconstruction, Inc. (unpublished PhD thesis, McGill University, Montreal, 2008).

Jason Lustig, Who Are to Be the Successors of European Jewry? The Restitution of German Jewish Communal and Cultural Property, in: Journal of Contemporary History 52 (2016), no. 3, 519–545.

Nancy Sinkoff, From the Archives. Lucy S. Dawidowicz and the Restitution of Jewish Cultural Property, in: American Jewish History 100 (2016), no. 1, 117–147.

Author

Bilha Shilo is PhD student at the Department of Jewish History and Contemporary Jewry at the Hebrew University of Jerusalem. She received her master's degree from the Hebrew University in 2016. From 2016 to 2019 she was a member of the team engaged in cataloguing the Hebrew University Historical Archives, a project funded by the Gerda Henkel Foundation in association with the Franz Rosenzweig Minerva Research Center and the German Literature Archive Marbach. *Selected Publications*: Bilha Shilo, "Funem Folk, Farn Folk, Mitn Folk." The Restitution of the YIVO Collection from Offenbach to New York, in: Moreshet. Journal for the Study of the Holocaust and Antisemitism 14 (2017), no. 12, 361–412.

ANNA HOLZER-KAWALKO

The Dual Dynamics of Postwar Cultural Restoration: On the Salvage and Destruction of the Breslau Rabbinical Library

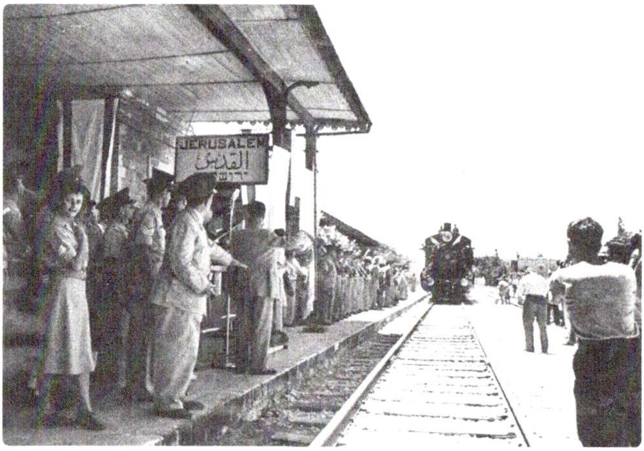

Fig. 1: The first Israeli train arrives in Jerusalem, carrying a large number of books salvaged from the looted Jewish libraries in Poland, August 1949.

In August 1949, less than a month after the final armistice agreement between the State of Israel and Syria was concluded to end the hostilities of the 1948 war, the first Israeli train arrived in Jerusalem, carrying thousands of books from the Nazi-looted Jewish libraries in Poland. Those local residents who came to the station on that sunny morning were doubtless greatly impressed by the celebrations laid on for the occasion. As depicted in the series of photographs taken by Edgar Hirshbain for the Hebrew University, the train was accompanied by a military entourage and welcomed by an orchestra and numerous distinguished guests, including the Minister of Transportation David Remez, and Prime Minister David Ben Gurion, who delivered a brief speech once the train had pulled into the station. The station building was vividly decorated with flowers and Israeli flags, and this contributed to the general festive atmosphere among the participants at the event (fig. 1).

The restoration of the railroad track and the first train journey from Tel Aviv to Jerusalem in the newly established State of Israel represented not only military and political prowess, but also a cultural achievement. For the representatives of the Hebrew University, who had worked tirelessly for the transfer of the Jewish book collections that were now finally being brought by the train to the National and University Library, the occasion was a

Contested Heritage, 91–102 | doi.org/10.13109/9783666310836.91

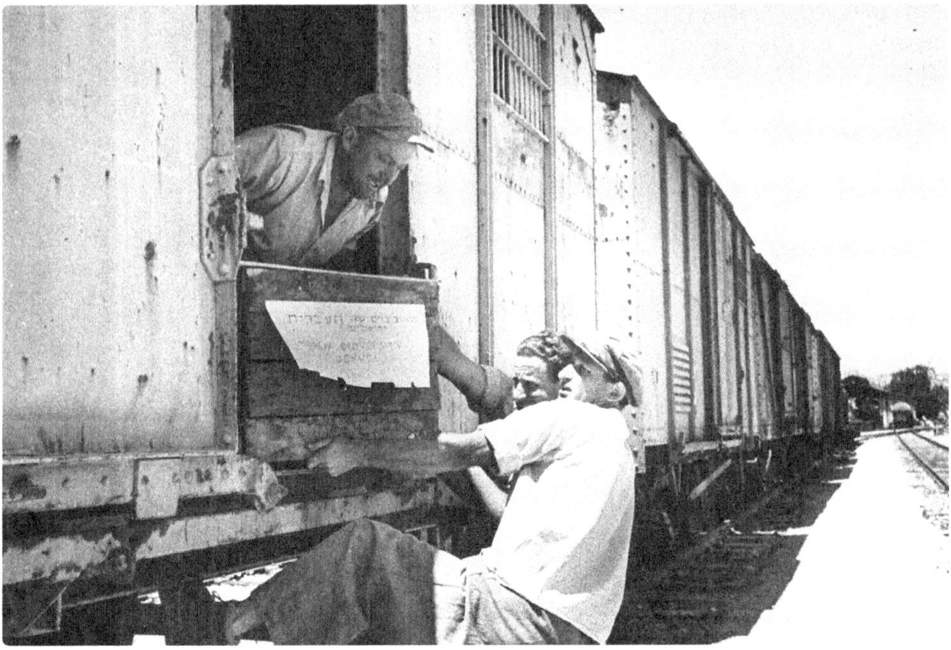

Fig. 2: The salvaged books are offloaded from the train, August 1949.

historic moment in the reconstruction of the heritage of the Jewish people and in "the renewal of their religious and cultural life in [...] the New Palestine."[1] In the coming years, the university received hundreds of thousands of rare volumes and manuscripts that originated mainly in German-Jewish libraries. Interestingly, while much was made of their significance for the future (re)creation of Jewish culture in Israel, the actual provenance of these materials became increasingly obscure. The university used to describe them collectively as the *Ozrot ha-Golah* (Diaspora Treasures), as if they had formed a single vast collection of unspecified volumes of Jewish origin (fig. 2).

However, as revealed by numerous documents dated between 1944 and 1951 which are currently kept in the Hebrew University Archives, the university was not interested in every single book of Jewish origin left on European soil, but rather sought to obtain very specific and carefully selected Jewish archives and libraries. Relying entirely on primary sources, I seek in this article to throw light on the university's endeavor to acquire one of the largest and most important German-Jewish libraries, namely the Breslau Rabbinical Library. In tracing its unique journey from the

1 The Archives of the Hebrew University (henceforth AHU), File 046/1948, Memorandum on the Policy of the Hebrew University concerning Jewish Books in Offenbach and Other Localities, n.d. (draft).

Wallstraße in Breslau to the train station in Jerusalem, I focus on the evolution of the Hebrew University's stance with regard to this particular library and to heirless Jewish cultural property in general. I furthermore examine how this stance helped determine the postwar fate of the Breslau collection and transform it from a concrete library of German-Jewish provenance into a part of the collective body of Diaspora Treasures. This examination will lead us to reflect on hitherto little explored dimensions of Jewish cultural restoration after 1945, in which cultural salvation is inevitably intertwined with cultural destruction. Before discussing these issues in depth, I shall briefly review the prewar history and the wartime fate of the Breslau library.

A Story of Survival: The Breslau Rabbinical Library and the Nazi Plunder of Jewish Books

Contrary to what one might expect, the pre-1945 history of the Breslau Rabbinical Library is not a narrative of destruction, but rather a tale of almost miraculous survival. The library was affiliated to the Jewish Theological Seminary of Breslau, an institution for the training of rabbis and teachers that promoted the intellectual values of the *Wissenschaft des Judentums* (the Science of Judaism) movement and provided its students not only with a Talmudic, but also with a philological and philosophical education. The foundation of the library was laid in 1854 with the purchase of the entire book collection of the famous Italian bibliophile Leon Vita Saraval of Trieste, which comprised 405 books, including 69 rare manuscripts and six incunabula. In the ensuing years the library's holdings grew rapidly as the seminary systematically acquired scientific literature and received additional book donations. By 1937, the library's collection contained some forty thousand volumes, including 433 manuscripts and 54 incunabula. The collection covered a wide range of disciplines and topics, from Bible and Talmudic literature to Christian writings; and from philology to physics and astronomy. As the Commission on European Jewish Cultural Reconstruction would note after the war, the Breslau library was regarded as "the most valuable Jewish-owned collection in Germany for ancient literature, Judaica and orientalia."[2]

Furthermore, against all odds and in the face of numerous challenges, a large part of the Breslau library survived the twelve-year long Nazi

2 The Research Staff of the Commission on European Jewish Cultural Reconstruction, Presentations and Reports. Tentative List of Jewish Cultural Treasures in Axis-Occupied Countries, 1946. The list was published as a supplement to the journal Jewish Social Studies 8 (1946), no. 1, <http://www.lootedart.com/MFEU4S32631_print> (1 August 2019).

cultural plunder between 1933 and 1945. Although some books were looted and destroyed during the pogrom of November 1938, the vast majority remained in the seminary building till July 1939, when they were seized by the Gestapo and transported to Berlin.

In the German capital, the Breslau collection was initially housed at the Freemason Lodge at Emserstraße, and then at the Grand Masonic Lodge at Eisenacherstraße, where Judaica plundered from various libraries was collected. At some point it was taken over by the Reichssicherheitshauptamt (Reich Main Security Office; RSHA) library, where Jewish forced laborers managed to keep the collection almost intact. In August 1943, as the war intensified, the Breslau library was rescued once again. Just before the Allied bombings almost completely destroyed the RSHA library, the collection was moved out of Berlin and divided among various locations in Lower Silesia and Sudetenland, where it was shortly thereafter discovered by the local authorities, the Soviet Trophy Brigades, and the Allied forces.

A Story of Destruction: The Hebrew University and the Transfer of the Breslau Rabbinical Library to Jerusalem

Less than a year after the plunder of the Breslau library in 1938, the first calls for it to be salvaged could be heard in Jerusalem. Gotthold Weil, the then-director of the National and University Library, wrote in 1939 to the Hebrew University Administration Office that "the Breslau library is the most important German collection [to be rescued]."[3] Weil furthermore stressed that the Hebrew University should forthwith stake its legal claim to the Breslau library and several other German-Jewish book collections, preferably with the help of the relevant authorities of the Yishuv. However, he failed to address the challenging question that his recommendation raised, namely: What were the grounds for such a claim? In other words, how could the Hebrew University justify its right to this specific cultural property that had belonged to Breslau Jewry?

It was precisely thorny issues of this kind that were thoroughly explored during the initial meetings of the Committee for the Salvaging of Diaspora Treasures *(Ha-va'ada le-hazalat Ozrot ha-Golah)*, after this body was set up by the university in 1944. Its members appear to have been fully aware of the numerous legal, but also political, moral, cultural, historical, and even technical complexities surrounding this issue. Significantly, at some

3 AHU, File 042/1939, Gotthold Weil to Hebrew University Administration Office, 30 May 1939.

point in their discussions, Julius Guttmann, who was a former lecturer at the Breslau Seminary, declared that, in light of the highly controversial status of the Nazi-looted libraries, "[the university] is not a legitimate body to decide what does and does not belong in Jerusalem."[4]

The Breslau library is a good example of the complications that confronted the Committee. Although a significant part of the library had survived, it was divided among different countries—Germany, Poland, and Czechoslovakia—and was therefore subject to three separate legal systems. Furthermore, the political situation in this region was still rather unstable and fluid, given the impacts of the crystallization of zones of occupation and the territorial changes endorsed at the Yalta and Potsdam Conferences. Finally, the issue of cultural restitution rapidly evolved into a fierce power struggle between the occupying forces, state authorities, local administrations, and Jewish restitution agencies, all of which presented competing solutions to the question of where the library should end up. Simply returning the books to Breslau was not a feasible option, for there appeared to be no legal heir to this precious legacy. The seminary and the local Jewish community had been destroyed during the war, and had left no successor to claim their property. Neither the law of the land nor the so-called escheat rule, which grants the state, as a universal heir, the right to inherit all heirless property found on its territory, was acceptable to any of the Jewish parties involved, for in many cases this would have resulted in leaving the property to the Holocaust perpetrators. Moreover, even had these conventions been accepted, in the case of the Breslau library a further controversy would have arisen as to which state—Poland or Germany—was entitled to receive the property.

The questions were many, and the answers few. It appears that at the beginning of the restitution struggle, the university adopted the argument first articulated by Cecil Roth in April 1943, at the Conference on the Restoration of Continental Jewish Museums, Libraries and Archives. In his opening lecture, in which he addressed the issue of Nazi plunder and cultural reconstruction, Roth maintained that the Jewish cultural property belonged to its original communal owners, and that as such it should be given in trust to the Hebrew University, as one of the largest and most important institutions of Jewish scholarship:

> "There is the problem of those objects whose owners cannot be traced, or which belonged to institutions—museums, synagogues, public collections, rabbinical seminaries, etc.—which are unlikely ever to be revived. I trust that there will be no objection from any quarter to my

4 AHU, File 042/1945, Minutes of the Meeting of the Committee for the Salvaging of Diaspora Treasures, 14 February 1945.

> suggestion that these should be placed in future in the custody of the Hebrew University of Jerusalem (I use the phrase 'in the custody of' advisedly, as I suppose there is the possibility that institutions which now seem to be dead may ultimately be revived)."[5]

This proposition appears to have rested on three major premises. First of all, as depicted by Roth, the Breslau library and other Nazi-looted book collections constituted the intellectual and cultural property of specific German-Jewish institutions of higher education. Their enormous value was thus a function not only of their actual content but also, and perhaps primarily, of this particular German-Jewish provenance. Secondly, the special status that Roth granted to the Hebrew University with regard to these treasures was strongly supported by purely practical considerations concerning the preservation of their historical value. Their temporary transfer to Jerusalem would prevent their further dispersion and ensure the proper identification of these collections, for which the university could provide the necessary experts. Furthermore, this measure was expected to facilitate the ongoing accessibility and scholarly use of these materials. Yet, on the other hand, this special role was subordinated to the possible future reconstruction of Jewish culture in Europe. From a letter by Judah Magnes to Selig Brodetsky, the then-president of the Board of Deputies of British Jews, one learns that the Hebrew University initially shared this vision:

> "The University pledges itself to make special provision for the care of these [Nazi-looted] collections and their use without distinction of race or creed, and undertakes to restore them to the communities or institutions which once owned them, should these ever be reconstituted."[6]

Lastly, as Roth himself explicitly spelled out, he did not consider the Nazi occupation of Europe to presage the end of Jewish life on the old continent, and believed in the postwar revival of local Jewish communities. However, over the following two years, when the overwhelming scope of the catastrophe had become apparent, the general view regarding the prospects of Jewish life in Europe after the war became markedly dimmer. Instead of Jewish reconstruction, a mass exodus appeared to be the most plausible scenario. Meanwhile, numerous other claims to rediscovered collections were submitted by both private individuals and public orga-

5 AHU, File 042/1944, Conference on the Restoration of Continental Jewish Museums, Libraries and Archives. Opening Address by Dr. Cecil Roth, 11 April 1943.
6 AHU, File 042/1945, Judah Magnes to Selig Brodetsky, 8 July 1945.

nizations, among which the Commission on European Jewish Cultural Reconstruction—established in 1944 in New York—was the most active and influential. Belying its name, the Commission's representatives lobbied for the transfer of Jewish books to what they saw as new centers of Jewish life in the United States and Palestine. The emergence of this American partner, which was often perceived as a rival and a "negative factor" (to quote Magnes's comment at a meeting of the Committee for the Salvaging of Diaspora Treasures in November 1945),[7] transformed the restitution discourse. While Roth appears to have understood this endeavor first and foremost as an attempt to salvage and preserve the Jewish past, the subsequent debates between the Hebrew University and the Jewish Cultural Reconstruction, Inc. (JCR)—the successor of the above-mentioned Commission—focused primarily on the Jewish future.

This shift was expressed in the innovative solution proposed to the ownership controversies, triggered largely by the issue of communal property, whose original owners were now replaced by the collective body of the Jewish people. Consequently, the Hebrew University's claim was no longer based on its role as spiritual heir to the Jewish-European tradition of scholarship, but rather on its responsibility as the representative "of the Jewish People in their Homeland."[8] From this perspective, set out by Magnes in his letter to Edward Warburg, who in 1948 served as chairman of the Joint Distribution Committee, the cultural restitution endeavor eventually evolved into a means of shaping the new Jewish culture in Palestine, with the Hebrew University playing a leading role in this process:

> "It is not of course a personal whim of mine or a narrow-minded desire on the part of the Hebrew University or of the Palestinian community to appropriate property, which has been left ownerless under such appallingly tragic conditions. Ours is, so we are deeply convinced, the approach which Jewish history entitles us to have. I would go further and say Jewish history lays upon us this great obligation. It must, so we think, be the innermost desire of the Jewish leaders of the world to do everything possible to enable the Jews of Palestine not only to develop their economic and political life, but perhaps, above all things, to deepen their cultural and spiritual existence."[9]

7 AHU, File 042/1945, Protocol from the Meeting of the Committee for the Salvaging of Diaspora Treasures, 5 November 1945.

8 AHU, File 046/1946, Memo re Religious Literature from Poland to Palestine, n.d., (draft).

9 AHU, File 046/1948, Judah Magnes to Edward Warburg, 16 January 1948.

This statement shows very clearly that the shift in emphasis from the Jewish communities to the Jewish people, and from cultural preservation to cultural creation was not merely a rhetorical figure of speech; rather, it implied a singular understanding of Jewish history, according to which the devastated Jewish-European communities were teleologically reinterpreted and written into the living body of the Yishuv in Mandatory Palestine and later into the State of Israel. This novel perspective on the historical relationship between European Jews and Jewish settlement in *Ereẓ Yisrael* (the Land of Israel) had far-reaching practical consequences for the status and allocation of salvaged libraries, as exemplified by the restitution of the bulk of the Breslau Rabbinical Library—containing over 11,000 volumes—that was gathered first in the archival depot in Offenbach and then transferred to the Central Collecting Point in Wiesbaden.

When the Breslau collection was discussed during the Board of Directors meeting at the JCR office in New York in October 1949, the representative of one of the participating organizations—the Council for the Protection of Rights and Interests of Jews from Germany—suggested that the Breslau books be kept intact and that they be donated, in toto, to the Jewish communities in Switzerland. Wind of this idea, which had not been formally approved, reached Wiesbaden, and the representative of the Hebrew University there, Shlomo Shunami, who immediately informed his superior and one of the university's professors, Gershom Scholem, of the plan. Two days later Scholem sent a formal letter to the president of the JCR, Salo W. Baron, in which he argued that the Breslau books should not be treated as a collection but should rather be divided among all interested parties, and that the Hebrew University should be the first institution allowed to exercise its stipulated right of selection.[10] In the reply that Scholem and Shunami received from Hannah Arendt, the then-executive secretary of the JCR, she reassured them that the JCR saw eye to eye with the Hebrew University on the matter of relocating the Breslau books, and stated:

> "I am very happy with your letter, because it confirms my opinion. […] During the Board of Directors meeting […] we stressed repeatedly that this is not the collection of the Breslau Seminary but remnants and that it would not make much sense to keep the collection intact."[11]

The discrepancy between the arguments articulated in Scholem's and Arendt's letters and the university's initial call to salvage these books

10 National Library of Israel, Archives Department (henceforth NLI), ARC. 4°793/288/55, Gershom Scholem to Salo W. Baron, 30 October 1949.

11 NLI, ARC. 4°793/288/62, Hannah Arendt to Shlomo Shunami, 7 November 1949.

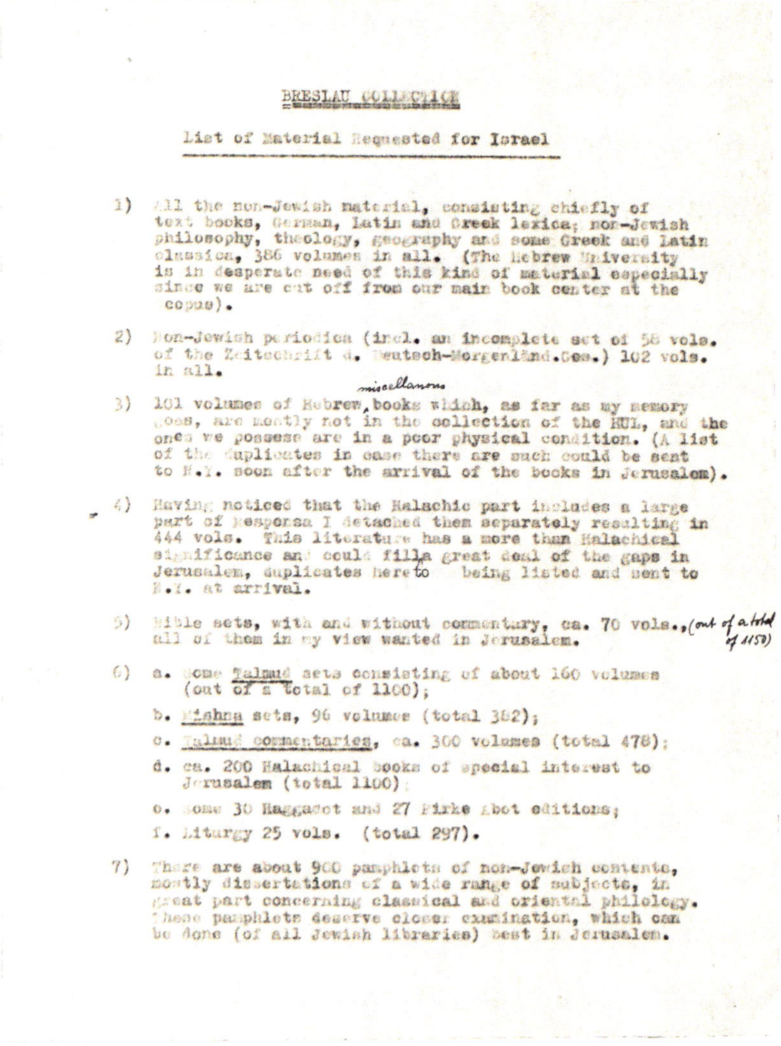
BRESLAU COLLECTION

List of Material Requested for Israel

1) All the non-Jewish material, consisting chiefly of text books, German, Latin and Greek lexica; non-Jewish philosophy, theology, geography and some Greek and Latin classics, 386 volumes in all. (The Hebrew University is in desperate need of this kind of material especially since we are cut off from our main book center at the copus).

2) Non-Jewish periodica (incl. an incomplete set of 58 vols. of the Zeitschrift d. Deutsch-Morgenländ.Ges.) 102 vols. in all.

3) 101 volumes of Hebrew, miscellanous books which, as far as my memory goes, are mostly not in the collection of the HUL, and the ones we possess are in a poor physical condition. (A list of the duplicates in case there are such could be sent to N.Y. soon after the arrival of the books in Jerusalem).

4) Having noticed that the Halachic part includes a large part of Responsa I detached them separately resulting in 444 vols. This literature has a more than Halachical significance and could filla great deal of the gaps in Jerusalem, duplicates hereto being listed and sent to N.Y. at arrival.

5) Bible sets, with and without commentary, ca. 70 vols., (out of a total of 1150) all of them in my view wanted in Jerusalem.

6) a. Some Talmud sets consisting of about 160 volumes (out of a total of 1100);
b. Mishna sets, 96 volumes (total 382);
c. Talmud commentaries, ca. 300 volumes (total 478);
d. ca. 200 Halachical books of special interest to Jerusalem (total 1100);
e. Some 30 Haggadot and 27 Pirke Abot editions;
f. Liturgy 25 vols. (total 297).

7) There are about 900 pamphlets of non-Jewish contents, mostly dissertations of a wide range of subjects, in great part concerning classical and oriental philology. These pamphlets deserve closer examination, which can be done (of all Jewish libraries) best in Jerusalem.

Fig. 3: The list of books from the Breslau collection requested by the Hebrew University (attached to a letter from Shlomo Shunami to Hannah Arendt), November 1949.

precisely because they were the only remaining part of the precious Breslau library, may at first appear rather surprising. However, one should bear in mind that according to this newly adopted historical perspective based on the notion of the Jewish people, the Breslau books were in fact no longer part of the Breslau library—namely the property of the concrete community of Breslau Jews—but had rather become part of the general heritage of the Jewish people, which should be equitably divided among its representatives. Eventually, the Board of Directors recommended that the Breslau books be redistributed among various Jewish institutions in

Israel, Switzerland, the United States, and South America. The Hebrew University was granted priority to claim parts of the collection and hastily submitted to JCR a detailed list of materials requested in Jerusalem (fig. 3).

The arrival of these books at the train station of Jerusalem therefore marked not only the beginning of a new Jewish culture in the State of Israel, but also the final act of the dissolving of the Breslau Rabbinical Library. Almost a century on from its establishment, having survived a series of misfortunes—the pogrom of 1938, the Nazi robbery, wartime bombings, evacuation, and numerous individual attempts at looting—the Breslau library finally fell prey to postwar Jewish cultural restoration. Significantly, the only part of the library that was not dismantled and survived as a single intact entity was the valuable Saraval collection, which had been overlooked by the Hebrew University and was discovered only in the early 1990s in Prague. But that is another story.

Final Remarks

After the Breslau collection together with thousands of books from the prewar Jewish-European libraries had been transferred to Jerusalem, a new chapter in its history began, which was shaped primarily by the new political circumstances in the aftermath of the 1948 war. The Diaspora Treasures were gathered, reshuffled, and redistributed once again, in accordance with the needs of various cultural and educational institutions in the State of Israel. Over the following years, the memory of their singular journey from Nazi-destroyed Europe to the newly established and war-torn Jewish state faded slowly into oblivion. Against this backdrop, the documentation of the cultural restitution held by the Hebrew University appears to be a valuable source for the yet-to-be-written history of the vast majority of German-Jewish libraries in the twentieth century, of which the Breslau Rabbinical Library is a prominent example. Furthermore, this episode offers unique insight into the evolution of the university's position with regard to the former Jewish communities and institutions

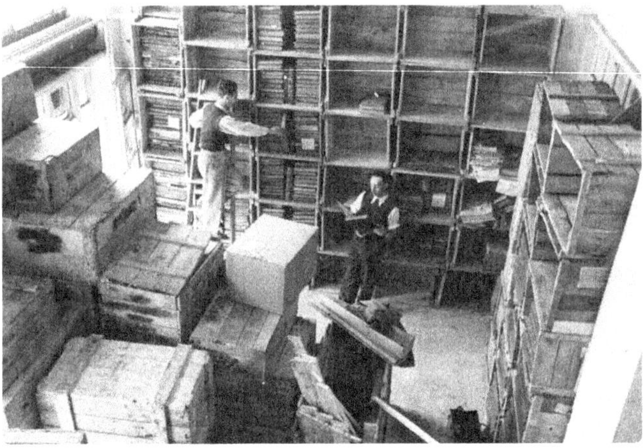

Fig. 4: The salvaged books are unpacked in one of the temporary premises of the Jewish National and University Library, December 1950.

in Europe, in which the university was intellectually rooted, and its place within the Jewish settlement in Palestine/Israel, which constituted the actual base for its activity. As I have sought to demonstrate, this position was profoundly influenced by the notion of the Jewish people as a universal heir to property and by the subsequent reinterpretation of both Jewish history in Europe and of the relations between the diasporic Jewish communities and the Jewish settlement in Palestine. Finally, the Hebrew University's struggle for the transfer of Nazi-looted libraries and book collections reflects the dual nature of the entire project of postwar Jewish cultural restoration, which seems to have oscillated constantly between the particular and the universal, the past and the future, and between the building and destruction of heritage (fig. 4).

Literature

Dan Diner/Gotthart Wunberg (eds.), Restitution and Memory. Material Restoration in Europe, New York/Oxford 2007.

Elisabeth Gallas, A Mortuary of Books. The Rescue of Jewish Culture after the Holocaust, New York 2019 (Germ. 2013).

Dana Herman, Hashavat Avedah. A History of Jewish Cultural Reconstruction, Inc. (unpublished PhD thesis, McGill University, Montreal, 2008).

Anna Kawałko, From Breslau to Wrocław. Transfer of the Saraval Collection to Poland and the Restitution of Jewish Cultural Property after WW II, in: Naharaim. Zeitschrift für deutsch-jüdische Literatur und Kulturgeschichte/Journal of German-Jewish Literature and Cultural History 9 (2015), no. 1–2, 48–72.

Dov Shidorsky, Burning Scrolls and Flying Letters. A History of Book Collections and Libraries in Mandatory Palestine and of Book Salvaging Efforts in Europe after the Holocaust, Jerusalem 2008 (Heb.).

Yfaat Weiss, Von Prag nach Jerusalem. Jüdische Kulturgüter und israelische Staatsgründung, in: Vierteljahrshefte für Zeitgeschichte 63 (2015), no. 4, 513–538.

Author

Anna Holzer-Kawalko is a PhD student at the Department of History of the Jewish People and Contemporary Jewry at the Hebrew University of Jerusalem. She earned her bachelor's degree at the University of Warsaw (2012), and completed her master's degree at the Hebrew University in Jerusalem (2015). Currently, she is working on her doctoral dissertation, which deals with German-Jewish book collections and nation-building in Czechoslovakia between 1918 and 1948. *Selected Publications*: East Meets East. Polish-German Coexistence in Lower Silesia through the Memories of Polish Expellees, 1945–1947, in: Jan Fellerer / Robert Pyrah (eds.), Lviv-Wroclaw: Parallel Cities? Myth, Memory and Migration, c. 1890—Present (forthcoming 2019); Lost on the Island. Mapping an Alternative Path of Exile in the Life and Work of Ernst Grumach, in: Jahrbuch des Dubnow-Instituts / Dubnow Institute Yearbook 16 (2017), Göttingen 2019, 493–518; Jewish Intellectuals between Robbery and Restitution. Ernst Grumach in Berlin, 1941–1946, in: Leo Baeck Institute Yearbook 63 (2018), 273–295.

ENRICO LUCCA

A Safe Home for German Jewry: Hugo Bergman, *Oẓrot ha-Golah*, and His Return to Europe

The period between 1946 and 1948 was of considerable significance in the life of Hugo Bergman (Prague 1883–Jerusalem 1975). A series of academic, institutional, and diplomatic missions he was asked to undertake on behalf of the Hebrew University took him within the space of two years first to Sweden (October–November 1946), then to Czechoslovakia (November 1946), to India (March–April 1947), and finally back to Sweden (July 1947–November 1948).

Bergman's mission to Prague at the end of 1946 as an emissary of the Committee for the Salvaging of Diaspora Treasures *(Ha-va'ada le-haẓalat Oẓrot ha-Golah)*—to claim for the Hebrew University the Nazi-looted libraries of European Jewish communities—should be analyzed in relation to his other concurrent activities, and, more specifically, against the backdrop of this singular historical moment. Bergman's visits to Europe coincided with the emergence of several major social and political processes: the shaping of a new geopolitical sphere in Europe in the aftermath of the war; the growing Sovietization of the countries of the Eastern Bloc and its impact on the remnants of Central and Eastern European Jewish communities; and on the other hand, the unstable situation in Palestine following the end of the British Mandate, the outbreak of the Arab-Jewish war, and the creation of the State of Israel. Observing Bergman's relatively brief sojourn in Prague within this context can help to understand how he began to consider the revival of a European Jewish culture in the aftermath of the Holocaust.

Back to Prague

Bergman landed in Prague on 6 November 1946. During the previous three weeks he had traveled all over Sweden lecturing and participating in official ceremonies and fundraising events organized by the Scandinavian chapter of the Friends of the Hebrew University. Although this

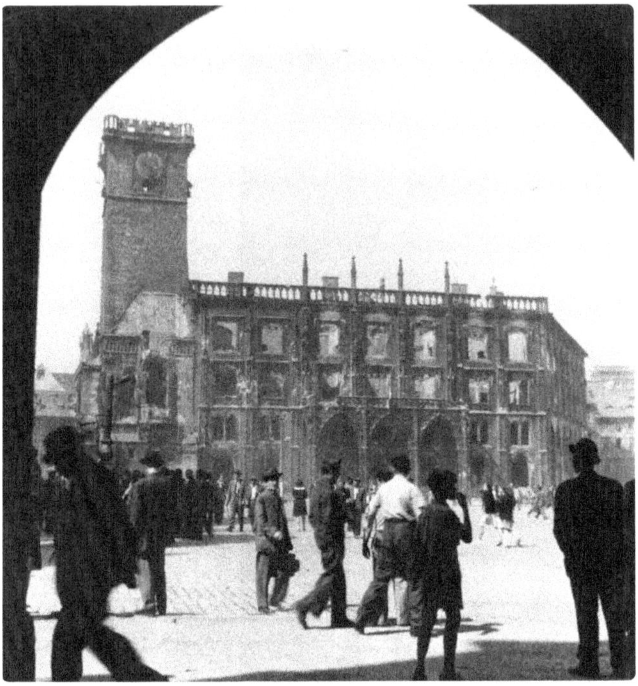

Fig. 1: Prague's old town square after the German withdrawal from the city, 11 February 1947.

trip was hastily arranged, Bergman's European mission was particularly significant as it marked his return to the continent for the first time after the outbreak of the war. Bergman's previous European destinations had been the same, Czechoslovakia and Sweden, which he visited in 1937 and 1938 respectively during his second and third terms as rector of the Hebrew University.[1] Yet Sweden and Czechoslovakia, and especially their Jewish communities, appeared now, after almost a decade, in a completely different light. In Stockholm Bergman encountered the distressing plight of a huge number of refugees, mostly German and Polish Jews who had come to Sweden during and after the war, and whose fate was still undecided. What he saw in Prague, for obvious biographical reasons, would have touched him even more deeply (fig. 1).

Bergman's transition from Sweden to Czechoslovakia left him with the impression that the two countries now belonged to different worlds. Shocked by the massive street parade celebrating the anniversary of the Russian Revolution that took place the day after his arrival, Bergman was even more depressed by the almost total absence of Jewish life in his home town. His first impression of the city was very similar to those gained by Leo Herrmann, the head of *Keren Hayesod*, who arrived in Prague already in September 1945,[2] and by Gershom Scholem, who visited Prague in June 1946 as the first emissary of the Hebrew University to pave the way for

1 Bergman visited Czechoslovakia (and Poland) in March 1937 on his way to the United States, and journeyed to Sweden in September 1938. More information on these trips can be accessed in the Archives of the Hebrew University of Jerusalem.

2 It is interesting to remark that in his travel notes Herrmann not only already mentioned the books stored in the Jewish Museum, but also suggested that the Hebrew University could send Hugo Bergman to Prague in order to secure the books for the Jewish National Library.

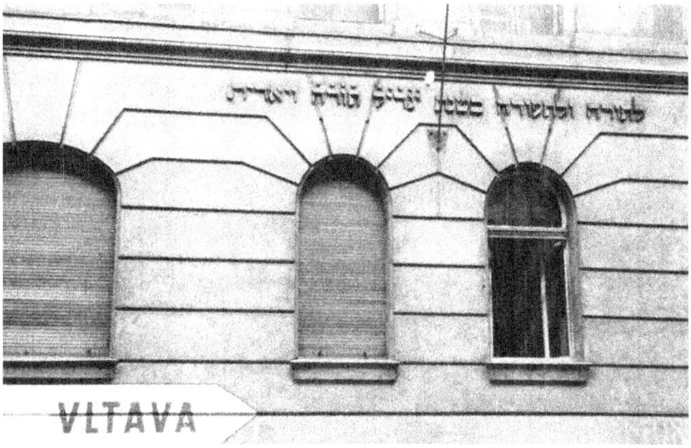

Fig. 2: Jewish Museum in Prague, 1947.

the restitution of looted Jewish books. "Tomorrow I am planning to go to the cemetery," Bergman wrote to his wife on the day of his arrival, "which I feel is the only thing in this city that still belongs to me."[3]

During his stay Bergman was able to meet up with surviving members of his family, and with friends and acquaintances from his early days in Prague. Yet, his first task was to win the trust of the local Jewish community in the Hebrew University. While in Prague, Scholem had sought to convince the members of the Council of the Jewish Religious Communities of Bohemia and Moravia-Silesia (henceforth Council) to secure for the Hebrew University some of the books from the Library of Terezín (Theresienstadt) that were moved to the Jewish Museum in Prague in autumn 1945 (fig. 2). Yet, although the Council had expressed its approval of Scholem's request at the end of June 1946, by mid-October no action had been taken on the matter. Scholem appears to have been particularly disturbed by what he perceived to be the unwillingness to cooperate on the part of the Prague Jewish community. He considered its attitude to be somewhat legalistic and cowardly and vented his feelings both in his report and in his personal notes. To be sure, Scholem's frustration is at least partially understandable. He was, moreover, unaware that at the Castle of Mimoň (Niemes) a large part of the looted Jewish collections originally stored at the Reichssicherheitshauptamt (Reich Main Security Office) in Berlin had been evacuated by the Nazis in 1943 as the war intensified. According to estimates, Mimoň Castle—one of four in the region between Liberec (Reichenberg) and Česká Lípa (Böhmisch-Leipa) where books had been assembled—housed more than 250,000 volumes that emanated from various Jewish communities and institutions both in Western and Eastern Europe. What is more, Scholem's hostility toward his partners was no doubt linked to his refusal to acknowledge the needs of the local Jewish community and the highly delicate political situation in which it found itself. For negotiations to advance, the presence of a figure familiar with

3 Hugo Bergman, Tagebücher und Briefe, ed. by Miriam Sambursky and with an introduction by Nathan Rotenstreich, 2 vols., Königstein/Ts. 1985, here vol. 1: 1901–1948, Königstein/Ts. 1985, 700.

Czech politics (and with the Czech language) was urgently needed. In this sense, there was none better than Bergman.

After moving to Palestine in 1920, Bergman maintained close relations with Czechoslovakian political leaders as well as with the local Jewish leadership. In 1919 he took part in the Paris Peace Conference as a delegate of the Czech Jewish minority. Subsequently, as director of the Jewish National and University Library, it was Bergman who accompanied President Masaryk during his visit to Palestine in 1927. He was a familiar figure among the Czech Jewish community, particularly following the successful visit he paid to Prague in 1937 as rector of the Hebrew University. On that occasion Bergman also met with President Edvard Beneš. Thus, in no sense was he perceived as a foreigner in Prague. Given these outstanding qualifications and his proven diplomatic skills, Bergman was able to establish a relationship of trust with leading local Jewish figures: Arnošt Frischer, president of the Council of the Jewish Religious Communities of Bohemia and Moravia-Silesia; his secretary Kurt Wehle; Karel Stein, leader of the Council of the Prague Jewish Community; Rabbi Hanuš Rezek (Rebenwurzel); and Hana Volavková, director of the Jewish Museum in Prague.

The Mission

A few days before arriving in Prague, Bergman was informed of a breakthrough in the negotiations. Following the resolution passed by the Council on 22 October 1946, the Jewish Museum Commission also agreed to the transfer of the Terezín books to the Jewish National Library, with the exception of books of Czechoslovakian origin.[4] At this time, Bergman was perturbed by the plan recently adopted by the US government (acting on the advice of the Commission on European Jewish Cultural Reconstruction) to transfer to the American zone all the looted Jewish material to be found on Czechoslovak territory. Perceiving this as a development that was very likely to seriously endanger the negotiations he was conducting, Bergman urged the Hebrew University authorities to warn the Commission on European Jewish Cultural Reconstruction of the potentially harmful consequences of its strategy. At the same time—acting in the belief that

4 Archives of the Jewish Museum in Prague (henceforth AJMP), Fond Židovské muzeum v Praze (1945–1960), File 5, Zápis o 9. schûzi museální komise [Minutes of the Ninth Meeting of the Museum Commission]. (I wish to thank Anna Holzer-Kawalko, who very generously allowed me access to relevant material from the archive of the Jewish Museum in Prague.)

this US plan would not apply to the books from Terezín—he directly approached the Czech political authorities.

Bergman was received by the Minister for Schools and Education, Jaroslav Stránský, with whom he reached an oral agreement concerning the transfer of the Terezín books to the Hebrew University, on the condition that both the head of the Prague University Library and the head of the Oriental Institute would formally approve this step.[5] Bergman then met with the director of the library, Josef Bečka, who probably remembered him from the time that Bergman worked as a librarian in Clementinum.[6] No documentation of this meeting has been found, and it appears that the question of the looted books was not the only issue at stake, and that both parties sought to renew friendly academic and cultural relations between the Jewish National Library and the Charles University Library. Bečka outlined his plan to transform his institution into one of Europe's leading libraries by virtue of the books that had fallen into the hands of the Czech government after the expulsion of the Germans. He stated, however, that he had no objection to transferring to the Hebrew University *Hebraica* and *Judaica* publications unrelated to Czechoslovakia. Bergman promised to donate modern Hebrew volumes and books on Palestine to the library in return.[7] As regards the Oriental Institute, it soon transpired that its approval of the transfer of books to the Hebrew University was no longer required (fig. 3).[8]

Yet Bergman's greatest achievement was perhaps to gain permission to inspect the books stored in Mimoň Castle. This visit proved to be particularly important in providing the Hebrew University with an idea

5 Archives of the Hebrew University (henceforth AHU), File 046/1946, Hugo Bergman, Din ve-ḥeshbon shel prof. Bergman al nesiato le-Prag [Prof. Bergman's Report on his Trip to Prague], December 1946.

6 To Luise Herrmann Bergman wrote that he was warmly welcomed in Prague and that in the library some of the long serving employees still recognized him. Josef Bečka (1894–1955) was listed as *Praktikant* in the Personalstand der Deutschen Karl-Ferdinands-Universität for the year 1919–1920 and as *Assistent* for the year 1920–1921. Although on leave *(beurlaubt)* in both these years, Bergman was still listed as *Bibliothekar II. Klasse.*

7 Following this meeting, copies of the Hebrew periodicals *Tarbiz* and *Kiryat Sefer* were regularly delivered to the Charles University Library. The Jewish National Library also requested publications on Czechoslovak history, economics, geography, and ethnology, as well as dictionaries and other types of publication. See AJMP, Fond Židovské muzeum v Praze (1945–1960), File 7, David Hartwig Baneth to the Sbor pro československé knihovny v zahraničí [Committee for Czechoslovakian Libraries Abroad], copy sent to Hana Volavková, 9 January 1947. See also the Archives of the National Museum in Prague (henceforth ANM), Fond Hana Volavková, File 2, Hugo Bergman to Hana Volavková, 3 December 1946.

8 ANM, Fond Hana Volavková, File 2, Hana Volavková to Hugo Bergman [11 January 1947] (draft).

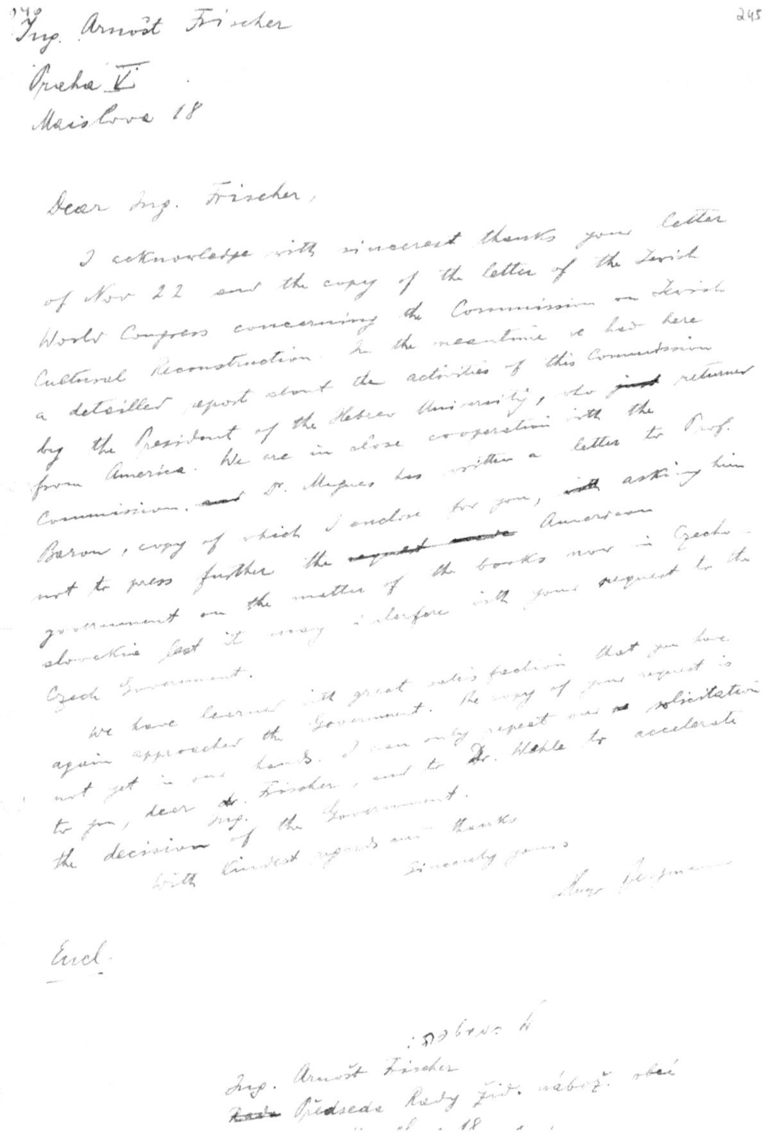

Fig. 3: Draft of a letter by Hugo Bergman to Ing. Arnošt Frischer, December 1946

of which books had been stored there. In the Castle Bergman spent several hours perusing the pile of Hebrew and Yiddish books he found there. Among these, he identified a number of boxes containing some 300 Yiddish volumes and newspapers originating from YIVO Vilna. Yet, as the memorandum he submitted to the Hebrew University Commission makes clear, Bergman was well aware of the many difficulties that lay ahead. These included practical issues, such as the need to arrange and catalogue the books, the question of packing them, and of how to fund the shipping. At this point he suggested that a further emissary be dispatched to Prague to handle the operation.

Unlike Scholem, Bergman apparently appreciated the efforts of Prague's Jewish leaders to protect their community in the face of serious challenges. It would thus be inaccurate to portray his trip solely as an assignment to salvage looted Jewish books. His broader mission was to renew the cultural ties between Palestine and the Czech-Jewish community. This emerges clearly from Bergman's correspondence following his return to Jerusalem. He supported, for example, Hana Volavková's idea of putting together a travelling exhibition that would be based in Israel, and referred her to Mordechai Narkiss, director of Bezalel Museum. He furthermore took charge of sending relevant publications to the Jewish Museum. And he encouraged the National Library in Jerusalem to establish contact and cooperate with the new Czechoslovak cultural and academic institutions, mainly through the exchange of periodicals. Finally, in response to Karel Stein's request Bergman engaged the help of his Prague acquaintances in Jerusalem to ship to Prague various *Hebraica* and *Judaica* publications for use by the local Jewish communities.

The Future of German Jewry

Regardless of all these efforts, Bergman was well aware that the radicalization of the struggle for political hegemony and the rise of nationalistic sentiments would soon altogether reshape the life of European Jewish communities. In the Czech territories in particular, German Jews were viewed with great suspicion by the local population after the war, and frequently suffered discrimination. On the other hand, the Communists' struggle to gain power in Czechoslovakia along with the expulsion of the German population from the country indicated that life in Prague would be very different to what it had been in the interwar period, and certainly during the First Czechoslovak Republic prior to the Nazi invasion.

As he surveyed the bleak scenery of contemporary Germany and Central Europe, Bergman would have pondered whether the cultural tradition of German Jewry could survive. It was with this in mind, in the midst of his Prague mission, that Bergman received an unexpected cable from Gunnar Josephson, president of the Stockholm Jewish community, inviting him to spend a year or two in Sweden to cater to the intellectual and spiritual needs of the local community. The invitation was conceived by Josephson together with renowned Rabbi Marcus Ehrenpreis in light of the deep impression that Bergman's lectures and personality had made on

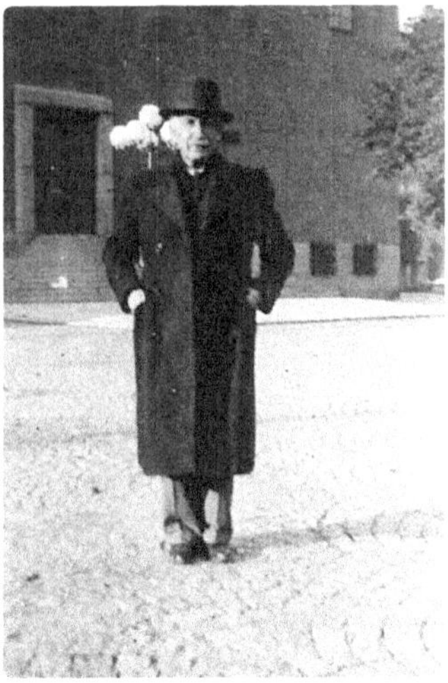

Fig. 4: Hugo Bergman in Stockholm, October 1946.

his Swedish audiences. One may assume that Bergman's concern about Prague was uppermost in his mind while he deliberated whether to accept the invitation to assume so important a role within a post-Holocaust European Jewish community (fig. 4).

Following negotiations with the Hebrew University administration, Bergman was initially given permission to remain in Stockholm only for nine months. In view of the escalation of violence in Palestine between the end of 1947 and the beginning of 1948, Bergman, who was joined in Sweden by his wife and two small daughters, asked the university to extend his stay. This request was granted, partly due to the cancellation of the summer semester. Bergman and his family spent almost sixteen months in Sweden before returning to Israel in mid-November 1948.

Among his diverse activities in Stockholm, Bergman delivered two series of public lectures, attended by an audience of Jews—mainly German-Jewish refugees—and non-Jews alike. Besides this and the lectures on philosophy he occasionally delivered at Swedish universities, Bergman preached at the Stockholm synagogue at least twice a month; set up a study group for young people dedicated to the discussion of religious topics; and promoted the formation of a liberal Jewish youth group at which he regularly lectured. In addition, he took a great interest in the expansion of the community library, and tried to breathe new life into the local Hebrew language study circle. All these different activities intersected with the need to reorganize the Stockholm Jewish community, which at that time confronted at least three important issues: the need to take care of a large number of refugees; tensions between the liberal and the orthodox factions; and the need to find a new rabbi who would take on the difficult task of replacing Marcus Ehrenpreis, who was now very old and unable to continue to fulfill his duties.

In Sweden, Bergman established contacts with various social and intellectual networks, beginning with the most prominent representatives of Swedish Jewry, on to the members of the local German-Jewish community, and finally with a number of Christian theologians with whom he engaged in stimulating dialogue that would later influence his positions on religious issues.

In late March 1948 Bergman was asked to return to Prague with a view to assisting Ze'ev Scheck, the fourth emissary sent by the Hebrew University to secure for the National Library of Jerusalem part of the looted Jewish books held on Czechoslovak territory. As the cable received by Bergman clearly stated, owing to new complications his immediate assistance was required: "Situation difficult intervention outstanding academic personality needed. Also represent University imminent Prague festival."[9] This time, however, Bergman declined the request. Apart from visa problems stemming from the imminent ending of the British Mandate, following the Communist coup—which took place in February of that year—the political situation in Europe appeared rather unstable as the antagonism between the Western and Eastern blocs escalated. Moreover, to represent the Hebrew University on the occasion of the jubilee celebrations of Charles University—as suggested in the cable—would certainly have generated tension between Bergman and his Scandinavian hosts, since the Swedish universities had decided to boycott the event.

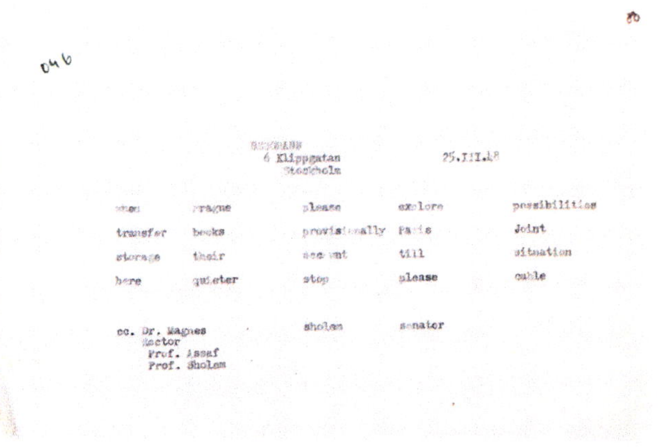
6 Klippgatan
Stockholm
25.III.48

prague please explore possibilities
transfer books provisionally Paris Joint
storage their account till situation
here quieter stop please cable

sholem senator

cc. Dr. Magnes
Rector
Prof. Assaf
Prof. Sholem

Fig. 5: Telegram sent by Hugo Bergman to the Hebrew University of Jerusalem, 1948.

Amid the uncertainties of this historical moment, Bergman continued to work tirelessly to ensure the survival of European Judaism, and in particular the spiritual legacy of German Jewry (fig. 5). Disenchanted with the course of events in Palestine, where the new political structure and the rise of nationalistic sentiment signaled, in his view, the approach of a dramatic religious crisis, Bergman was also well aware of the grave risks and problems that bedeviled the new European political configuration. It may appear somewhat surprising that he still considered Europe to be a place where the tradition of German Jewry could scatter its seeds in the hope of regenerating itself, given that the bleak climate of postwar Germany left little room for optimism; and that in light of the recent political events Czechoslovakia had turned eastward, and would move ever closer to Soviet Russia. It is against this backdrop that Bergman's energetic endeavors to secure the *Oẓrot ha-Golah* for the Hebrew University should be appreciated. Yet he believed that at least the Scandinavian countries, and Sweden in particular, could still provide a safe haven, and that their Jewish communities were well disposed toward his pedagogical and intellectual efforts to revive European Jewish cultural and spiritual life.

9 AHU, File 046/1948, Cable from the Hebrew University Authorities to Hugo Bergman, 23 March 1948.

A letter from Bergman's correspondence at the time is rather revealing in this respect, and is worth quoting here in conclusion. Shortly before he received the cable from the Hebrew University asking him to travel to Prague, Bergman wrote to Kurt Wilhelm, one of his closest friends in Jerusalem and the rabbi of the Rechavia liberal community *Emet ve-Emunah*. Although Bergman considered Wilhelm to be eminently suitable to replace Ehrenpreis as the rabbi of Stockholm and had warmly endorsed him before the members of the local community, it appears that Wilhelm was reluctant to leave Palestine, even though in February 1948 his house on Ben Yehudah Street in Jerusalem had been almost completely destroyed by a bomb. Intended to instill in Wilhelm the courage to embark on this new mission, Bergman's words can be also read as the epitome of his postwar experience. Facing the old continent's desolate post-Holocaust landscape and in the midst of turbulent times for the Jewish Yishuv in Palestine and uncertainty as to its future, Bergman continued to view Europe as a highly significant location in which to keep the cultural and spiritual legacy of Judaism alive:

> "I know very well what would you lose by leaving Jerusalem. And yet the evolution of our politics during the last months proved personally to me how incredibly important the Diaspora is for us. I would dare to think that Nordic countries, if only we could manage to overcome their ignorance in Jewish things, could acquire a very specific significance in this sense. The tradition of German Jewry, that—as long as I can see—in America and in England can be carried on only with extreme difficulty, and that in Palestine is endangered—and perhaps even more than that—by the excessive politicization, might be further fostered by the Jews of this place [...]. Under this point of view, it would be extremely sad for me if my work here won't find an adequate successor."[10]

10 National Library of Israel, Archives Department, ARC. 4° 1502, Hugo Bergman Papers, File 01/1281, Hugo Bergman to Kurt Wilhelm, 22 March 1948.

Literature

Hugo Bergman, Tagebücher und Briefe, ed. by Miriam Sambursky and with an introduction by Nathan Rotenstreich, 2 vols., Königstein/Ts. 1985.

Elisabeth Gallas, A Mortuary of Books. The Rescue of Jewish Culture after the Holocaust, New York 2019 (Germ. 2013).

Peter Heumos, Rückkehr ins Nichts. Leo Herrmanns Tagebuchaufzeichnungen über seine Reise nach Prag und die Lage der Juden in der Tschechoslowakei im Herbst 1945, in: Bohemia. Zeitschrift für Geschichte und Kultur der böhmischen Länder/A Journal of History and Civilisation in East Central Europe 27 (1986), no. 2, 269–304.

Dov Schidorsky, Burning Scrolls and Flying Letters. A History of Book Collections and Libraries in Mandatory Palestine and of Book Salvaging in Europe after the Holocaust, Jerusalem 2008 (Heb.).

Yfaat Weiss, Von Prag nach Jerusalem. Jüdische Kulturgüter und israelische Staatsgründung, in: Vierteljahrshefte für Zeitgeschichte 63 (2015), no. 4, 513–538.

Author

Enrico Lucca studied philosophy, history, and Jewish thought at the universities of Milan, Modena, and Chicago. He received his PhD from the University of Milan in 2012. From 2012 until 2017 he was affiliated with the Franz Rosenzweig Minerva Research Center at the Hebrew University of Jerusalem. Since January 2018 he is Research Associate at the Leibniz Institute for Jewish History and Culture – Simon Dubnow in Leipzig. He is engaged in writing an intellectual biography of Hugo Bergman. *Selected Publications*: Vom Gott der Aufklärung zum Gott der Religion. Franz Rosenzweigs Brief an Rudolf Ehrenberg vom September 1910 und sein Kampf gegen die Geschichte als Theodizee, in: Naharaim. Zeitschrift für deutsch-jüdische Literatur und Kulturgeschichte/Journal of German-Jewish Literature and Cultural History 10 (2016), no. 2, 303–319 (with Roberto Navarrete Alonso); Franz Rosenzweig. Réception, in: Salomon Malka (ed.), Le Dictionnaire Rosenzweig. Une étoile dans le siècle, Paris 2016, 305–313 (with Ynon Wygoda).

3. Forming Archives: Personal Estates and Institutional Collections

AMIT LEVY

A Discipline in a Suitcase: The Scientific *Nachlass* of Josef Horovitz

The untimely death of Prof. Josef Horovitz—chair of Semitic Languages at the University of Frankfurt, and simultaneously director of the School of Oriental Studies at the Hebrew University of Jerusalem—dealt a devastating blow to both institutions. In March 1931, a month after his demise in Frankfurt, Horovitz's junior colleague there, the orientalist Martin Plessner (1900–1973), vented this feeling in a letter to one of his orientalist colleagues in Jerusalem: "Although, obviously, I cannot estimate what Horovitz's students, and particularly the ones in Jerusalem, have lost, my own loss is painful enough to make me understand them."[1]

Plessner's sentiments point to Horovitz's importance and the influence he exerted in the academic circles of Germany and Palestine alike. The following offers a glimpse into this longstanding connection between Frankfurt and Jerusalem, as materially manifested in Horovitz's scientific *Nachlass*, which was transferred from Frankfurt to Jerusalem in 1934. This special relationship is traced through documents found in personal and institutional papers held at the archives of the National Library of Israel and the Hebrew University. The path taken by the suitcase that contained the *Zettel*—tens of thousands of densely handwritten research notes—was, it may be argued, emblematic of the migration of German-Jewish Orientalism from German universities to the Hebrew University; in many respects, so was the archival fate of these *Zettel*.

1 "Wenn ich natürlich nicht abschätzen kann, was die Schüler von Horovitz, und nun gar die Jerusalemer, verloren haben, so ist doch mein eigener Verlust schmerzlich genug, um Ihnen nachfühlen zu können." National Library of Israel, Archives Department (henceforth NLI), ARC. 4° 1911/03/18, Shelomo Dov Goitein Collection, Martin Plessner to Fritz Goitein, 4 March 1931.

Josef Horovitz and the Inception of the School of Oriental Studies in Jerusalem

Born in 1874 in Lauenberg (nowadays Lębork in Poland) to a German-Jewish orthodox rabbinical family, Josef Horovitz grew up in Frankfurt and studied in Berlin, where he wrote his PhD dissertation on early Muslim historiography under the supervision of Eduard Sachau (1845–1930). He had wide-ranging research interests, which included early Arabic poetry and Qur'anic studies. The seven years (1907–1914) he spent in India as a teacher of Arabic in the Muhammedan Anglo-Oriental College of Aligarh and as the curator of Islamic inscriptions for the British government made a crucial impact on his political views, spurring a strong anti-colonial sentiment. Upon returning to Germany, Horovitz was appointed professor of Semitic Languages, heading the Oriental Seminar *(Orientalisches Seminar)* in Frankfurt. He held this position until his death, tutoring many students who would become leading orientalists.

Despite his family's anti-Zionist leanings, Horovitz was profoundly involved in the establishment of the Hebrew University of Jerusalem. He was a member of its Board of Governors and attended the university's inauguration ceremony in 1925, at which he was one of the speakers. In that same year Horovitz was asked by the university's chancellor, Judah Magnes (1877–1948), to draft a paper setting out a proposal for the establishment of an Institute of Arabic and Islamic Studies. This document became the founding memorandum of the School of Oriental Studies at the Hebrew University, which was opened in 1926 and headed by Horovitz himself, who once again came to Jerusalem and taught a condensed seminar. Maintaining his position in Frankfurt and never moving to Jerusalem, Horovitz functioned as director in absentia. He nevertheless supervised every aspect of the school's management and activities, receiving updates and delivering instructions via daily correspondence with Magnes and the school's initial members of faculty—Leo Aryeh Mayer (1895–1959), David Zvi (Hartwig) Baneth (1893–1973), Levi Billig (1897–1936), Yosef Yoel Rivlin (1889–1971), and Shelomo Dov (Fritz) Goitein (1900–1985), the latter two having previously been Horovitz's doctoral students in Frankfurt.

It is thus hardly surprising that the school's first two research projects were determined by Horovitz, on the strength of his personal interest in them. These were the preparation of a concordance of classical Arabic poetry, which was painstakingly classified on index cards; and the editing and publishing of the Arabic manuscript of the seminal work of the famed ninth-century historian Al-Balādhurī, *Ansāb al-Ashrāf* (Genealogies of the Nobles). The latter was carried out in collaboration with the Preußische Staatsbibliothek (Prussian State Library) in Berlin, which delivered to Jerusalem photos and copies of the original manuscript. All this points to the fact (often cited by the School of Oriental Studies' critics in British Mandate Palestine) that by and large, this new institute preserved its German-Jewish scientific legacy during the initial years of its existence, both in terms of research interests (classical Arabic, early Islamic history) and scientific methods (meticulous philology and version comparison).

Finding a New Home for the Scientific *Nachlass*

Horovitz's sudden death in 1931 (he had not suffered from any known illness) forced the oriental institutes in Frankfurt and Jerusalem to regroup.[2] A well-known successor was brought to Frankfurt—Gotthold Eljakim Weil (1882–1960), who until then had served as director of the Oriental Department at the Preußische Staatsbibliothek (which he has founded in 1918). Weil also inherited the School of Oriental Studies from Horovitz, and became its new director. But things were no longer the same: With Horovitz gone, and Weil's epistolary involvement less frequent, the scholars in Jerusalem grew more independent.

Having passed away at the age of 57, Horovitz left behind several research projects that had not come to fruition. His wife, Laura Horovitz (née Scheier, 1881–1933), was well aware of this, and offered to provide information on her late husband's completed and uncompleted work. With the help of Horovitz's former student Ilse Lichtenstädter (later Lichtenstadter, 1907–1991), an index of his research notes (which was either created by Horovitz himself or, perhaps more likely, by Lichtenstädter) was sent to another former student of his, Shelomo Dov Goitein, now a faculty member at the School of Oriental Studies in Jerusalem. Goitein was informed that if he wished to view research materials pertaining to one of the topics in the index, the relevant packet of research notes would be sent to him upon his request. This offer was probably linked to Goitein's work on an obituary of Horovitz, which was published in 1934, during the course of which he corresponded with Horovitz's brother, Rabbi Jacob Horovitz, asking him for biographical documents relating to his late brother Josef.[3]

2 As Plessner described, it was an "immediate death on the street due to heart failure" ("der Tod trat auf der Straße durch Herzschlag ein"). NLI, ARC. 4°1911, Plessner to Goitein, 4 March 1931.

3 NLI, ARC. 4°1510/16, Josef Horovitz Collection, Jacob Horovitz to Shelomo Dov Goitein, 25 October 1933.

While the index itself is rather unremarkable, it is an excellent source of information about Horovitz's research interests and projects (fig. 1). It is divided into more than a dozen categories, among them *Eschatologie*, *Sprachgebrauch*, and *Altarabische Poesie*. Each category comprises several enumerated items, which represent the various topics contained within it.[4] For example, the category *Eschatologie* includes 16 items, such as "6. Paradies," "27. Himmel," "26. Erde," and "17. Gericht" (the lists are not ordered numerically). Alongside some of the items, a note indicates that some other scholar was working on the material. In the category *Gebet, Liturgie u. religiöse Dichtung*, for example, the index mentions that both of its items were "taken by Dr. Billig." Not all categories, however, represented unfinished work: The category *Vorlesungen u. Referate*, for example, comprised 13 items pertaining to various—not only scientific—themes that Horovitz had studied, including "The political prospects of Zionism."

Whatever Goitein's involvement with the index may have been, the materials themselves remained in the possession of Laura Horovitz. Yet before long, in February 1933, she too passed away. Since the couple were childless, in her last will made in November 1932 Laura stipulated that her late husband's scientific *Nachlass* be donated to the Oriental Seminar in Frankfurt, on condition that

> "my husband's successor to the Chair of Oriental Languages, and particularly Mr. Prof. Dr. Gotthold Weil [...] are going to supervise that this *Nachlass* will continue to be examined and used, namely in suitable cooperation with my husband's students, who work on different parts of the scientific *Nachlass* anyhow. Also extra care should be taken to hand the scientific *Nachlass* and the documents only to people where it is clear that the material is going to be used in an adequate manner—with references and within the general framework of the use of the *Nachlass*'s other scientific material."[5]

4 NLI, ARC. 4°1510/16, untitled index.

5 "[...] der Nachfolger meines Mannes auf dem Lehrstuhl für Orientalische Sprachen, und insbesondere Herr Professor Dr. Gotthold Weil [...] die Aufsicht darüber übernimmt, dass dieser Nachlass weiter nachgeprüft und verwertet wird, und zwar in tunlichster Zusammenarbeit mit den Schülern meines Mannes, die ohnehin andere Teile des wissenschaftlichen Nachlasses bearbeiten. Insbesondere möge darauf geachtet werden, dass der wissenschaftliche Nachlass und die Unterlagen nur an Persönlichkeiten ausgegeben werden, bei denen klarsteht, dass die Verwertung des Materials auch unter Hinweis auf dieses Material und im Gesamtrahmen der Verwertung des sonstigen wissenschaftlichen Materials aus dem Nachlass in entsprechender Weise erfolgt." The Archives of the Hebrew University (henceforth AHU), School of Oriental Studies, File 226/1934, Rechtsanwalt [Abraham] Horovitz to the Hebrew University, 10 April 1934.

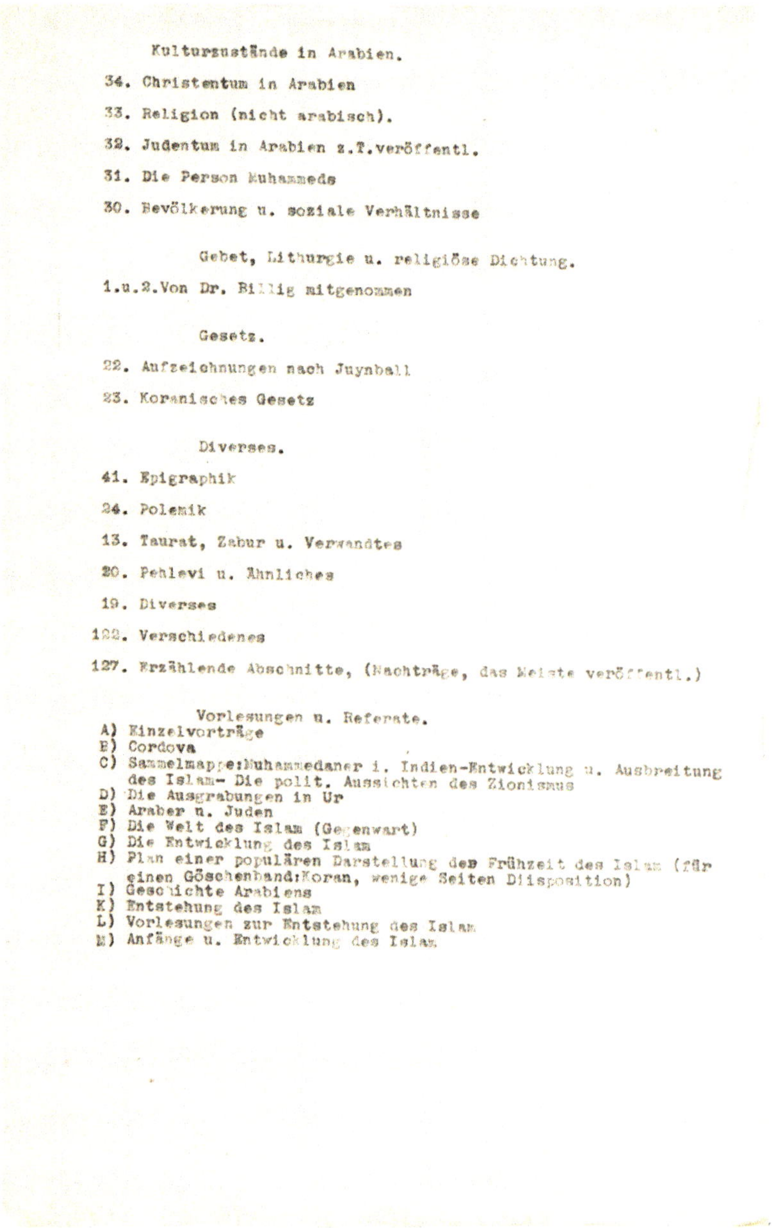
Kulturzustände in Arabien.

34. Christentum in Arabien

33. Religion (nicht arabisch).

32. Judentum in Arabien z.T.veröffentl.

31. Die Person Muhammeds

30. Bevölkerung u. soziale Verhältnisse

Gebet, Lithurgie u. religiöse Dichtung.

1.u.2.Von Dr. Billig mitgenommen

Gesetz.

22. Aufzeichnungen nach Juynball

23. Koranisches Gesetz

Diverses.

41. Epigraphik

24. Polemik

13. Taurat, Zabur u. Verwandtes

20. Pehlevi u. Ähnliches

19. Diverses

122. Verschiedenes

127. Erzählende Abschnitte, (Nachträge, das Meiste veröffentl.)

Vorlesungen u. Referate.

A) Einzelvorträge
B) Cordova
C) Sammelmappe:Muhammedaner i. Indien-Entwicklung u. Ausbreitung des Islam- Die polit. Aussichten des Zionismus
D) Die Ausgrabungen in Ur
E) Araber u. Juden
F) Die Welt des Islam (Gegenwart)
G) Die Entwicklung des Islam
H) Plan einer populären Darstellung des Frühzeit des Islam (für einen Göschenband:Koran, wenige Seiten Diisposition)
I) Geschichte Arabiens
K) Entstehung des Islam
L) Vorlesungen zur Entstehung des Islam
M) Anfänge u. Entwicklung des Islam

Fig. 1: A page of the index of Horovitz's scientific *Nachlass*, c. 1932.

Subject to these conditions—supervision by Weil, cooperation with Josef Horovitz's students, and use of the material and the intellectual property only by persons who would make it known that it had been obtained from the *Nachlass*—it was up to the executor of the will, Josef's younger brother, the lawyer Abraham Horovitz (1880–1953), to deliver the *Nachlass* to the university in Frankfurt.

By that time, however, the political and intellectual climate in Germany had changed: The NSDAP had risen to power. While Professor Gotthold Weil was able to remain in his post, other Jewish scholars such as Martin Plessner were dismissed. While this was not explicitly stated, it was probably due to these circumstances that at the beginning of 1934 the Board of Directors *(Kuratorium)* of the university in Frankfurt informed Abraham Horovitz that "the Oriental Seminar is not in a position to fulfill the assigned tasks and therefore cannot accept the inheritance."[6] Abraham now had to find another home for his late brother's scientific *Nachlass*.

Following a conversation he held on the subject with Gotthold Weil, Abraham decided to approach the Hebrew University, acknowledging his brother's strong connection to that institution. On 10 April 1934, he wrote to the Hebrew University citing Laura Horovitz's will and explaining that the University of Frankfurt had declined the offer, and enquired whether the Hebrew University would agree to take possession of the *Nachlass* subject to the abovementioned conditions. He stressed that he required a prompt answer, since his sister—Mrs. Alfred Bermann (referred to as Sofie or Sophie in the letters; 1891–1964), was about to travel to Palestine, presumably not merely to visit but to migrate. Abraham hoped that she could take "the suitcase that contains the scientific *Nachlass*" with her.

Abraham's offer elicited a mixed response among the faculty of the Hebrew University. Professor L. A. Mayer, who had become a leading figure in the School in the years following Horovitz's death, sent a brief note to the Hebrew University's administrator, Moshe Ben-David (1898–1948), in which he noted that the School of Oriental Studies had never taken upon itself the "Behandlung dieses Nachlasses" (handling of this legacy); while the note was written in Hebrew, these three words were written in German, presumably to underscore that this request had been made from the Frankfurt end.[7]

The university's response to Abraham Horovitz, albeit polite, stressed this very point: The university's vice-chancellor, Max Schloessinger (1877–1944), thanked Abraham Horovitz, going as far as to declare that the latter "could not find a place where the memory of [his] brother and his wife would be more cherished and beloved than by the School of Oriental Studies of the Hebrew University in Jerusalem." But he stated plainly that the school would not necessarily work on the material: "We cannot promise, however, that

6 AHU, School of Oriental Studies, File 226/1934, Rechtsanwalt [Abraham] Horovitz to the Hebrew University, 10 April 1934.

7 AHU, School of Oriental Studies, File 226/1934, L. A. Mayer to [Moshe] Ben-David, n. d.

we will publish this material, be this for lack of scholars who will have the time to bring it to a point that it can be published, be this for lack of funds to publish it, or for any other reason." Nevertheless, the university—represented by Schloessinger—agreed to the other terms in Laura Horovitz's will, promising not to "hand out this material to scholars who would not comply with the terms mentioned in your letter, and Professor Weil's general supervision may serve as an additional guarantee of our conscientious compliance with the regulations laid out in your letter."[8]

This was, apparently, good enough for the Horovitz siblings. Perhaps it was the turbulent present—and the uncertain future—of Jews in Germany that led them to deliver the *Nachlass* irrespective of this reservation, knowing that it may not be handled in the way that Laura Horovitz had stipulated; yet leaving it in the hands of former students of Josef Horovitz was still a relatively safe option. And so, on 5 September 1934, Sofie Bermann wrote to the Hebrew University, informing it that the material "has now arrived here at Haifa."[9] She regretted that she would be unable to come to Jerusalem to hand it over in person, and it was soon arranged that someone would be dispatched from Jerusalem to receive it. In early October 1934 the suitcase was already in the possession of the Hebrew University.[10] The process of knowledge transfer, which began when Josef Horovitz founded the School of Oriental Studies, was now completed by means of a material transfer, by a suitcase that carried his scientific heritage from Frankfurt to Jerusalem.

What is Left?

The year 1934 is also the point at which the archive fell dormant. We do not know precisely what happened to the *Nachlass* over the years, or how well the documents it contained survived the university's moves around Jerusalem after the Hebrew University had to leave Mt. Scopus in 1948, scattering its departments and personnel around Western Jerusalem and later building a new, alternative campus on Giv'at Ram. The *Nachlass* eventually ended up as a collection (ARC. 4°1510) in the Jewish National and University Library (which later changed its name to the National Library of Israel) (figs. 2 and 3). An inventory entry for December 1976 merely

8 AHU, School of Oriental Studies, File 226/1934, Max Schloessinger to Rechtsanwalt [sic] Horovitz, 21 May 1934.

9 AHU, School of Oriental Studies, File 226/1934, Sophie Bermann to the Hebrew University, 5 September 1934.

10 AHU, School of Oriental Studies, File 226/1934, M[oshe] Ben-David to Sofie Bermann-Horovitz, 8 October 1934.

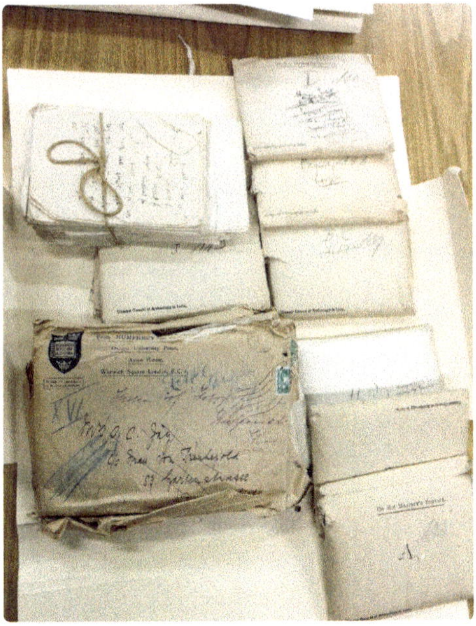

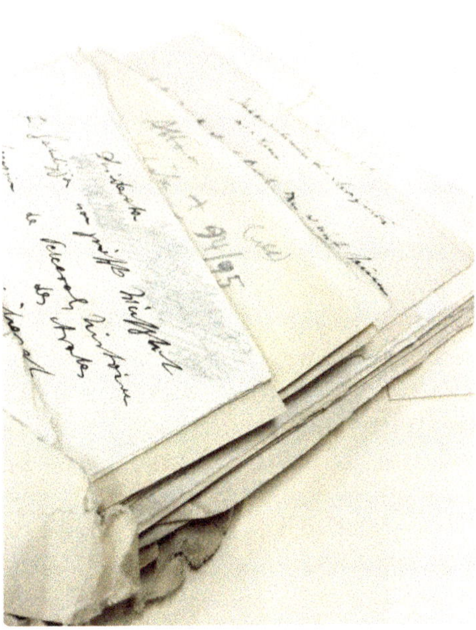

Fig. 2 and 3: Packets of handwritten research notes and documents from the scientific *Nachlass*.

mentions that this collection is the archive of "the orientalist, Prof. Josef Horovitz (Frankfurt). Includes only notes and lists in German and Arabic."

For years, this collection has been virtually unusable for research purposes. The orientalists who were familiar with the research materials at first hand, namely Horovitz's students, either left the School, retired, or died; and there was no index attached to the collection. The packets of handwritten notes contained in yellowing envelopes—some of whose topics were undecipherable—were simply forgotten. Researchers who wished to inspect this collection, whose origins were (as the inventory note indicated) uncertain, could do little without a user guide. Scholars in Germany speculated that Horovitz's research papers had gone missing during World War II.

Luckily, the fortunes of the Horovitz collection changed in 2016. During the course of work on the joint German-Israeli project, "Traces and Treasures of German-Jewish History in Israel," the collections of German-Jewish orientalists at the National Library of Israel were sorted and catalogued. Among the documents that were found and reevaluated was the abovementioned list that Laura Horovitz and Ilse Lichtenstädter had sent to Shelomo Dov Goitein back in 1932. From their notes and the topics in the list it became clear that the list could be used as an index for the Horovitz *Nachlass*. All that remained was to match the entries in the list to the actual packets. Some packets were missing—either because they were lost during the journey, handed over to students of Horovitz in Frankfurt, or used in Jerusalem at some point. Yet large parts of the collection remained intact. With the help of the index, it was possible to create a catalogue of the *Nachlass*, a task completed in 2016. More than seventy years after they were shipped to Jerusalem in a suitcase, Josef Horovitz's research notes can finally be put to use again.

The topic of German-Jewish Orientalism and its transplantation to Palestine/Israel has gained scholarly attention in recent years, with studies on different aspects of this multilayered case study of knowledge transfer currently being contemplated. One of the principal questions that emerges from this study addresses the extent to which German scientific themes, methods, and academic habitus influenced the evolution of oriental studies in Palestine/Israel. The School of Oriental Studies (today's Institute of Asian and African Studies), the oldest oriental institute in Palestine/Israel, obviously constitutes one of the focal points for scholars who attempt to unravel the question of influence and other issues related to this research topic.

While the spatial and chronological path of the Horovitz *Nachlass* should not be considered analogous to the transplantation of the entire discipline, since it represents only a single case of transference among many, it is tempting to view it as emblematic of a broader phenomenon. It was imperative that the *Nachlass* should leave Germany, just as German-Jewish scholars, among them orientalists, had to do. Some of them, such as Max Bravmann and Martin Plessner, also ended up in Jerusalem; and while other German-Jewish orientalists had arrived earlier, after 1933 the option of returning to Germany was no longer available to them either. As Horovitz's dominant influence waned after his demise, some of the scholars at the School of Oriental Studies began looking for other research projects, and as a result his research materials—just as his scientific heritage—were no longer accorded a high priority, to say the least. The field of Oriental studies was undergoing a gradual disciplinary change in Palestine, as it was in other oriental institutions that had European roots. The United States offers, perhaps, the clearest example, where one discerns an inclination to engage in contemporary topics with immediate political relevance. Perhaps the lingual shift within the discipline and in parts of the academic world in general—from German to English as its lingua franca—did not add to the appeal of these densely handwritten German *Zettel*. In British Mandate Palestine, some orientalists turned their attention to Oriental (especially Yemenite) Jews and to modern Arabic literature. Students at the School of Oriental Studies—many of whom were either born in Palestine or had arrived from non-German-speaking lands and who did not necessarily read German—were not that interested in ancient poetry, and sought to gain conversational skills that would help them find employment in the multilingual job market.

Eventually, in light of contesting orientalist traditions and political and security needs in Mandate Palestine and all the more so in the State of Israel, the *Nachlass* was buried in closed, virtually inaccessible storage rooms—just like the legacy of Horovitz itself, which has been largely confined to the realm of the subconscious within Israel's academia. (It is generally Goitein—perhaps the scholar who made the most radical changes to his research topics and methods following his emigration from Germany—who is remembered in Israel today as the founding father of oriental studies in Palestine/Israel.) Only in recent years have Horovitz and his *Nachlass* resurfaced and gained recognition as an important component in the reconstruction of the history of oriental studies in Palestine/Israel.

Perhaps above all, this intriguing story of the physical transfer of knowledge—in the form of *Zettel*, research notes—illustrates the point that this was not entirely a matter of one-way traffic. The Jerusalem orientalists have, from the very beginning, for the most part adopted an orientation different to that of Horovitz, who remained a somewhat shadowy presence among them. Accepting the Horovitz *Nachlass* but using little of it to construct their new research projects; and respecting his legacy without committing to it, were stepping stones in the process of forging a new disciplinary amalgam: Israeli Orientalism.

Literature

Shelomo Dov Goitein, Josef Horovitz, in: Der Islam 22 (1934), 122–127.

Gudrun Jäger, Der jüdische Islamwissenschaftler Josef Horovitz und der Lehrstuhl für semitische Philologie an der Universität Frankfurt am Main 1915–1949, in: Jörn Kobes/Jan-Otmar Hesse (eds.), Frankfurter Wissenschaftler zwischen 1933 und 1945, Göttingen 2008, 61–79.

Hava Lazarus-Yafeh, The Transplantation of Islamic Studies from Europe to the Yishuv and Israel, in: Martin Kramer (ed.), The Jewish Discovery of Islam. Studies in Honor of Bernard Lewis, Tel Aviv 1999, 249–260.

Sabine Mangold-Will, Gotthold Weil, die Orientalische Philologie und die deutsche Wissenschaft an der Hebräischen Universität, in: Naharaim. Zeitschrift für deutsch-jüdische Literatur und Kulturgeschichte/Journal of German-Jewish Literature and Cultural History 8 (2014), no. 1, 74–90.

Menahem Milson, The Beginnings of Arabic and Islamic Studies at the Hebrew University of Jerusalem, in: Shaul Katz/Michael Heyd (eds.), The History of the Hebrew University of Jerusalem. Origins and Beginnings, Jerusalem 2000, 575–588 (Heb.).

Author

Amit Levy studied history and political science at the Hebrew University of Jerusalem, where he receiced his master's degree in 2016. He is a fellow at the Mandel School PhD Honors Program and the research coordinator of the "Traces and Treasures of German-Jewish History in Israel" project. His dissertation focuses on the transplantation of oriental studies from Germany to Palestine/Israel and the role of the School of Oriental Studies in that process. *Selected Publications*: The Archive as Storyteller. Refractions of German-Jewish Oriental Studies Migration in Personal Archives, in: Jahrbuch des Dubnow-Instituts/Dubnow Institute Yearbook 17 (2018) (forthcoming); Orientalist Collections at the National Library of Israel, in: Geschichte der Germanistik 49/50 (2016), 147f.; A Man of Contention. Martin Plessner (1900–1973) and His Encounters with the Orient, in: Naharaim. Zeitschrift für deutsch-jüdische Literatur und Kulturgeschichte/Journal of German-Jewish Literature and Cultural History 10 (2016), no. 1, 79–100.

ADI LIVNY

A History of Adversity: The Historical Archive of the Hebrew University of Jerusalem

At the beginning of 2016, we (a group of research students at the Hebrew University) began work on a project dedicated to the Historical Archive of the Hebrew University.[1] This project combines the preservation and systematic cataloguing of the materials of the archive for the years 1918–1948, with a study of the history of the Hebrew University in the pre-state era.

Some of us were already well acquainted with the archive and were aware of the historical treasures it contains. As an institutional archive, it includes the materials of the university's different administrative bodies, its departments and institutes, and the personnel files of faculty and administrative staff. There, within what often seems very ordinary and mundane, one can gain a vivid picture of university life in Mandate Palestine. The materials depicting the university's newly established departments serve as valuable source for a *Wissenschaftsgeschichte* of Palestine. The archive furthermore includes traces of the distinct period in which the university was established, alluding to both the national conflict in Palestine and World War II as they were experienced within the Jewish community in Palestine and elsewhere. It also reflects the transnational movement of scholars and potential students, making it a prime source of documentation on Jewish émigrés and refugees in the years preceding and following World War II.

Yet, the archive's importance is somewhat overshadowed by some striking limitations. Among these are the poor state of some of the materials, which spill out from their dusty and sometimes torn boxes onto the large metal shelves on which they lie in the basement of the Administra-

1 The project "The Historical Archive of the Hebrew University: German-Jewish Knowledge and Cultural Transfer, 1918–1948" is a joint endeavor of the Franz Rosenzweig Minerva Research Center for German-Jewish Literature and Cultural History, the Archive of the Hebrew University, and the Deutsches Literaturarchiv Marbach, and is supported by the Gerda Henkel Foundation. I would like to thank Ofer Tzemach, the archive's director, for his valuable assistance.

Contested Heritage, 129–138 | doi.org/10.13109/9783666310836.129

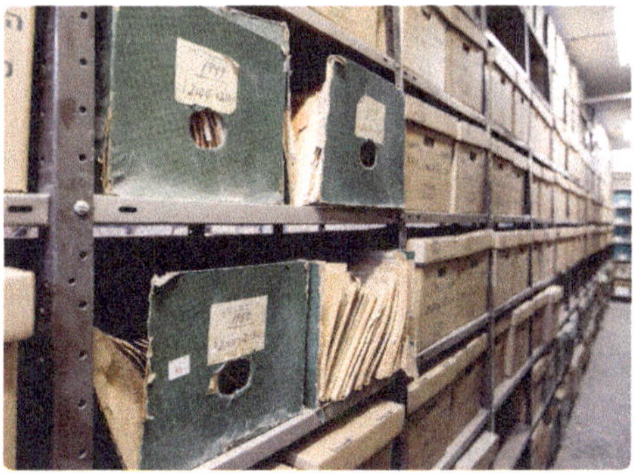

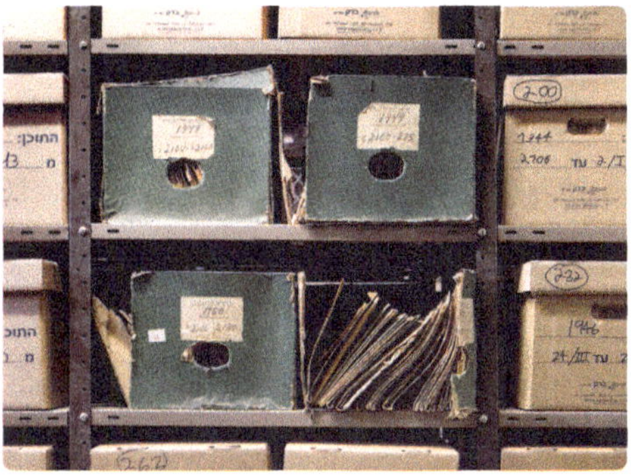

Fig. 1 and 2: The Historical Archive of the Hebrew University.

tion Building at the Hebrew University's campus on Mount Scopus (figs. 1 and 2). Accordingly, a major task of the project is the material preservation of the archive. Another task is to enhance its accessibility to scholars: Its current finding aid, which is partially hand-written, offers only a general description of files and is available only in Hebrew, making the archive de facto inaccessible to most international scholars.

Five percent of the material, so we were told when the project began, was lost or destroyed when the university was forced to vacate its original site on Mount Scopus during the 1948 War and during its subsequent return following the recapture of the Mount in the 1967 War. This is far from unprecedented: Archives frequently have been and continue to become victims of war. As the project proceeded and we examined the archive's files year by year, we found some clues as to the fate of the lost items. A sequence of missing files for the year 1933, for example, led us to conclude that an entire box was missing. Presumably, though, most of the lost material is indiscernible. Only seldom does that which is absent leave a trail—especially in this archive, given the inadequacy of its current finding aid (figs. 3 and 4).

Seeking to gain a fuller picture of the archive's history, I turned to its self-documentation, namely to the records that relate to the archive itself; in other words, I listened as the archive told its own history. While the records do not fully account for the archive's history, leaving many "gaps" or "silences" (to borrow Derrida's rather overused phrase), they nonetheless provide us with a self-deciphering tool. Apart from the textual recollection that the records provide, the archive's materiality—its physical condition and state of preservation—in itself constitutes a further source of decoding.

While the Historical Archive of the Hebrew University was officially established in 1925, this short article focuses on its history during and following the 1948 war—examining in particular the effects of "external" political events on its fate. References to the "archive" in the following

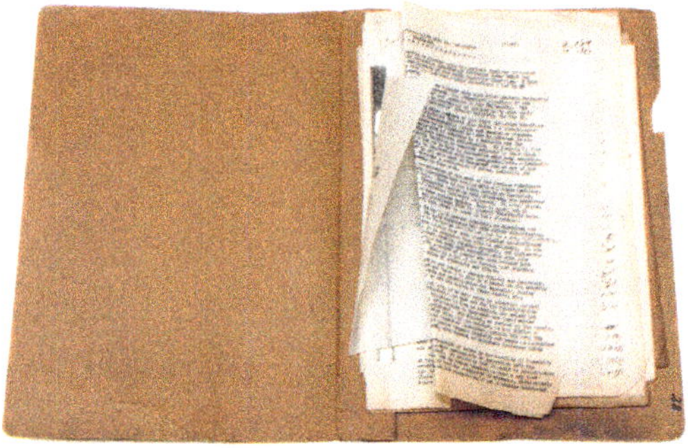

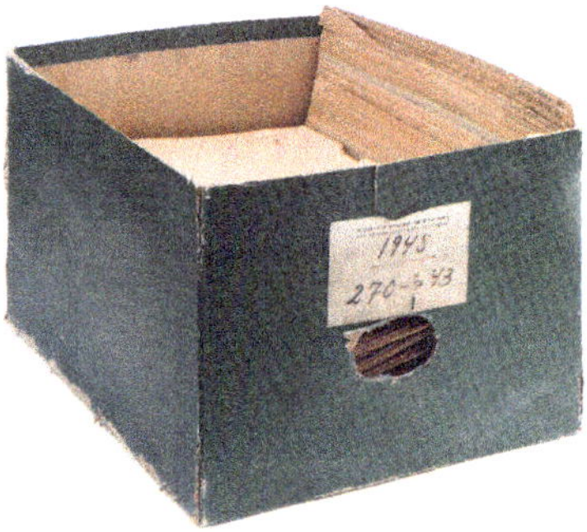

Fig. 3 and 4: One of the boxes and files in the archive containing documents from 1948.

cover its various components; not only the bulk of its collections, but also the office of the archive, which at times remained separated from its stacks.

Year Zero: 1948

Beginning in December 1947, the Hebrew University's regular activity was disrupted by the events that were to become known as the 1948 War, which commenced with several armed attacks on vehicles making their way to Mount Scopus from the city center. Thus, already in January 1948, the academic and administrative activity of the university was transferred to the city center. While the archive's stacks remained on Mount Scopus, its operation and staff were quickly relocated to an office on the central Ben Yehuda Street, in the building of the Kupat Milve bank ("Loan-Fund Bank").[2]

The university functioned there for no more than a few weeks before the bombing of 22 February 1948. At 6:30 in the morning, three British army trucks were blown up by Arab irregulars assisted by British deserters on Ben Yehuda Street. In the bombing, in which 49 people were killed and 140 injured, four buildings collapsed and others were damaged—among them the building that housed the archive's office. This event quickly led to a change in the plan—drawn up only a few weeks previously—to continue to operate the archive from the building on Ben Yehuda Street.[3] After the bombing, though, a different location had to be found for the archive. "The office was not badly damaged, but everything there was upside down,"

2 The Hebrew University of Jerusalem, Avraham Harman Institute of Contemporary Jewry, History of the Hebrew University Collection I, File 117/23, Interview with Yehoshua Rivlin, 1983; The Archives of the Hebrew University (henceforth AHU), File 81/1948, Yitzhak Hoffmann to Noah Sheffer, 9 February 1948 (all sources cited here are translations by the author from the Hebrew).

3 AHU, File 81/1948, Yitzhak Hoffmann to Noah Sheffer, 9 February 1948.

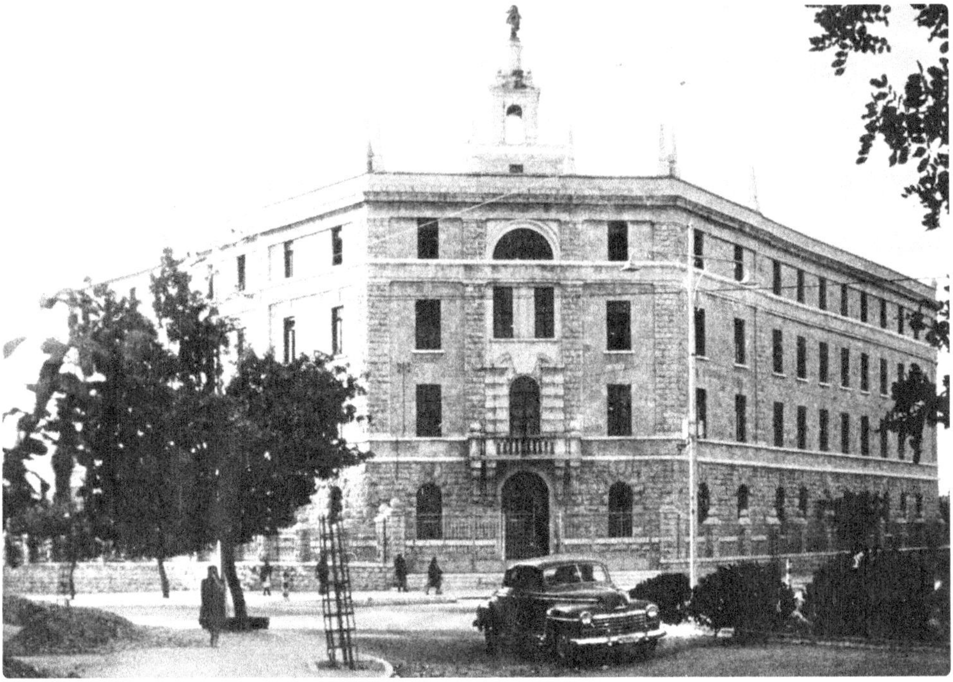

Fig. 5: The Hebrew University's temporary building at Terra Santa, 1949.

recalled Yehoshua Rivlin, who worked in the archive and was soon to become its director, in a 1983 interview. It was moved to a private residence not far from there, at 26 King George Street. "It is especially important, in these days, to precisely maintain the regular archival procedures," wrote the archive's director, Noah Sheffer, only a few days after the bombing and its ensuing relocation.

While many still hoped to return to Mount Scopus after the 1948 War, the Hebrew University's detachment from Mount Scopus became—at least for the time being—an unavoidable fact. As the lengthy deliberations over the location of a new campus dragged on, the university operated in thirty different places in central Jerusalem. A major locus of its activities was the Terra Santa compound (fig. 5), which was leased to the university in 1948. Originally known as Terra Sancta, the compound was built in 1926 by the religious Italian S. Paolo Association, and initially housed the Opera Cardinal Ferrari School. After its closure in 1929, it became home to the Terra Santa College, which consisted of an elementary school and a high school.

Among the administrative and academic units that functioned in the building was the archive. Located on the ground floor of the building, it shared its space with a cleaning supplies storage, which was located within the room of the archive itself. Noah Sheffer, the archivist, complained about the inconvenience of this arrangement, "adding to the noise and pervasive pungent odors that cause headaches, the cleaning personnel," he maintained, "wander around in the archive room, and the person in charge of materials draws up his lists in our room." Given the university's general lack of space, one may assume that few departments were happy with the new arrangements. Perhaps in light of these circumstances, Sheffer proposed that if the storage room could not be relocated, the archive should return to its previous rooms. A few months later it was reported that the "problem of space in the archive is extremely severe." "After carefully looking into the matter," the university's administrative secretary was indeed willing to agree that "it is impossible to continue working at all without solving this matter."[4]

In a complex round of musical chairs, the university's economic director suggested that the office of the archive be moved from the ground floor in the Terra Santa compound to two small rooms to be built on the third floor. For storage, the archive would be assigned a "space beneath the stairs leading from the third to the fourth floor." Yehoshua Rivlin, now the archive's director, strongly objected to this suggestion. Arguing that the proposed office could not possibly accommodate the archive's six employees, he announced that it was his duty "to reject a deterioration in the already trying working conditions." Rivlin furthermore argued against the use of a separate space (beneath the stairs between the floors) as storage for the contents of the archive, protesting at the prospect that the "secret archive and personnel files would stand outside, accessible to all."[5]

The archive's records for the following years do not reveal how this conflict over the archive's location was resolved. Whatever arrangement was reached, a year later Rivlin was still dissatisfied: The archive's records for 1953 once again include a reference to the overcrowding in the archive's 35-square-meter office, with Rivlin complaining that "two cabinets are now placed outside [the office]." Toward the end of 1953, Rivlin submitted yet another complaint about the conditions, protesting "that within the various arrangements in the administration building the archive is discriminated against." The archive's employees, he reported, "are working in a very cramped space, the cabinets placed in the office are inadequate, it is cold in the rooms, and there are always coats laid on the doors and cabinets."[6]

4 AHU, File 81/1949, Noah Sheffer to Yochanan Carl Sulman, 30 August 1949; AHU, File 81/1950, Yitzhak Hoffmann to Yochanan Carl Sulman, 17 January 1950.

5 AHU, File 81/1951, Yochanan Carl Sulman to the Committee on Facilities Distribution (Vaadat Halukat Ha'shtachim), 23 December 1951; Yehoshua Rivlin to Yitzhak Hoffmann, 28 December 1951.

6 AHU, File 81/1953, Yehoshua Rivlin to Yitzhak Hoffmann, 16 January 1953; Yehoshua Rivlin to Yitzhak Hoffmann, n. d. [3 November 1953].

Although these documents make no direct reference to the archive's location, it is possible that these poor—yet seemingly recent—conditions were the result of yet another transfer of the archive across the street from Terra Santa to the building of the Social Security Institute—which Rivlin mentions in an interview he gave in 1983.

A New Beginning

The inauguration of the university's spacious new campus at Givat Ram in April 1958 finally put an end to the university's wanderings. Planned by the architects Richard Klarwein, Heinz Rau, and Richard Kaufmann, the new campus reflected the latest trends in the modernist "international style." The archive, Rivlin recalled in his 1983 interview, was among the first university divisions to relocate to the new campus, some time before the campus' official opening.

The transition, however, did not put paid to what its workers regarded as unsatisfactory working conditions. In a letter written by the archive's staff to its director in February 1958, stored in the archive's records for that year, they report that they were now working "in a closed basement, sealed off from any sunlight and with a minimal amount of air…" Many of them, they continued, "have recently begun to suffer from headaches and eye complaints and are consequently forced to take sick leave."[7]

This document is revealing, since it offers the first report on the archive's state and working conditions from someone other than its director. This is not to suggest that director Rivlin saw things any differently. In light of his frequent and pressing complaints in the years to come, Rivlin himself may well have encouraged or even instructed his workers to pen an official complaint about the conditions. Rivlin forwarded the letter to the university's administrator, noting his deep concern about "the archive's good name" and wondering "how much longer they can take it." Rivlin, who had worked at the university since 1935, added the persuasive argument that he had been taken ill over the preceding year more often than in all of his years of service at the university. Similar references to the impact of the conditions at the archive on the employees' health continued to appear in Rivlin's persistent complaints to the administration about the enclosed space and lack of natural light.[8]

7 AHU, File 81/1958, The Archive's Staff to Yehoshua Rivlin, 19 February 1958.

8 AHU, Yehoshua Rivlin to Asher Reshef/Yitzhak Hoffmann, 20 February 1958; Yehoshua Rivlin to Asher Reshef, 8 April 1958; AHU, File 160/1959, Yehoshua Rivlin to Yitzhak Hoffmann, 6 January 1959.

Once again, we do not know how the problem was resolved this time. The archive continued to function for a good twenty years. By this time Rivlin, who served as the archive's director for almost forty years (he retired in 1985 and continued to volunteer in the archive thereafter),[9] had guided the archive through its last transition—back to Mount Scopus.

Mount Scopus was recaptured during Israel's swift occupation of the West Bank and Gaza Strip. By July 1967, the university had already decided to return to the Mount. This move would take a while longer, but the archive was one of the first administrative organs to return to Mount Scopus, sometime in 1979.[10]

Presumably, with its return to Mount Scopus the archive could finally incorporate all its former records. During the period of the enclave, the university managed to lay its hands on the contents of the archive that remained on Mount Scopus. As Rivlin revealed in his 1983 interview, the university had eventually managed to bring out all its personnel and student files. Under the terms of the demilitarization agreement concluded in 1948, Israel was permitted to deploy a small police force on the Mount to protect and maintain the university's property. Convoys taking a complement up to the Mount and bringing another back down would travel from West Jerusalem once a fortnight, subject to a UN escort and supervision. These "policemen" were in fact soldiers, and in 1954 a special unit was formed to perform the designated tasks that service on Mount Scopus called for.

"Following the separation from Mount Scopus in 1948," a subsequent official memorandum read, "we managed to bring it [the archive] down to town bit by bit, 'stealthily' in the Mount Scopus convoys, and they [the contents] were moved between several places in town until returning to their first home on the Mount. During these wanderings, a small quantity of files was lost."[11]

It is perhaps paradoxical that, just as the archive's office managed to reassemble its collections and finally settle back into the location it had been forced to leave more than thirty years earlier, it was confronted with yet another threat. At least this is the impression gained by an inspector from the Israel State Archives who paid a visit to the university's archive in 1983. Moshe Mossek, director of the Department of Records Management

9 AHU, Personal Record of Yehoshua Rivlin, Yehoshua Rivlin to Hanoch Gutfreund, 7 March 1994.

10 The Personal Record of Yehoshua Rivlin dated 5 March 1979 reveals that in February and March 1979 he was approved overtime for working on Mount Scopus in preparation for the archive's return to the Mount. See AHU, Personal Record of Yehoshua Rivlin, 5 March 1979.

11 AHU, File 160/1983, N.a., A Historical Archive for the University, 9 May 1983.

in the State Archives, summarized his impressions in a lengthy, stern letter to the head of the Hebrew University's Administration Department. Mossek reports that during his visit he discovered that the records for the years 1925–1956 were stored in the basement of the students' dorms, above which ran the pipes of the building's heating system. "It is hard to conceive how such important documentary material was placed in a basement that lacks elementary conditions for the day-to-day maintenance and the physical safety of the material," Mossek commented, suggesting that "if the university cannot take care of its records, the State Archives will be willing to take them." The problem of dampness was not the only one that Mossek identified. There was an urgent need, he argued, to replace the cardboard boxes in which the materials were stored, which, according to Mossek, were of poor quality: "Many of them are torn, the folders are spilling out of them onto the shelves and onto the floor of the hall." Mossek concluded that

> "Universities younger than the Hebrew University, whose materials cannot be compared to the materials of the Hebrew University in terms of historical and scholarly value, care for their materials more responsibly and facilitate more efficient and convenient use of the material by the university's institutions and scholars."[12]

Mossek was seemingly unaware that the nightmare scenario that he invoked was already beginning to unfold. As a single document reveals, on 16 May 1983, only a few months before Mossek's visit, "the archive was surrounded by water flowing from the ceiling. Many files became wet," and Rivlin—still the archivist—"could not yet determine the damage."[13]

To mark the sixtieth anniversary of the founding of the Hebrew University, it was decided to collect material that would form the basis for an historical archive of the university. Rivlin, about to retire after fifty years of service to the university, was invited to continue working as a volunteer on the construction of this historical archive. It was then, in 1985, that the section known as the "historical archive" was built.[14] It included the archive's thirty or so first boxes, containing materials for the years 1925 to 1930. These boxes, assembled and organized by Rivlin for the occasion, were found to be in better shape than some of the materials from later years.

Universities, as this example well illustrates, tend to show interest in their history, and by implication also in their archive, especially leading up to an anniversary or some other festive occasion. In the case of the Hebrew University's archive, the university's sixtieth anniversary arrived at an

12 AHU, File 160/1983, Moshe Mossek to Eli Gonen, 5 December 1983.
13 AHU, File 160/1983, Yehoshua Rivlin to Akiva Sobol, 19 May 1983.
14 AHU, File 160/1983, A. Shachar to Yehoshua Rivlin, 11 August 1983.

opportune moment, and marked the end of its long saga of misfortune. As we have seen, like many other organs of the university the archive's functioning was seriously disrupted by the university's departure from and subsequent return to Mount Scopus. It faced its greatest adversity during the early 1950s, when the archive's office had to make do with a confined and inadequate space, which it shared with uninvited roommates in the cramped Terra Santa compound, separated from its records, which remained on Mount Scopus. Some of its later woes, it bears repeating, were not visited upon it by the circumstances of war or geopolitics. The university's relocation to the new spacious campus at Givat Ram did not redeem its employees from what they perceived to be highly inadequate working conditions; nor did its return to the old-new campus on Mount Scopus—and the long-awaited reunification of the archive with its collections—put an end to problems of space and storage and their attendant minor disasters, which belong squarely in the realm of the mundane.

Literature

Uri Cohen, Conflict in Academia. The Hebrew University during the War of Independence, 1947–49, in: The Journal of Israeli History 22 (2003), no. 2, 96–129.

Diana Dolev, An Ivory Tower in the National Precinct. The Architectural Plan for the University Campus in Giva'at Ram, in: Zmanim. A Historical Quarterly 96 (2006), no. 4, 86–93 (Heb.).

David Kroyanker, The Terra Santa Compound, Jerusalem. Biography of a Place—Profile of a Period, 1926–1999, Jerusalem 1999 (Heb.).

Ron Makleff, Sovereignty and Silence. The Creation of a Myth of Archival Destruction, Liège, 1408, in: Archive Journal (2017), <http://www.archivejournal.net/essays/sovereignty-and-silence> (1 August 2019).

Yair Paz, Political and Symbolic Perspectives on Mount Scopus, 1948–1967, in: Cathedra. On the History of Eretz Israel and Its Yishuv 163 (2017), 64–104 (Heb.).

Ernst Posner, Effects of Changes of Sovereignty on Archives, in: The American Archivist 5 (1942), no. 3, 141–155.

Yfaat Weiss, "Nicht durch Macht und nicht durch Kraft, sondern durch meinen Geist." Die Hebräische Universität in der Skopusberg-Enklave, in: Jahrbuch des Simon-Dubnow-Instituts/Simon Dubnow Institute Yearbook 14 (2015), 59–90.

Author

Adi Livny is a PhD student at the Department of Jewish History and Contemporary Jewry, and a fellow of the Mandel School for Advanced Studies in the Humanities at the Hebrew University of Jerusalem. She studied towards her master's degree (2013) in political science in Jerusalem and Freiburg (Germany). Her dissertation deals with the spatial history of the Hebrew University (1925–1948), exploring its relations and affiliations in the Middle East and within the British Empire. From 2016 to 2019 she was the academic coordinator of the project "The Historical Archive of the Hebrew University: German-Jewish Knowledge and Cultural Transfer, 1918–1948." *Selected Publications*: Conscientious Objection and the State. Contextualizing the Israeli Case, in: Armed Forces & Society 44 (2018), no. 4, 666–687; Raketengetrieben. Wie die post-israelische Generation um ihr Leben kämpft, in: Kursbuch 181 (2015), 117–130; "An Order is an Order?" Conscientious Objection in Cold War West Germany, in: Hayo Haya. A Young Forum for History 10 (2014), 94–113 (Heb.).

4. Shifting Centers: Rebuilding Jewish Culture

YFAAT WEISS

The Tricks of Memory: Salo W. Baron, Cecil Roth, and the Salvaging of Jewish Property in Europe

The draft manuscript of the autobiography that Salo W. Baron dictated close to his death has remained unpublished and lies among his papers in the special collections archive at Stanford University. In it, Baron gives a lengthy account of the Jewish Cultural Reconstruction (JCR) enterprise he headed in the late 1940s. This umbrella organization, which sought to salvage Jewish cultural property in Europe after the Holocaust, has recently aroused considerable scholarly interest. Like many autobiographies written in the first person, and perhaps all the more so when it comes to dictated texts when the author has little opportunity to revise the draft and thus to curb his self-aggrandizement, Baron speaks of JCR virtually as his own exclusive enterprise, and writes as follows:

> "As the war progressed it became clear to everybody—even the large majority of people which never anticipated the Holocaust—that the Jewish communities of the continent would be utterly destroyed qua organizations. It was also taken for granted that the great treasures, books, manuscripts, and other materials of intellectual value would have been either destroyed or confiscated by the hostile administration. We all agreed that a much greater effort would have to be made to reconstruct Jewish life in the occupied territories than had been done after World War I. I, for one, felt that the sooner we start making preparations for some such reconstruction of Jewish cultural and religious life, the more we would be in a position to salvage whatever might have remained and start dividing plans for additional needs for reconstruction with regard to schools, libraries, and so on. I personally began agitating in this direction soon after the beginning of the war, and intensified my efforts as its duration extended far beyond all predictions by so-called experts."[1]

1 From the manuscript of Salo W. Baron's unpublished autobiography, Stanford University Libraries, Department of Special Collections and University Archives (henceforth

Contested Heritage, 141–152 | doi.org/10.13109/9783666310836.141

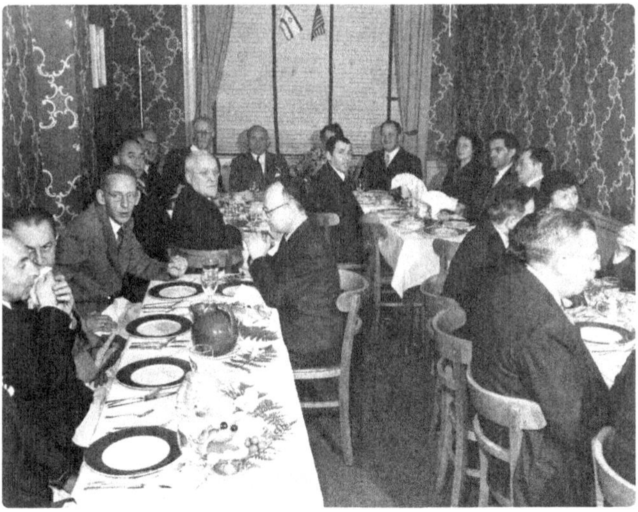

Fig. 1: JCR members in New York, 1951. From left to right: Wolf Blattberg, Philip Friedman, Irvin Weintroub, Joseph Reider, Aaron Margalit, Lawrence Marwick, Chaim Wormann, Alexander Marx, Salo W. Baron, Hannah Arendt, Jacob Novak-Schwimmer, Isaac E. Kiev, M. Gruber, Isaac Goldberg, Jacob Dienstag, Sylvia Landress, David Rosenstein.

Baron proceeds to name several principal figures who engaged in this task. All, apart from Judah Magnes, were Jews who resided in the USA, among them Jerome Michael, a professor of law at Columbia University who served as head of the legal team and briefly as head of the organization, and Hannah Arendt, who served as its executive secretary from 1949 to 1951. Baron next describes how the group in New York compiled a preliminary inventory of Jewish cultural treasures in Europe prior to the Holocaust, subsequently known as the *Tentative List*, which appeared in several issues of the periodical *Jewish Social Studies* that Baron founded and edited (figs. 1 and 2). He then provides a long list of organizations that worked together under the auspices of JCR.

> "All the Jewish international and national organizations of note, like the Jewish Agency, the Joint Distribution Committee, the World Jewish Congress, the American Jewish Committee, etc., and the European Organizations, like the Board of Deputies of British Jews, the Anglo-Jewish Association, the Alliance Israelite, the Hebrew University, and two newly organized groups of Jews in Germany."[2]

Yet there is something missing from this description, which in any event is at odds with the content of two thin files housed in the archives of the Hebrew University in Jerusalem.[3] These files document the approach made by the Jewish Historical Society of England to the Hebrew University in Jerusalem, calling upon it to join the effort to gather information on the location of Jewish cultural property in Europe on the eve of the Holocaust. This request was submitted to the university in early February 1944 on behalf of the society's chairman, Professor Cecil Roth, by Oskar Rabinowicz,

SUL/SCUA), Salo W. Baron Papers, M0580, Box 379, Folder 5, 285 (minor typing errors in the original typescript corrected).

2 SUL/SCUA, Salo W. Baron Papers, M0580, Box 379, Folder 5, 295 (errors in the original typescript corrected).

3 The Archives of the Hebrew University (henceforth AHU), Documents of the Ha-va'ada le-hazalat Ozrot ha-Golah 042, Files 1944I–1944II.

honorary secretary of the committee tasked with the "reconstruction of Jewish museums, libraries and archives in continental Europe." In his letter, Rabinowicz included a print-out of a lecture delivered by Cecil Roth at the inaugural gathering of the initiative of the Jewish Historical Society of England in April 1943 (fig. 3). He likewise provided general instructions on how to register information about the prewar location of this cultural property. The files kept in the Hebrew University Archives clearly indicate that it was the request by the English association, and none other, that prompted the Hebrew University to consider the issue and to take action. It was this request that dictated the method by which information was collected and that led to the founding in Jerusalem of the Committee for the Salvaging of Diaspora Treasures, which, shortly thereafter, became a major player in the salvaging of Jewish cultural property in Europe.

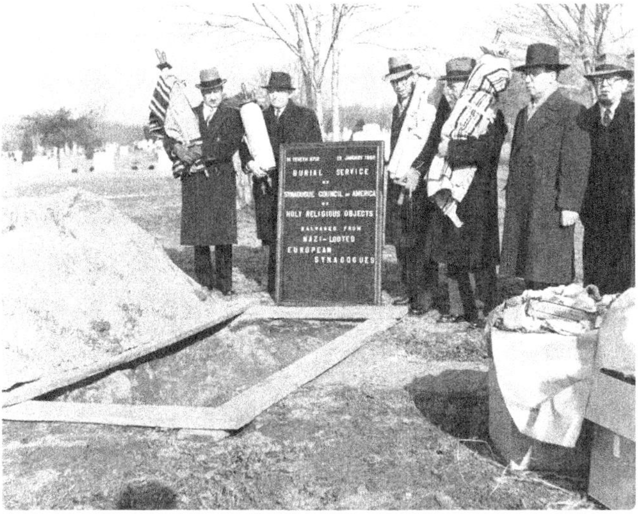

Fig. 2: Burial of the looted Torah scrolls by Salo W. Baron and the Synagogue Council of America, 1952.

From the outset, the English initiative sought international cooperation. A few days after the convention in April 1943, Cecil Roth was quick to bring Salo W. Baron into the picture, informing him of the content of the convention's discussions, noting that "collaboration will be essential," and asking Baron to share with him his views on the matter. He furthermore sent Baron a report on the convention that was due to appear in the *Jewish Chronicle*.[4] Two months later, Roth again wrote to Baron, promising to send him the official declaration adopted at the close of the convention, happy to tell him of various inter-continental contacts and quick to note that "you are surely the proper coordinating authority."[5] It appears that the letter was held up in the post, as Baron had still not received the materials by October 1943, but Roth's overture was generally positive and he demonstrated his goodwill. Baron, for his part, informed Roth that the organization he headed, the Conference on Jewish Relations, had for

4 SUL/SCUA, Salo W. Baron Papers, M0580/19/22, Cecil Roth to Salo Baron, 16 April 1943.
5 See SUL/SCUA, Jewish Social Studies Papers, M0670/13/55(f), Program of the Conference on Jewish Relations (Second Meeting): The Resuscitation of Jewish Cultural Life in Europe.

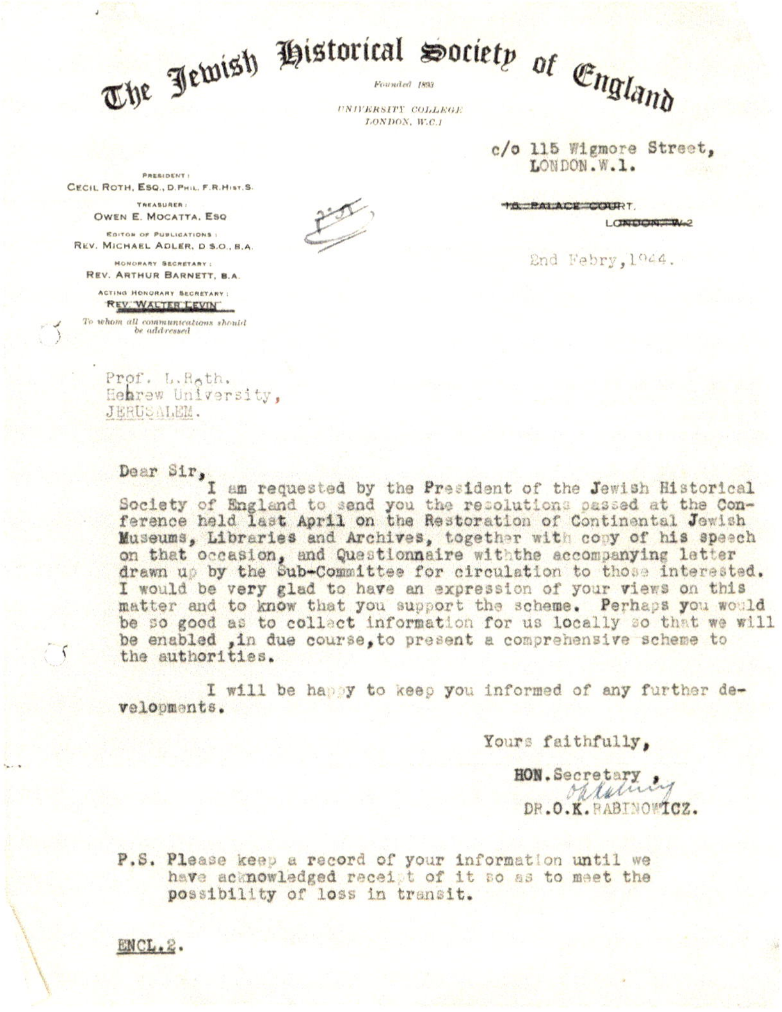

The Jewish Historical Society of England
Founded 1893
UNIVERSITY COLLEGE
LONDON, W.C.1

c/o 115 Wigmore Street,
LONDON.W.1.

~~15, PALACE COURT.~~
~~LONDON. W.2~~

PRESIDENT: CECIL ROTH, ESQ., D.PHIL. F.R.HIST.S.
TREASURER: OWEN E. MOCATTA, ESQ
EDITOR OF PUBLICATIONS: REV. MICHAEL ADLER, D.S.O., B.A.
HONORARY SECRETARY: REV. ARTHUR BARNETT, B.A.
ACTING HONORARY SECRETARY: ~~REV. WALTER LEVIN~~
To whom all communications should be addressed

2nd Febry,1944.

Prof. L.Roth.
Hebrew University,
JERUSALEM.

Dear Sir,

I am requested by the President of the Jewish Historical Society of England to send you the resolutions passed at the Conference held last April on the Restoration of Continental Jewish Museums, Libraries and Archives, together with copy of his speech on that occasion, and Questionnaire with the accompanying letter drawn up by the Sub-Committee for circulation to those interested. I would be very glad to have an expression of your views on this matter and to know that you support the scheme. Perhaps you would be so good as to collect information for us locally so that we will be enabled ,in due course,to present a comprehensive scheme to the authorities.

I will be happy to keep you informed of any further developments.

Yours faithfully,

HON.Secretary ,
DR.O.K.RABINOWICZ.

P.S. Please keep a record of your information until we have acknowledged receipt of it so as to meet the possibility of loss in transit.

ENCL.2.

Fig. 3: Oskar Rabinowicz to Leon Roth, 2 February 1944.

some time been considering embarking on a similar project.[6] Baron was most probably referring to a conference titled "The Resuscitation of Jewish Cultural Life in Europe," which took place in December 1943 at the New School for Social Research. Replying to Roth's letter, Baron announced that he would be very glad to collaborate with his group.

The Jewish Historical Society of England was by several months the first Jewish body to recognize the problem presented by Jewish cultural

6 SUL/SCUA, Salo W. Baron Papers, M0580/25/11, Salo Baron to Cecil Roth, 5 October 1943.

property following the Nazi annihilation, and was, in any event, the first to formulate guidelines for its location and salvage two years before the end of the war. Yet it appears that the British colleagues soon lost the distinction of being the first. They found it difficult to preserve the society's status vis-à-vis the umbrella organization of British Jewry, the Board of Deputies of British Jews, which from an early stage preferred to deal directly with the Jewish-American initiative. They likewise struggled to keep up with the pace at which Baron and his associates worked, most notably with the work of the jurists. As a result, by the spring of 1945 New York had taken hold of the reins. In early April 1945, Roth noted in a letter to Rabinowicz that only the Hebrew University was mentioned in a report on the initiative to salvage Jewish cultural property that appeared in Bloch's Book Bulletin.[7] Rabinowicz, by the way, was already suspicious. He had in the past noticed that the Hebrew University tended to use obscure terminology, and his suspicions were now confirmed. With a blend of indignation and satisfaction, he told Roth that "after all, I know these 'Germans' better than you," referring of course to the senior management of the Hebrew University.[8] Roth's suspicions grew when, a month and a half later, on 14 May 1945, just a week after the end of the war, the Hebrew University, which neglected to reply to the English associates and took its time fulfilling its part in locating the required information pertaining to prewar cultural property, tried to change the rules of the game and reverse the roles by now demanding information from the British committee. Roth was now quick to express his indignation and sense of insult to the president of the university, Judah Magnes. It appears that Roth's and Rabinowicz's distrust was not unfounded. The minutes of meeting of the Committee for the Salvaging of Diaspora Treasures reveal that at that time, two days before the end of the war, the first signs of a clash of interests between the associates in Jerusalem and in London appeared. Gershom Scholem, for example, expressed his apprehension that "the Jewish Historical Society of England will demand books to replace their bombed out library," and regarded these and similar demands as "a means" to denigrate the Hebrew University.[9] Roth's disappointment grew stronger when in spring 1946 he realized that Gershom Scholem and Avraham Ya'ari had been sent by the university to draw up an inventory of European culture in Europe without bothering to coordinate their visit with the English society, and, so he

7 See Central Zionist Archive (henceforth CZA), Oskar Rabinowicz Collection, A87/333, Correspondence between Cecil Roth and Oskar Rabinowicz, April–May 1945.

8 CZA, Oskar Rabinowicz Collection, A87/333, Oskar Rabinowitz to Cecil Roth, 18 April 1945.

9 AHU, File 042/1945, Minutes of Meeting of the Committee for the Salvaging of Diaspora Treasures, 6 May 1945.

believed, unaware of the list being prepared at the same time in the USA. One gains a sense of the magnitude of the affront felt by Roth in his letter to Oskar Rabinowicz:

> "How the deuce the Zionist leaders think they could run a Jewish Commonwealth when they en't shew [sic] sufficient discipline to control a trivial matter like this I cannot conceive. The great quality of we English, which saved us from disaster, is that we are a superbly disciplined people; us Jews should learn from them—before it's too late."[10]

One can well imagine the indignation felt by Roth and his colleagues, all the more so since it was they who, as early as in spring 1943, suggested that the Hebrew University should be the exclusive inheritor of the heirless Jewish cultural property after the war, at a time when the university had yet to consider the issue and certainly before it regarded itself as the rightful heir.

For a while, so it appears, the Jewish Historical Society of England continued to engage in a rearguard battle to try to bolster its status. In August 1945 it drafted a memorandum on the topic of "Jewish cultural art and objects" on behalf of the Committee for the Restoration of Jewish Museums, Libraries and Archives in Continental Europe. By means of this memorandum the society sought to influence policy on Jewish cultural property in Europe.[11] We do not know whether the memorandum was submitted to any of the relevant governments. Interestingly, the committee based its claim to representation on the convention held in London in 1943, attended by representatives of English, French, Dutch, Austrian, and German Jewish organizations, and which preceded the English society's approach to the Hebrew University and to Baron; namely, at the stage when this was a purely European initiative and before the society's members had joined forces with colleagues in the USA and in Palestine. It appears as though the English committee had failed to grasp the sharp decline in the status of England in particular and Europe in general as a consequence of the results of the war. Oblivious to the overarching geopolitical developments, it looked on in dismay as its initiatives were carried forward by others and it became largely superfluous. It is hardly surprising that, given the new circumstances, the committee displayed little enthusiasm for col-

10 CZA, Oskar Rabinowicz Collection, A87/352, Cecil Roth to Oskar Rabinowicz, 14 April 1946.

11 Central Archives for the History of the Jewish People (henceforth CAHJP), Judah Magnes Collection, P3/20159, Memorandum Regarding Jewish Art and Jewish Cultural Objects Submitted to the Committee for the Restoration of Jewish Museums, Libraries and Archives in Continental Europe, 20 August 1945.

laboration with the New York colleagues. In June 1946, for example, Jerome Michael scolded Cecil Roth for not informing them of the memorandum, and complained that the Jewish Historical Society of England had not checked the drafts of the first *Tentative List* that Hannah Arendt submitted to them several months earlier. The Hebrew University's estrangement from the English colleagues and the growing mistrust between the English committee and the Jewish colleagues in the USA reflected the new global political constellation that evolved as the war ended. It was no longer Britain but the USA that was the dominant power with regard to the multitude of both international and Jewish issues. Given that the large majority of the remaining Jewish cultural property in Germany was located in the US occupation zone, the ties with the US administration in Washington and with the American occupation authorities in Germany became decisive. As was the case with all the central issues affecting the lives of Jews after the Holocaust, on this matter too, the USA's growing international stature and its new position as the dominant Western power in Europe raised the status of US Jewry. This development did not, of course, go unnoticed by Salo W. Baron and his associates, nor by the Jerusalem scholars. Given these circumstances, the top echelon of the Hebrew University and its president, the American Judah Magnes, looked to New York rather than to London. While Roth and his colleagues failed to receive the full backing of the British Jewish organizations, alongside the major issues this aspect was most probably of little importance.

The part played by the English committee in the overall effort to reclaim heirless Jewish cultural property diminished from year to year. The lead was taken by Baron's organization, and he maintained this position through the establishment of the Jewish Cultural Reconstruction umbrella organization in 1947. Roth vented his frustration in a letter he wrote to Hannah Arendt in October 1949, in which he noted that:

> "It is very often overlooked that it was our English Committee which started the ball rolling, and that your people in the U.S.A. only arrived on the scene much later, and through a 'stroke of luck' were enabled to head the work, in view of the fact that the books were found in the American Zone."[12]

By late 1949, apparently, Baron and his American associates had forgotten about the contribution of the English initiative. "I can testify," Baron wrote to Roth, "that I was the first to discuss the problem of cultural

12 As cited in Katharina Rauschenberger, The Restitution of Jewish Objects and the Activities of Jewish Cultural Reconstruction, Inc., in: Leo Baeck Institute Yearbook 53 (2008), 191–211, here 204.

reconstruction after the war in a lecture at the local branch of the Union of American Hebrew Congregations in November 1939." He continued:

> "The Conference on Jewish Relations appointed a committee to deal with these matters and held public meetings on the subject all through 1941 and 1942. [...] Since no one could anticipate at that time the extent of the Jewish catastrophe we called our group the Commission on European Jewish Cultural Reconstruction, a name carried over into JCR."[13]

In his letter to Roth, Baron proceeded to list the steps he and his associates had taken and noted their success in initiating talks with the US administration and persuading the US occupation authorities to establish the depot at Offenbach in 1946. Baron continued:

> "When we learned some time thereafter, of the existence of your committee and of a similar group at the Hebrew University, we immediately took the *Initiative* in trying to arrange for concerted action. However, we continued to have the entire burden of research, diplomatic negotiation, personnel and, last but not least, financing."[14]

On the basis of this description, Baron rejected out of hand the status that Roth claimed for himself, and put him and his associates firmly in their place as no more than a subsidiary of Jewish Cultural Reconstruction, Inc., alongside a long list of other organizations. Roth naturally utterly rejected this version. In a lengthy detailed letter to Baron he laid out his version of the events, noting that: "We apparently have now the diverting spectacle of two historians giving conflicting accounts of events in which they themselves played a part!"[15]

The dates and chronological unfolding of the events according to Roth were totally different to those that Baron noted, and certainly match the documentation found in Israeli archives. In the letter Roth claimed recognition as having been the first to propose the survey of Jewish cultural property, recognition of the contribution made by the questionnaires drawn up by the English committee in producing the tentative list, and of the equal status that Baron granted the English committee in the introduction to the first list he penned at the time. Roth believed that the American partner owed its dominance to historical chance, and concluded bitterly:

13 CZA, File A87/64, Salo Baron to Cecil Roth, 22 November 1949.

14 CZA, File A87/64, Salo Baron to Cecil Roth, 22 November 1949 (emphasis underlined in the original).

15 SUL/SCUA, Salo W. Baron Papers, M0580/43/5, Cecil Roth to Salo Baron, 7 December 1949.

> "I frankly admit that the discovery in the U. S. A. Zone of the tremendous deposit of material at Offenbach placed the J. C. R. in a very special position in connection with our work. However, had conditions been reversed and this deposit been found in the British Zone, I can assure you that *our* attitude to you would have been unaffected."[16]

The issue of who came first may appear to be secondary, if not downright petty. In articulating his grievances, Roth seems oblivious to the substantive aspects that played into the hands of the New York initiative, namely the growing international stature of the USA and of US Jewry in particular, the brilliant legal team employed by the New York initiative, and its success in gaining official recognition of JCR as a successor organization. One doubts whether Roth would have been equally successful had he operated in the British occupation zone in Germany, both in light of the weak position of the English committee within the Jewish organizations of Britain, and in view of Britain's refusal, given the political circumstances in the Middle East, to lend a hand to processes that could imply recognition of the existence of a Jewish nation. The question of who was first is both a complex and minor matter. What is more important is that Roth was quick to recognize the essence of the historical event, whereas Baron, because of a combination of reasons and circumstances, failed to realize its significance. Baron's tragedy, notes Michael Brenner in the chapter that addresses Baron and Roth's historiographical enterprise in the same breath, was "to have sought to oppose the conception of Jewish history as one of suffering precisely at a time that produced more suffering than any earlier period."[17]

Yet the tragedy, as I see it, is far deeper, and perhaps the reverse, and lies in the fact that Baron's fundamental historiographical conception, known as his "anti-lachrymose" version of Jewish history, was what blinded him to the historical event that played out in front of him. As Robert Liberles has shown, Baron erred in his historical assessments throughout World War II. In May 1940, and again in October of that year, for example, he invoked the historical precedent of tolerance toward Jews in multi-national states to predict that the attitude of the Third Reich toward the Jews would improve in the wake of its invasion of Czechoslovakia.[18] In mid-1942 Baron considered the hypothetical possibility that the war would end suddenly and unexpectedly, and would be followed not by a peace conference but by

16 SUL/SCUA, Salo W. Baron Papers, M0580/43/5, Cecil Roth to Salo Baron, 7 December 1949 (emphasis underlined in the original).

17 Michael Brenner, Prophets of the Past. Interpreters of Jewish History, Princeton, N. J, 2010, 131.

18 Robert Liberles, Salo Wittmayer Baron. Architect of Jewish History, New York 1995, 274–282.

an armistice without a peace treaty and a lengthy transitional period and process of reconstruction, in which the Jewish communities would take charge of the revival of Jewish religious life and educational institutions.[19] At that time he still predicted that "even shattered European Jewry may, in the course of fewer years than we now dare to hope, reconstruct its existence on a basis more solid than that upon which it had lived during the present generation."[20] It is not Baron's inability to foresee the event—namely the annihilation of the Jews by the Nazi regime—that calls for an explanation, argues David Engel, but rather the fact that "the failure of his prediction did not undermine his belief in his overall approach to the study of the Jewish past, even though his erroneous forecast was largely attributable to this approach."[21] Whether it was the apprehension he felt about his parents and sister who remained in Tarnów that blurred his vision, or whether his fundamental view of Jewish history could not contain the Nazi train of extermination, faced with the flood of events and reports, Baron continued to adhere to a vision of the revival of Jewish life in Europe during the war,[22] and largely clung to this view during the initial postwar months once its results became known, declaring in an article that appeared in *Commentary* that "the destiny of European Jewry will, of course, be settled in Europe."[23]

This steadfast belief in the continuity or renewal of life in Europe could not have informed Roth's vision, as manifested in April 1943; a vision that fully recognized that Jewish life had come to an end in most parts of Europe. While the means at his disposal to realize his vision and his reading of the international map were limited, Roth's historical perception of the fate of Europe's Jews was more alert and clear-sighted than that of his colleague in New York. Baron, it would appear, refused to recognize this, either in private or in public. In the obituary he issued upon Roth's death in 1970, Baron noted Roth's rare qualities as a collector (fig. 4), "a fine detective talent for unpublished documents," was how he phrased this.[24] Perhaps Baron knew in his heart that it was his vast experience in locating documents that led Roth to his early understanding? At the

19 Salo W. Baron, The Second World War and Jewish Community Life, in: idem, Steeled by Adversity. Essays and Addresses on American Jewish Life, Philadelphia, Pa., 1971, 469f.
20 Salo W. Baron, Reflections on the Future of the Jews of Europe, in: Contemporary Jewish Record 3 (1940), no. 4, 355–369, here 367.
21 David Engel, Mul har ha-ga'ash. Hoqrei toldot yisrael le-nokhah ha-shoah [Confronting the Volcano. Students of Jewish History in the Face of the Holocaust], Jerusalem 2009, 70f.
22 Liberles, Salo Wittmayer Baron, 281.
23 Salo Baron, The Spiritual Reconstruction of European Jewry, in: Commentary 1 (1945), 5.
24 SUL/SCUA, Salo W. Baron Papers, M0580/244/7, Obituary for Cecil Roth by Salo Baron.

end of the eulogy Baron noted that a bibliography of Roth's research appears in a volume that the Jewish Historical Society of England published in his honor, and in an accompanying sentence he explained that Roth had served as president of the society for eight years, including "the critical period of World War II." Baron made no mention of Roth's efforts to salvage cultural property. Thus did Baron eulogize Roth, revealing some of the truth and obscuring other parts of it, and finally putting to rest his colleague's singular contribution to the Jewish Cultural Reconstruction enterprise.

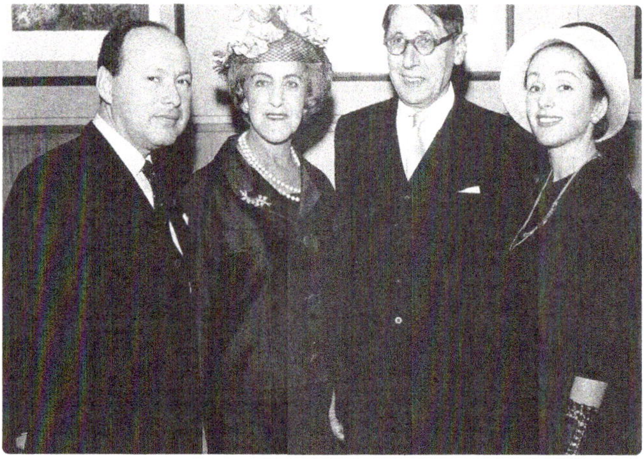

Fig. 4: Cecil Roth (third from the left) with his wife Irene Rosalind Roth (second from the left), and Fred and Joy Cherry Weinberg, who secured the acquisition of the Cecil Roth collection for the Museum at Beth Tzedec Synagogue in Toronto, 1964.

Literature

Michael Brenner, Prophets of the Past. Interpreters of Jewish History, Princeton, N.J., 2010.

Dan Diner, Rituelle Distanz. Israels deutsche Frage, Munich 2015.

David Engel, Mul har ha-ga'ash. Hoqrei toldot yisrael le-nokhah ha-shoah [Confronting the Volcano. Students of Jewish History in the Face of the Holocaust], Jerusalem 2009.

Elisabeth Gallas, A Mortuary of Books. The Rescue of Jewish Culture after the Holocaust, New York 2019 (Germ. 2013).

Dana Herman, Hashavat Avedah. A History of Jewish Cultural Reconstruction, Inc. (unpublished PhD thesis, McGill University, Montreal, 2008).

Robert Liberles, Salo Wittmayer Baron. Architect of Jewish History, New York 1995.

Dov Shidorsky, Burning Scrolls and Flying Letters. A History of Book Collections and Libraries in Mandatory Palestine and of Book Salvaging Efforts in Europe after the Holocaust, Jerusalem 2008 (Heb.).

Author

Yfaat Weiss is professor of Jewish history at the Hebrew University of Jerusalem, director of the Leibniz Institute for Jewish History and Culture – Simon Dubnow, and professor of Modern history, especially Jewish history, at Leipzig University. From 2010 to 2017 she was director of the Franz Rosenzweig Minerva Research Center for German-Jewish Literature and Cultural History in Jerusalem. In 2001, she founded the Bucerius Institute for Research of Contemporary German History and Society at the University of Haifa, which she headed until 2007. She studied history and modern German literature at the University of Hamburg, and received her PhD from Tel Aviv University. *Selected Publications*: Sovereignty in Miniature. The Mount Scopus Enclave 1948–1967, in: Zion. A Quarterly for Research in Jewish History 83 (2018), no. 2, 151–174; "Nicht durch Heer oder Kraft, sondern durch meinen Geist." Die Hebräische Universität in der Skopus-Enklave, in: Jahrbuch des Simon-Dubnow-Instituts / Simon Dubnow Institute Yearbook 14 (2015), 59–90; Von Prag nach Jerusalem. Kulturgüter und Staatswerdung, in: Vierteljahrshefte für Zeitgeschichte 63 (2015), no. 4, 321–346.

GIL S. RUBIN

Aftermath: Salo W. Baron in the Postwar Jewish World

In May 1946, the eminent historian of the Jews, Salo W. Baron, left his home in New York City to spend a few months in Johannesburg and Cape Town as a guest of the South African Jewish Board of Deputies (fig. 1). On his way to South Africa and back to New York, Baron made several stops, among them in Paris, where he attended a conference on Jewish educational reconstruction, and in Jerusalem, where he participated in a meeting on Jewish cultural reconstruction. Baron's first international trip after the war offered him an opportunity to encounter first-hand many of the major centers of Jewish life—the United States, Europe, and Palestine, as well as the small but vibrant Jewish community in South Africa. As his writings and letters from the period indicate, Baron was deeply disturbed by the fixation of Jewish communities around the world on Zionist political aspirations in Palestine at the expense of what he regarded as the far more important task of rebuilding Jewish life and culture throughout the vast Jewish diaspora. This paper seeks to contribute to this volume by showing how Baron's multi-centered approach to Jewish cultural reconstruction—insisting that Jewish cultural property be transferred to the United States and Palestine, as well as serve to reconstitute Jewish communities in Europe—should be understood as part of his broader approach to the question of the political future of Jews after the war.

In early 1944, Baron founded the Commission of European Jewish Cultural Reconstruction. Under his directorship, the organization sought to locate, salvage, and distribute Jewish cultural assets in Europe. In Baron's view, salvaged Jewish cultural property should serve primarily to reconstruct Jewish communities in Europe. This conception fitted with Baron's broader vision for Jewish postwar reconstruction during the first years of the war. Baron believed that the majority of European Jews would survive the war and seek to rebuild their communities in their prewar countries of residence. Europe was thus to remain the main center of Jewish life after the war.

By late 1944, however, Baron had started to come to terms with the extent of Jewish extermination in Europe. The scale of Jewish destruc-

Contested Heritage, 153–162 | doi.org/10.13109/9783666310836.153

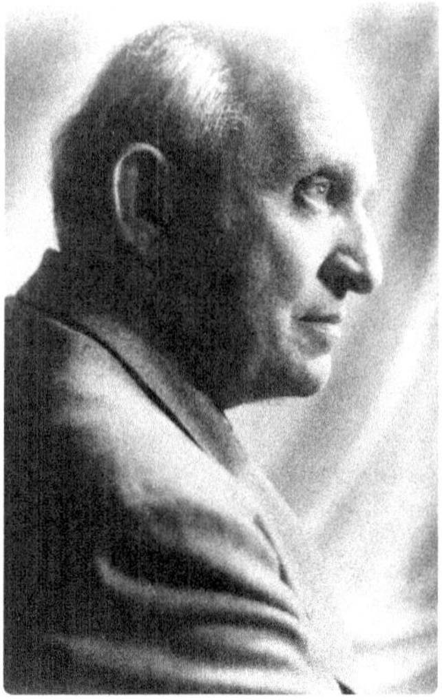

Fig. 1: Salo W. Baron, undated.

tion convinced Baron that the United States, home to a population of 4.5 million Jews, would emerge as the major Jewish population center after the war. As he put in a November 1944 speech, though "we shall not despair of the physical and cultural resurrection of European Jewry [...] despite the physical extinction of multitudes [...], from the Jewish point of view America alone now outranks all countries."[1] This massive demographic shift necessitated, in Baron's view, a change in political priorities. In place of his previously European-centric approach, Baron came to envision a new postwar Jewish world with a thriving American Jewish community at its center that would serve as a shining example for Jewish communities across the diaspora on how to develop and maintain a vibrant Jewish cultural and communal identity. This new conception went hand in hand with a new approach to the distribution of salvaged Jewish cultural property. By 1945, Baron argued that Jewish cultural property should be distributed to the United States and Palestine, as well as to various Jewish communities in Europe, and serve as the cultural repository of the Jewish collective.

As the war drew to an end, Baron became increasingly fearful as to the future of Jewish collective identity. Before the outbreak of war, he argued, collective Jewish identity was preserved through the existence of social, legal, and economic disadvantages that prevented the masses of Jews of East Central Europe from assimilating into the societies in which they lived. Western European and American Jewish identity was shaped by a sense of a philanthropic and diplomatic commitment to ameliorate the conditions of the Jews of the "East." Constant waves of migration of Jews from East to West meant that Jewish societies across the globe remained largely inseparable: A great number of American Jews in the interwar period, for example, had either immigrated themselves from Eastern Europe, or were direct descendants of Eastern European Jewish immigrants. The destruction of the Eastern European Jewish center created a radically new postwar world in which most Jews now lived in societies in which they enjoyed meaningful legal equality and faced few impediments to social integration. Based on this assessment, Baron argued that the main challenge Jewish communities faced in the postwar period was how to preserve Jewish collective identity under these new conditions of social and legal equality. American Jewry, Baron insisted, should lead the way in meeting this challenge by directing its energies in the postwar period

1 Salo W. Baron, At the Turning-Point, in: Menorah Journal 33 (1945), no. 1, 1–10.

to developing a thriving Jewish culture. The mantle of leadership in the Jewish world, Baron observed in December 1945, had now been thrust upon American Jews, "even if somewhat too suddenly and without preparation." And though American Jews should continue in their historic role of defense of Jewish rights abroad and philanthropy, above all, world Jewry looked to the American Jewish community "for cultural and spiritual guidance."[2]

Baron's vision for the postwar Jewish world encountered resistance among American Jews. During the war the American Jewish street was swept up by a commitment to a maximalist vision of Zionism. Baron viewed himself as a Zionist, but insisted that the postwar fixation of Jews on the Yishuv's political aspirations in Palestine misconstrued the priorities of Jewish life in the postwar world. In 1946, the Jewish Yishuv in Palestine numbered only around 600–650 thousand Jews, a small center compared to the 4.5–5 million Jews who lived in the United States; smaller than the number of Holocaust survivors in East, Central, and Southeastern Europe, who numbered around 850,000, and roughly comparable in size to the Jewish population of Great Britain and France combined. When Baron first publicly laid out his vision for the postwar Jewish world in a December 1945 speech, and insisted that the main task of American Jews was to build a thriving culture at home rather than direct their energies toward Palestine, he was widely attacked. Several Jewish leaders publicly decried Baron's views. Baron received several letters in response to his speech. A certain Julius Haber, a former "Galician landsman," lamented that Baron had come to espouse the view of a "small minority group who are against us [...]. If you weren't the man who is respected by all of us," Haber charged, "I would use the words 'You too Brutus?'"[3] A certain Rabbi Jacob Agus wrote a letter of support to Baron in the wake of the controversy. "I am very happy," Agus wrote, that "a scholar of your ability and reputation" has become a champion against "the hysterical brand of Jewish nationalism that is sweeping the country."[4]

Baron's vision for the postwar Jewish world further crystallized during his first international trip in the summer of 1946. In May 1946, he left New York to spend a few months in South Africa as a guest of the South African Board of Jewish Deputies, and made stops in Paris and Jerusalem. Paris cemented Baron's conviction that Jews would have a bright future

2 Stanford University Libraries (henceforth SUL), Department of Special Collections and University Archives, Salo W. Baron Papers, Box 48, Salo W. Baron, World Jewry Looks to America. Address at Temple Emanu-El, December 1945.

3 SUL, Department of Special Collections and University Archives, Salo W. Baron Papers, Box 29, Julius Haber to Salo W. Baron, 30 December 1945.

4 SUL, Department of Special Collections and University Archives, Salo W. Baron Papers, Box 27, Jacob B. Agus to Salo W. Baron, 7 January 1946.

in Europe. As he wrote his wife Jeanette shortly after his arrival in the city, "in general Paris looks little changed. They are tearing up too many streets to the chagrin of taxi drivers, but this, too, is a healthy sign of progressive recovery." Baron was elated during his days in Paris. In his letters to Jeanette he constantly referred to their two vacations in the city during the 1930s. Baron walked down Rue Lavoisier, where he and Jeanette had once lodged, and enjoyed a cup of coffee and a cherry tart at a café at which they had once dined. After meeting with several members of Jewish organizations, Baron grew optimistic about the future of French Jewry. As he wrote Jeanette, "I had the distinct feeling that things are picking up in France and that the French Jews are beginning to take care of themselves. They still need financial assistance, but are trying to do things on their own."[5] Baron's time in Paris clouded his perception of the fate of Jews in Europe. The conditions in Paris were a world apart from those in his native town of Tarnów, Poland. Just one month after Baron sent his letter to Jeanette, the Kielce Pogrom broke out in Poland, spurring the flight of thousands of Jews to displaced persons (DP) camps in Germany. The situation in Poland was no doubt foremost on Baron's mind. In early 1946, a few months before he embarked on his trip, Baron received news that his father and sister had been murdered by the Nazis in 1942 and in the following years sought to ascertain further facts about their deaths.[6]

After spending a week in Paris, Baron traveled to South Africa, landing in Durban on 14 June. "Flying over the marshy, but rich plateau of Uganda," Baron reported to Jeanette about his flight, "I began feeling sorry for the Zionist refusal in 1903 to accept the British offer, there is ample room in what appears to be a fertile country." In South Africa Baron hoped to find a Jewish community that would serve as a model for his vision of the postwar Jewish world—a small but thriving group of people with a vibrant Jewish culture. Instead, Baron encountered a community overwhelmingly consumed by the future of Palestine while disregarding its own fate. Indeed, when Baron delivered several speeches emphasizing the importance of cultural and political reconstruction of Jewish life throughout the diaspora, he was met with hostility. On 18 June, Baron wrote Jeanette that after proposing in a lecture "that Jews in many European countries will continue rebuilding their communities" after the war, he felt as if he had raised "a red flag to a bull." A week later Baron observed that "the Zionists here, as elsewhere, were making propaganda that there is no future for the Jews

5 SUL, Department of Special Collections and University Archives, Salo W. Baron Papers, Box 73, Salo W. Baron to Jeanette Baron, 2–4 June 1946.

6 SUL, Department of Special Collections and University Archives, Salo W. Baron Papers, Box 27, Salo W. Baron to Commission of Internal Revenue, 19 February 1947.

of Europe […] they were naturally displeased with my analysis." He then summarized his experience in South Africa:

> "I am afraid that I am out of step with the present mood of Zionist youth all over the world, which indeed has traveled very far from my Vienna days, when we considered Zionism as the great representative movement in Judaism to accrue to the benefit of Palestine and world Jewry alike. […] In its dire straits and despair the Palestinian *Yishuv* […] sees only its own really terrifying problems. […] Today they are even more prepared to sacrifice the entire galut for the attainment of their political goals."[7]

A few weeks later, in a report he drafted on his stay for the South African Jewish Board of Deputies, Baron reiterated these observations:

> "While talking with many leading Jews in many of parts of the country […] I have received the definite impression that South African Jews are far more concerned about happenings in Palestine than about antisemitism and the future Jewish status in this country."[8]

In early September, Baron embarked on a "five-thousand mile trip in a British flying boat" from South Africa to Palestine, passing "through the entire coast of Africa." During the summer of 1946 Palestine was engulfed in violence. In June, the British authorities arrested thousands of members of the Yishuv in an effort to quash the Jewish insurgency. In July, the Irgun bombed the King David Hotel in Jerusalem, killing 91 people. Given the militant Zionism he encountered in South Africa and the United States, Baron expected to find a Palestine that had become a world "storm center" marked by "'terroristic' acts of all kind," but instead soon discovered "that not all is drama in Palestine." In an unpublished account of his nine days in Palestine, Baron shared his detailed thoughts on the Yishuv. He spent most of his days on Mount Scopus and devoted most of his account to describing his amazement at the growth and intellectual vitality of the Hebrew University. The university campus was now "twice the size" it had been during his last visit nine years previously (fig. 2); the students "enjoy an enviable reputation for diligence and ardent scholarship," and the professors "display that serene spirit of self-confidence and genuine belief in the worthiness of their work."[9]

7 See SUL, Department of Special Collections and University Archives, Salo W. Baron Papers, Box 73, Salo W. Baron to Jeanette Baron, 18, 25 and 27 June 1946.
8 SUL, Department of Special Collections and University Archives, Salo W. Baron Papers, Box 48, Salo W. Baron, Memorandum, 26 August 1946.
9 SUL, Department of Special Collections and University Archives, Salo W. Baron Papers, Box 382, Salo W. Baron, Some Palestine Impressions, n.d.

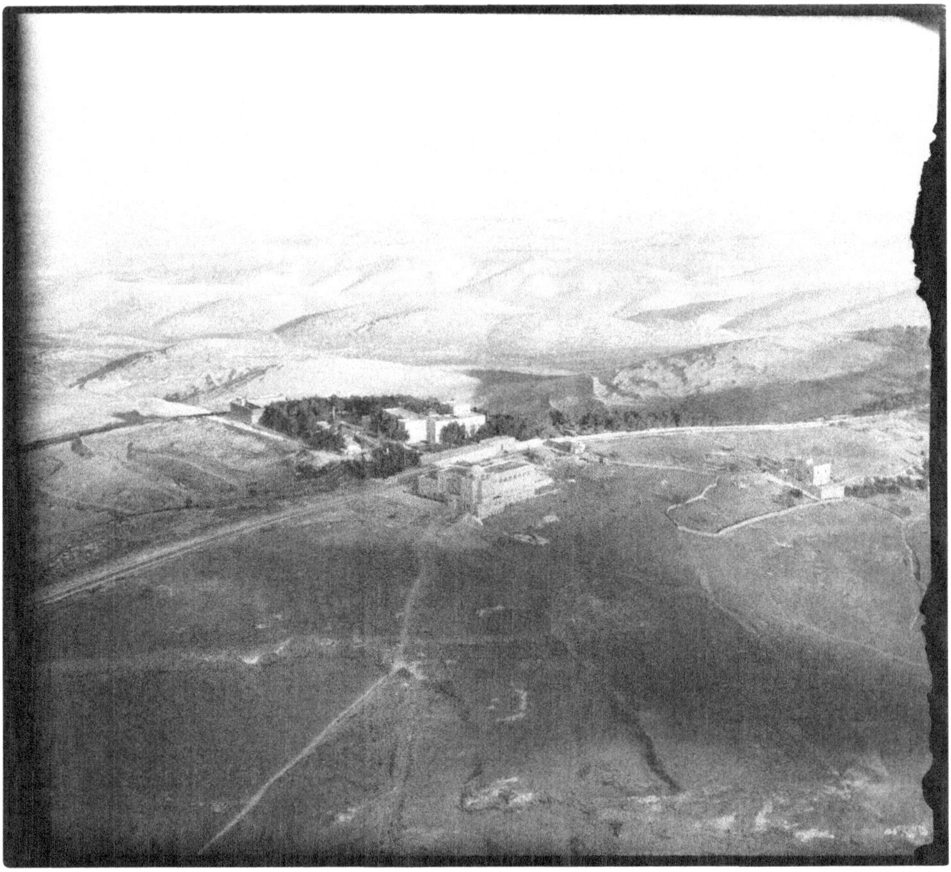

Fig. 2: Aerial view of the Hebrew University campus on Mount Scopus, Jerusalem, 1925 till 1946.

At a meeting with the leadership of the *Ha-va'ada le-hazalat Ozrot ha-Golah* (Committee for the Salvaging of Diaspora Treasures), a Jerusalem-based organization dedicated to salvaging Jewish cultural property from Europe, Baron engaged in conversation with many of the university's renowned professors—Martin Buber, Ben-Zion Dinur, and Gershom Scholem, among others. During the war, Baron and the members of the Jerusalem committee had sharply disagreed over the future fate of looted European Jewish property. Baron, as noted above, insisted that Jewish cultural artifacts serve first to reconstitute Jewish communities in Europe, whereas the members of the Jerusalem committee argued that Jewish cultural assets be transferred to Palestine and serve the Zionist project of Jewish political regeneration. After the war, however, Baron envisioned Palestine too as a major center to which salvaged Jewish property should be transferred. As Baron noted at the meeting, "the main question […] is the question of distribution: what will be done with the collections and how will they be distributed after they will be salvaged?" Baron assured the members of the *Oẓrot ha-Golah* committee that most of the members of his New York organization were Zionists, and thus that the Hebrew University professors would find ardent support for their views in New York.[10]

Despite Baron's admiration for the cultural and intellectual spirit of the Yishuv, he remained deeply critical of the dominance of the Zionist political project in the postwar Jewish world. Whenever Baron ventured out of the university campus, he registered his agitation at the political turmoil in Palestine, repeatedly noting the "numerous road blocks and other fortress-like establishments manned by a military on a war footing" that dotted the country. Shortly after he arrived in Palestine, Baron met with his friend Aharon Ze'ev Ashkoli to discuss his preparations for the Conference on Jewish Educational Reconstruction in Europe that he was about to attend in Paris the following week. At the meeting, the two discussed a plan for rebuilding European Jewish educational institutions and among other topics spoke about how Zionist emissaries in Europe were spreading propaganda about "the negation of the galut" as well as the indifference among many Zionists to the fate of Jews in postwar Europe.[11]

Baron left Palestine during the second week of September but was held up in Cairo for several days on his way to Paris, arriving at the Conference on Jewish Educational Reconstruction only toward its end. The conference addressed the themes closest to Baron's heart, and laid out a plan for training rabbis and teachers and for providing books and teaching materials to help reconstruct devastated Jewish communities in Europe.

During his stay in Paris, Baron was caught up in a major international event—the Paris Peace Conference (fig. 3), convened by the Allied victors in the summer of 1946 to draw up the terms of peace with Nazi Germany's wartime European allies—Hungary, Romania, Bulgaria, and Italy, home to over 700,000 Jewish survivors of the Holocaust. Representatives of nine Jewish organizations arrived in Paris in early July, hoping to replicate the achievement of Jewish leaders at the 1919 Paris Peace Conference, where Jews secured international guarantees for minority protection. Jewish leaders at the conference submitted elaborate demands for new minority rights guarantees, human rights provisions, and reparations. Yet, unlike in 1919, in 1946 none of the demands of Jewish leaders were accepted, or even officially discussed by the Allies. Lamenting their failure, many Jewish leaders

10 SUL, Department of Special Collections and University Archives, Salo W. Baron Papers, Box 39, Ha-va'ada le-haẓalat Oẓrot ha-Golah Minutes of Meeting, Jerusalem, 8 September 1946. (I thank Elisabeth Gallas for sharing this document with me.)

11 SUL, Department of Special Collections and University Archives, Salo W. Baron Papers, Box 27, Conference on Jewish Educational Reconstruction, Paris, 12–18 September 1946. Report of Conference, 1946, I.

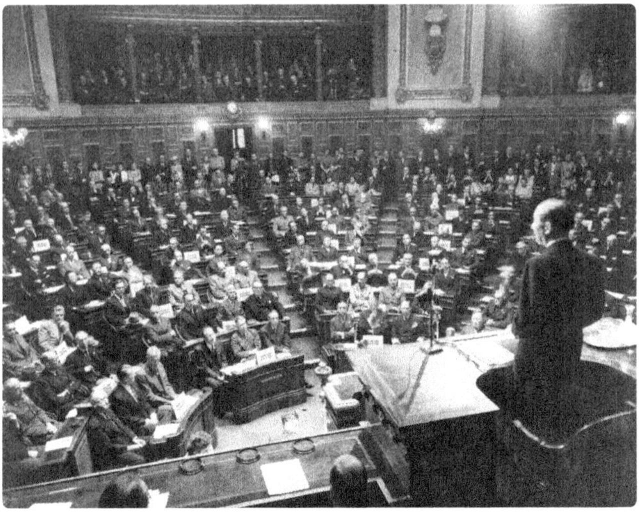

Fig. 3: French President Georges Bidault welcomes delegates to the Peace Conference, Paris, 29 July 1946.

described the conference as marking the end of a century of prolonged struggle for Jewish collective rights in Europe. Baron offered a diametrically opposite assessment. Though even "the most casual observers," Baron acknowledged in an unpublished 1946 essay, "could not but help noticing the pitiful role played by Jewish representatives" in Paris, he insisted that the conference should nonetheless be viewed as a major achievement for the Jews. Indeed, Baron argued that Jewish observers had simply failed to take note of what they had achieved at the conference without a battle. For the first time in the modern history of the Jews, no state in Europe opposed Jewish equality as such. At the 1919 Paris Conference, Baron reminded his readers, the Allies had to force Jewish equality on states such as Poland and Romania against their will, but in 1946, Jewish equality was beyond dispute—a political fact accepted by all states. "The prediction seems [...] not too rash," Baron dramatically declared in his essay, "that future historians may well consider the present post-war period as the incipient stage of a truly world-wide Jewish equality."[12] This analysis reflected Baron's general vision for the postwar period. In his view, Jews had entered a new period in their history, in which the main challenge Jews faced was no longer that of combating legal disadvantages, but rather how to maintain a thriving collective identity under conditions of worldwide legal equality and the prospect of successful social integration.

In mid-September, Baron returned to New York. Alarmed by the mood of fatalism among Jews over the prospects of Jewish life in the diaspora and the fixation of the Jewish street on Zionist political aspirations in Palestine, he decided to write a series of three essays that would lay out his alternative vision for the postwar Jewish world. In late 1946, Baron sent a draft of these essays to the pro-Zionist magazine *Commentary*. After a lengthy exchange, Elliot Cohen, the journal's editor, rejected Baron's contributions. For

12 SUL, Department of Special Collections and University Archives, Salo W. Baron Papers, Box 412, Salo W. Baron, Final Stages of Jewish Emancipation.

Baron, this was another indication of how his vision radically departed from that of the Jewish street and Jewish intellectuals of his day. Baron did not submit these essays to any other journal and in subsequent years remained largely silent on the topic of the postwar Jewish world.

In his 1946 essays, Baron was the first to observe that the postwar period augured a new era in Jewish history—a "golden age" of worldwide physical and legal security, an era that previous generations would have celebrated as "the ushering of the messianic era."[13] He observed that this new political period also implied a new political project—no longer fighting discrimination, but protecting Jewish collective identity from the allure of legal equality and social integration. Yet perhaps Baron was too adamant in insisting that the Jewish postwar fixation on Palestine came at the expense of building a thriving Jewish culture throughout the diaspora. Indeed, Baron did not consider the possibility that, much like the plight of the Jews of East Central Europe had been prior to the war, the fate of Jewish Palestine would in turn become a new issue around which postwar collective Jewish identity would crystallize, particularly among American Jewry.

Literature

Michael Brenner, Prophets of the Past. Interpreters of Jewish History, Princeton, N.J., 2010.

David Engel, Crisis and Lachrymosity. On Salo Baron, Neobaronianism, and the Study of Modern European Jewish History, in: Jewish History 20 (2006), no. 3/4, 243–264.

Elisabeth Gallas, A Mortuary of Books. The Rescue of Jewish Culture after the Holocaust, New York 2019 (Germ. 2013).

Robert Liberles, Salo Wittmayer Baron. Architect of Jewish History, New York 1995.

Natan Sznaider, Jewish Memory and the Cosmopolitan Order. Hannah Arendt and the Jewish Condition, Cambridge, Mass., 2011.

13 SUL, Department of Special Collections and University Archives, Salo W. Baron Papers, Box 412, Salo W. Baron, The Crisis of Emancipation.

Author

Gil Rubin is the Geoffrey H. Hartman Fellow at the Fortunoff Video Archive for Holocaust Testimonies, Yale University. He completed his PhD at Columbia University in 2017 and was an Israel Institute Postdoctoral Fellow at Harvard University, 2017–2019. His research focuses on Jews in Eastern Europe, the Holocaust, and the history of pre-state Palestine and the State of Israel. He is currently at work on his book manuscript, *The Future of the Jews. Planning for the Postwar Order 1919–1948. Selected Publications*: The End of Minority Rights. Jacob Robinson and the "Jewish Question" in World War II, in: Jahrbuch des Simon-Dubnow-Instituts/Simon Dubnow Institute Yearbook 11 (2012), 55–71; From Federalism to Binationalism. Hannah Arendt's Shifting Zionism, in: Contemporary European History 24 (2015), no. 3, 393–414.

YEHUDA DVORKIN

Saga of a Chandelier: A Jewish-English Debate of Cultural Restitution

Toward the end of World War II, as the Allies and liberated nations turned their attention to restoring property and cultural property to their countries of origin, a question arose regarding Jewish cultural property.[1] While it was clear that art that was looted in Italy and transferred to Germany or to a salt mine in Poland should return to Italy, it was far from clear to where Jewish cultural property should be returned. Most of the prewar Jewish communities had been annihilated in the Holocaust. Survivors who returned to them were not seen as representing the former community. International Jewish organizations stepped in and called for property to be restituted to the Jewish people, creating a precedent whereby property formerly owned by a group of citizens of a state was restituted to the ethnic or religious group they had belonged to, even if this entailed removing the property from its original location. This circumstance created an opportunity for the British Jewish community in the British zone in Germany.

When the war ended, Britain's Jewish community found itself in a unique position as it was one of only a few European communities that had remained outside Nazi Germany's sphere of influence. The British community had already begun to address the question of the restitution of Jewish property during the war, in particular at the groundbreaking conference convened in 1943 by Prof. Cecil Roth on the Restoration of Continental Jewish Museums, Libraries and Archives, and had begun to consider various restitution models to be applied after the war. In this paper I discuss the different models and their ideological and sociological background. I begin by reviewing the position of British Jews in the context of the status of the British Empire at the end of the war. I then address the issue of how the war impacted British Jewish continentalism and the idea of local compensation. I next demonstrate how British Zionism impacted the

1 In writing this paper I used documents found in archives in England and in Israel. I wish to thank the Deutsches Literaturarchiv Marbach for granting me a research scholarship and Da'at HaMakom for its cultural property cataloguing project, in which I was fortunate to take part.

restitution discussions. Throughout this paper I examine which restitution models the relevant British Jewish organizations and their prominent members proposed. This paper concludes with an example of an actual restitution process to demonstrate how those ideals were translated into action.

The fact that Britain was one of the four major powers after the war enabled the British Jewish community to view itself as a part of the victorious alliance rather than as a victim along with its fellow Jewish communities. As a result, various Jewish organizations that had not previously dealt with questions of restitution, compensation, and restoration now viewed themselves as giving voice to the Jewish communities on the continent. Given that Britain controlled Palestine as well as areas of Germany and Austria and still had the Empire, and that Britain's chief rabbi still bore the title "chief rabbi of the British Empire" and functioned as such up until 1953, the Jewish community tended to behave as though it were an imperial force within world Jewry. British Jews found it difficult to adjust to their altered position alongside the new centers of Judaism in North America and Palestine/Israel, and to the fact that they were not viewed as representatives of the Jews in the occupied areas in Germany and Austria or in Palestine/Israel.[2] Even after they became aware of their changed circumstances, they continued to perceive themselves as an equal partner with American Jewry, at least until the mid-1950s.

The Jewish activists and champions of relief had seen themselves as representing not only the Jewish community in England or Britain, but as representatives of the British Empire. As such, they oversaw the wellbeing of Jews in the colonies and whereever the British Empire became involved. The fact that the British army was an occupying force in Germany and that British Jews had played an active role in most wartime conquests, at least in the European arena, led to an interesting shift in the British Jewish orientation toward other European communities. Now it was a British Jew who came to the aid of the German or Austrian Jew and took their matter to the British officer in charge of the area. Petitions to government offices in London were now submitted not only from a distant colony or Mandatory Palestine but by the Jewish remnant in continental Europe. This gave rise to a sentiment one may term Continentalism, which led those who harbored it to view Britain as a part of Europe.

British Continentalists thus viewed Britain as a part of the European community. Within the Jewish community, it was the Anglo-Jewish Association (AJA) that adopted this approach most enthusiastically. The

2 Bernard Wasserstein, Vanishing Diaspora. The Jews in Europe since 1945, Cambridge, Mass., 1996, 72.

AJA was a long-standing organization that promoted education in the Jewish community along the model of the English elite school and aided Jewish communities worldwide to provide a decent education for their children. Its members sought to reconstitute the former European Jewish communities where possible and to support any community that sought assistance. They were not alone in proclaiming the idea of a reconstructed Europe. Individuals affiliated with other organizations likewise sought to position Britain within a broader European Jewish community and refused to accept the void created by the Holocaust. We may equate this standpoint to the British army's desire to rehabilitate Germany economically and politically. The British Section (BS) of the World Jewish Congress vied for dominance with the Board of Deputies (BoD) in their mission to represent the Jewish community and to advocate for Jewish national rights as a minority "wherever they are." The BS issued a memorandum stating that while it continued to pursue its Zionist agenda for the resettlement of displaced persons (DPs), it also sought to support and initiate the religious rehabilitation and reconstruction of the Jewish communities across Europe, including the restitution of religious property and books to these communities.[3] This approach is evident in other organizations as well. The Jewish Historical Society of England (JHSE), for example, saw itself as representing all Jewish museums and scholarly historical Jewish institutes in Europe that had no-one left to speak on their behalf. Even before the war had ended, in an internal memo dated 10 January 1945, the JHSE sought to ensure that the British military forces understood that it would represent the interests of those institutes within the Inter-allied-restitution commission until such time as they could rebuild themselves.[4]

But imperial pride and continentalism were not the only sentiments triggered in Britain during the war. A patriotic desire for compensation for the losses that Britain had suffered during the war at the hands of Germany was widespread among the British public. While the British government sought compensation for its losses in the form of money, goods, and cultural property, the Jewish community strove to replace property it had lost during the war. The concept of substituting cultural effects with artifacts and books from Germany appeared first in the initiative to rebuild the Mocata Library in London.[5] While it was not suggested that the Jewish community should be content merely to replace those items ruined during

3 University of Southampton, Hartley Library, MS 283/2/22, World Jewish Congress British Section, Guiding Principles of a Jewish Post-War Programme, 11 November 1944.
4 University of Southampton, Hartley Library, MS 156 A1080 2/5, N.a., Letter to Cecil Roth, 10 January 1945.
5 See, e. g., London Metropolitan Archives, C11/8/2/1, Cecil Roth to Adolph G. Brotman, 29 June 1945.

the war in England, this concept demonstrated that the British Jewish communities were keen to receive restituted artifacts from Europe to mark their identification with the lost European communities.

In general, the British political establishment was disinclined to view the Jewish people worldwide as a single entity, let alone as a national unit with a right to inherit Jewish property. Within the Jewish community, the AJA's approach to restitution was very similar to that of the British authorities, and was based on a similar rationale. At first, the AJA believed that the majority, if not all, of the cultural property should remain in Europe. Only later, when it came to understand that the local communities were unable to inherit and preserve everything, did it agree to consider a more complex restitution model. Nevertheless, the AJA was critical of the BoD over its support for Zionist causes, and left the BoD over this issue.

British Zionists found themselves in a delicate position following the war. On the one hand, almost all of them agreed that the Jews in the DP camps should be allowed to enter Palestine. On the other hand, they were unwilling to clash with the British authorities. The JHSE, which set up the Committee on Restoration of Continental Jewish Museums, Libraries and Archives during the war in order to promote cultural restoration, argued that the bulk of heirless cultural property should be transferred to Israel/Palestine through the agency of the Hebrew University. Although Roth was no longer president of JHSE after the war, nor did his committee actively participate in the restoration debate, the JHSE's approach to cultural restitution prevailed in most of the discussions held within the Jewish community. Roth and his committee advocated that the Hebrew University and the National and University Library in Jerusalem should become the main repository of Jewish books and that Israel should receive the lion's share of the Jewish cultural property located in Europe. This position was widely accepted, not only by active Zionists but also by those who favored the idea of a "Jewish Home" in Palestine under the British Empire either as a dominion, as a member state of the Commonwealth, or merely as a Jewish population center that would welcome the Holocaust survivors. Moreover, given the growing trend toward secularization in the British Jewish community at that time, the notion of a "Palestinocentric Hebrew culture," in which the religious Jewish society would be replaced with a cultural community, won a measure of support.[6] Accordingly, the transfer of what had once been religious objects to Palestine/Israel would help to transfer their cultural significance to objects of Hebrew or Jewish culture, and would alter their context.

6 Stephan Wendehorst, British Jewry, Zionism, and the Jewish State, 1936–1956, Oxford 2012, 235–240 and 285f.

It is important to distinguish between the approach of the Hebrew University, which dealt directly with restitution through the Committee for the Salvaging of Diaspora Treasures (*Ha-va'ada le-haẓalat Oẓrot ha-Golah*), and the British approach. Roth, the Diaspora Treasures Committee and other bodies that followed their lead viewed the Hebrew University in a different light. First, they considered it a trustee rather than an "eternal receiver." Second, one should note that many British Jews, and in particular British Jewish academics and government officials, tended to view the Hebrew University as a British university as it was sanctioned by the Mandate authorities and to some extent supervised by them. Given that the university operated according to the British model as an independent research institution; that British Mandate officials had accompanied the university during its early years; and that the Board of Governors initially convened in London,[7] many gained the impression that the Hebrew University was essentially a British institution. Whether this had some basis in reality or not, this belief was still held by many British Jews.

Therefore, according to this conception, by transferring cultural property to the Hebrew University the committee not only supported Zionism and the idea of a Jewish home, but also preserved these cultural treasures within the British realm. For at least some of the Jewish leaders who advocated this solution, restitution to the Hebrew University might have served as a way to link their patriotism with their Zionism. While "patriotic Zionism" was no longer the force it had been before the British government showed signs of reneging on the Balfour Declaration, British Jews still aspired to reconcile its conflicting components.

In a letter dated 29 June 1945 Roth himself proposed that most of the retrieved cultural property be transferred to the National Library and the Hebrew University. Yet he also asserted that British synagogues and the Moccata Library should receive compensation for damage suffered during the war, even if this should take the form of European cultural property.

Most of the cultural property that was restituted was not located in the British zone of occupation in Germany, and although the British Jewry had been the first to float the idea of claiming it for itself, it was the American community that took the lead in this matter. The different and at times contradictory approaches and agendas within the British Jewish community had not been reconciled by the time the Jewish Trust Corporation (JTC) was established in 1950, after a restitution law was enacted in the British sector of Germany. The JTC established the Advisory Council

7 David N. Myers, A New Scholarly Colony in Jerusalem. The Early History of Jewish Studies at the Hebrew University, in: Judaism. A Quarterly Journal of Jewish Life and Thought 45 (1996), no. 2, 142–159.

on Jewish Cultural and Religious Objects in the British Zone of Germany. The council's members were chosen in a way intended to represent the different views that competed within British Jewish circles on the question of restitution. It is thus no surprise that its discussions regarding the restitution of artifacts reflected their ideological differences.

It should be noted that the British authorities demanded that the local communities be represented on the JTC executive board. When the advisory council was established, however, the local communities were not invited to sit on it, although the committee stipulated that communities be consulted and be invited to choose the cultural artifacts, Judaica, and books they required for their routine activity. This step was probably taken in part for fear that the JTC's access to cultural property would be jeopardized. It was nevertheless in line with predominant views within British circles that had advocated local restitution since the end of the war.

An instructive example of the complex and contradicting views on cultural property is provided by the fate of the Altona chandelier. The JTC first learned of the chandelier in 1951 when the Altona museum reported, under the terms of the new law that required every organization to declare all Jewish property in its possession, that it had the chandelier. The disclosure was accompanied by a request on the part of the museum to retain the chandelier in the museum so that future visitors could learn about the Jewish community. The chandelier is described in the letter as part of the heritage of Altona-Hamburg. While the idea that a Jewish community's heritage is part of its city's heritage could not be discounted, the JTC was disinclined to grant the museum the chandelier as its overriding mission was to return the cultural property to Jewish hands.

Interestingly, even though the JTC had excluded representatives of the local communities from the advisory council, it took account of the communities' interests on multiple occasions. The balance between the local communities and the JTC was delicate. There were those within the JTC that believed that cultural property should first be allocated in accordance with the immediate needs of the local communities and only then be distributed outwardly especially since the Jewish Cultural Reconstruction, Inc. (JCR), the American Jewish restitution organization that dealt with the majority of the Jewish cultural property, did not, as a rule, grant British zone communities religious items. Some within the JTC, the advisory council, and British Jewry in general continued to believe during the 1950s that the European Jewish communities could be reconstructed to some degree, and that the British community should aid those communities and should take cognizance of their wishes in all matters.

In January 1952, the Altona community agreed to transfer the chandelier to a community in England. The community indicated that it deemed it proper that the chandelier function not only as a relic that honored the memory of the 6 million, but also as a symbol of the lost cultural world.[8] It is important to note that the British authorities demanded that restitution should not harm the local communities. In the case of the chandelier, letters exchanged between JTC officials indicate that some members of the council, while agreeing to consult the local community, did not believe the relic should remain in Germany, as there were no large Jewish communities left there.[9] Oskar Rabinowicz, a prominent British Zionist and secretary of the JHSE, lobbied for the transfer of the chandelier to England and specifically to the Great Synagogue in London, which had been destroyed by the Germans.[10] It appears that Rabinowicz felt that the chandelier would also serve to restore the eminence of the West London synagogue.

Following legal consultations, on 23 June 1953 the JTC executive board met in London and decided to grant the chandelier to

> "the Great Synagogue, Duke's Place, London, in commemoration of Jews who lost their lives through the Nazi regime. Should it not be found practicable to place the chandelier there, it was decided to donate it, after having the Chief Rabbi's advice, to another principal synagogue in this country, or in Israel."

This was not a binding decision but rather a listing of priorities that emerged from the discussion among the board members and others.[11]

This decision led to a lengthy sequence of letters, memos, and further decisions in which the various parties involved sought to find an appropriate location for the chandelier. Feeling responsible for the interests not only of Jews in England but also of those who resided in the British zone in Germany, the chief rabbi's office initially requested an expression of support in writing from the local community for the transfer,[12] and a similar acquiescence on the part of the Association of Jewish Refugees (AJR).[13] This course of action shows not only that the chief rabbi's office felt that the local communities possessed a moral right to inherit the cultural property but that it also felt that the refugees should have a greater say in the matter

8 Central Archive for the History of the Jewish People (henceforth CAHJP), Jewish Trust Corporation—London (JTC/LON) 575, Ernst Lowenthal to Charles Kapralik, 19 January 1953.

9 CAHJP, JTC/LON 575, Charles Kapralik to Hans Reichman, 16 January 1953.

10 CAHJP, JTC/LON 575, Oskar Rabinowicz to Charles Kapralik, 15 January 1953.

11 University of Southampton, Hartley Library, MS 137 AJ/6/5/35, JTC Minutes of the Council Meeting.

12 CAHJP, JTC/LON575, Letter by Erna Goldshmidt (recipient unknown), Hamburg, 3 June 1953.

13 CAHJP, JTC/LON575, Charles Kapralik to Erna Goldshmidt, 13 May 1953.

than "ordinary" British Jews. Several months later, when the blueprints of the new West London synagogue were completed, it transpired that the chandelier would not fit into it. The chief rabbi's office now issued another set of letters and requests for approval to donate the chandelier to a different synagogue in England. Yet this option was also discarded after no postwar-reconstructed synagogue in England was found fit for the chandelier owing to its considerable size and the exorbitant cost of installation. When this impasse was reached in mid-1955, the chandelier had still not been transferred to Israel as the original 1953 decision stipulated. First, the Jewish community in Frankfurt was asked if it could accommodate the chandelier in its synagogue.[14] It was only when this proposal was turned down that the chandelier was offered to Israel, where it was finally accepted by the Ministry of Religious Affairs in July 1957.[15]

The saga of the Altona chandelier is not typical of the fate of small retrieved objects, but it does bear similarities to what befell cultural artifacts of great financial, historical, or cultural value. It also demonstrates that while the British Jewish community was certainly supportive of the transfer of cultural property to Palestine/Israel, it displayed a vast array of opinions regarding other destinations, and its members offered very different justifications for the transfer to Palestine/Israel. The fact that the Palestine/Israel option eventually triumphed does not indicate that the community had abandoned its Continentalist or patriotic orientations. This ideological debate continued for years thereafter.

Literature

Roy Bainton, The Long Patrol. The British in Germany since 1945, Edinburgh 2003.

Richard Bolchover, British Jewry and the Holocaust, Oxford/Portland, Oreg., 2003.

Charles I. Kapralik, Reclaiming the Nazi Loot. The History of the Work of the Jewish Trust Corporation for Germany, London 1962.

Dalia Ofer/Françoise S. Ouzan/Judy Tydor Baumel-Schwartz (eds.), Holocaust Survivors. Resettlement, Memories, Identities, New York 2012.

Stephan Wendehorst, British Jewry, Zionism, and the Jewish State 1936–1956, Oxford 2012.

14 CAHJP, JTC/LON575, Erna Goldshmidt to Charles Kapralik, 24 June 1955.

15 CAHJP, JTC/LON575, Erna Goldshmidt to Zerach Warhaftig, 19 July 1957.

Author

Yehuda (Udi) Dvorkin is a PhD Student at the Hebrew University of Jerusalem. His research deals with questions of cultural restitution by British Jewish organizations and within the British occupation zone in Germany. Yehuda is a graduate of Yeshivat Hadar and Yeshivat Siach Yitzhak. He is the founding-director of the initiative Mechadshey Kedem. *Selected Publications*: The Revival of Liberal Judaism in Berlin after the Holocaust. The Pestalozzistrasse Synagogue as a Case Study, in: Moreshet. Journal for the Study of the Holocaust and Antisemitism 14 (2017), no. 12, 291–329.

5. Transfer, Rupture, Continuity: Reflecting Materiality

ADA WARDI

Reflections on Books as Vehicles of Cultural Transaction: The Design Work of Moshe Spitzer

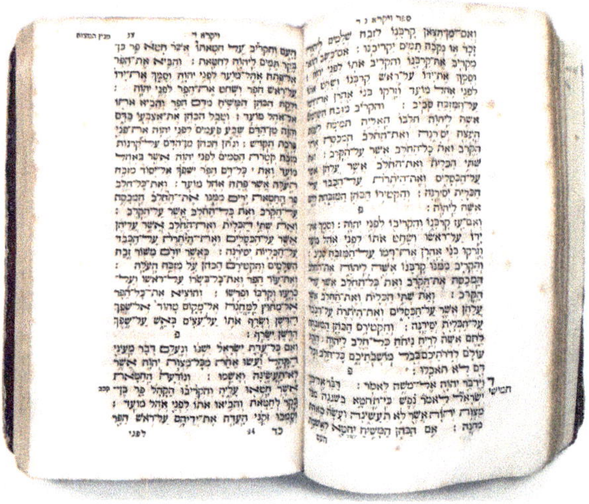

Fig. 1: Double-page spread (DPS) from Pentateuch, Book of Leviticus, printed in 1852 by printer and bookseller Eliezer Menachem Ottolenghi, Livorno, Italy.

One generally doesn't need to begin to read a printed page in order to recognize the format of the text. One doesn't have to be a typographer or a book designer to identify the form of the page, its genre, or even the period in which it was printed. Different texts have their own distinctive layouts, which one immediately associates with their content, recognizing them as poetry or prose, for instance. The most familiar example of this matching is the traditional typesetting and design of a bible page, which has retained its form unaltered: The text is set in one block, with no indents, and the verses are numbered in the margins of the text. This format applies not only to the Hebrew Bible but to most of its translations as well (fig. 1).

Yet what happens when the layout of the Bible page changes? When one looks at a page of the German translation of the Buber-Rosenzweig edition, one is reminded of a page of poetry or song; there is nothing here that identifies this as the sacred text with which we are familiar from a page of the traditional Bible (fig. 2).

Moshe Spitzer (1900–1981), erudite book designer, typographer, and publisher, was deeply engaged with this question—how does the choice of a new design for a book transmit to the reader a new meaning, a different interpretation of the text? Furthermore, how does this choice impart

Contested Heritage, 175–183 | doi.org/10.13109/9783666310836.175

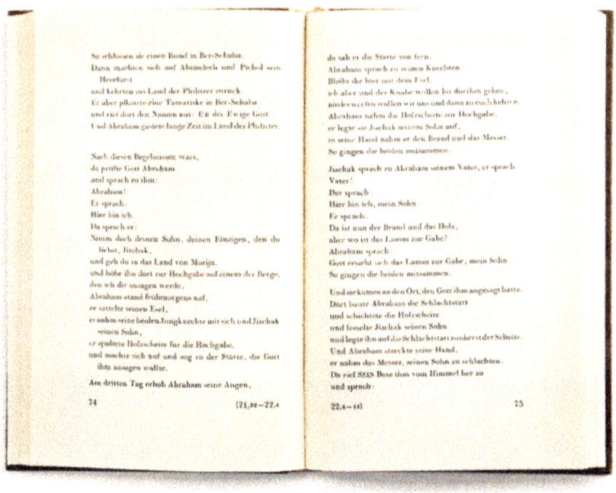

Fig. 2: Revolutionary page layout of the Bible as spoken text, Book of Genesis, Buber-Rosenzweig Edition, Verlag Lambert Schneider.

to the content of the text a unique visual identity and a different and fresh cultural significance?

In this article I attempt to trace the various ways in which Spitzer used form and design to add a further cultural element to the books he published. For this purpose, I use the first Hebrew translation of *Michael Kohlhaas*, which he published in Jerusalem in the 1950s.

Spitzer returned to Berlin in the late 1920s, after completing his doctoral dissertation in Sanskrit Studies at the University of Kiel. Upon his return, he resumed his activities in the Zionist Youth Movement, served as principal of an evening Hebrew language school for youngsters, and taught Hebrew to Salman Schocken's children. At that time, the publisher Schocken was involved in the preparation of a new translation of the Bible into German, begun by Buber and Rosenzweig. After Rosenzweig's death, Schocken searched for an assistant to Buber and hired Spitzer for this task. Spitzer had met Martin Buber when he was active in the Zionist Youth Movement, and they had corresponded over the years.

Martin Buber had a clear concept of how he wished to present the Hebrew Bible to the German public: It should be read as spoken text, without indications of sanctity. Thus, the typographic setting of the page bears no resemblance at all to the traditional layout of a bible page. The numbering of the verses appears at the bottom of the page, so as not to disturb the flow of reading. The lines are broken according to the rhythm of reading, taking account of pauses to take breath. All this is done in order to facilitate a "clean" reading devoid of previous associations, and as close as possible to the spoken word.[1]

This "translation philosophy" of Buber's as expressed in the page layout was the first time that Spitzer had come across the impact of visual form on the perception of content; a nexus that was to become the basis of Spitzer's work with books.

Another illustration of the use of form to create a new context is the cover design of the books published by the Schocken Library. Spitzer

1 For a discussion of this subject, see Halit Yeshurun, An Unfinished Conversation with Dr. Moshe Spitzer, in: Hadarim. Poetry Journal, Winter (1982/83), 52–55 (Heb.).

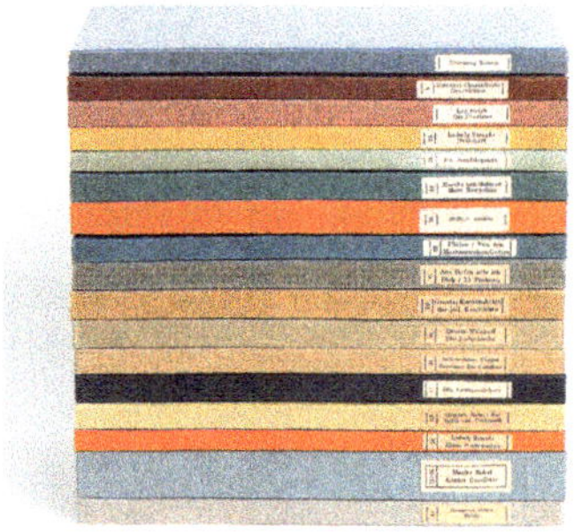

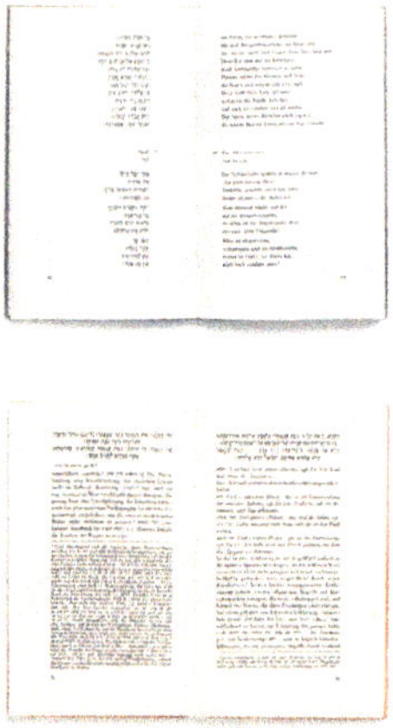

Fig. 3: Left: Book covers of the Schocken Library series, Schocken Verlag, Berlin 1933–1938; upper right: DPS from *Out of the Depths Have I Called unto Thee, O Lord*, a bilingual collection of Psalms translated by Martin Buber, Schocken Library series, vol. 51, 1936; lower right: bilingual edition of the Passover Haggadah, designed by Moshe Spitzer and Max Malte Müller, Schocken Library series, vol. 54, 1936.

served as editor and designed some of the books in the series. The Schocken Library was envisaged as a means of cultivating a bond with Jewish tradition among German Jews, as well as offering them a source of support at a time of discrimination and persecution. The format chosen for the library was almost identical to that of the German Insel Library. It likewise served to further Schocken's quest to find a suitable outfit for the evolving Hebrew language culture (fig. 3).[2]

Upon gazing at Buber's Bible translation, which erased symbols of sanctity, and at the minimalistic monochromatic covers of the Schocken Library, which disclose nothing of the Jewish content of the books, one realizes that both employ design styles to offer their readers a different and innovative reading. These dual elements—the choice of titles to match the theme of the narrative, and the choice of a visual language that added content to one's readers—characterize Spitzer's work in Israel as well from the 1940s, when he established his own publishing house Tarshish. Yet the purpose and form of the design and content he used in Jerusalem were precisely the opposite of those he had used in Germany.

In Germany, Spitzer urged his readers to look inward into their Jewish heritage and become acquainted with it, while lending a modern German appearance to the books to shield their content, as it were, from the hostile environment; while in Jerusalem, he intended his books to reveal the outside world to his Hebrew readers, and thus produced for each a cover that suited its content. The design of each book is derived from the text, serves the text, and thus gives each book its unique individual appearance; each book—an entire world. We can deduce this from the biblical name Spitzer chose for his publishing house, "Tarshish," which in the Bible refers to ships that carry treasures and valuables. The emblem he chose—a ship—once again echoes the Insel publications, which served as a source of inspiration to him, and perhaps a model.

2 For more on this topic, see Stefanie Mahrer, Tradition and Modernity. Salman Schocken and the Aestheticization of the Everyday, in: Ada Wardi (ed.), New Types. Three Pioneers of Hebrew Graphic Design, Jerusalem 2016, 69–86.

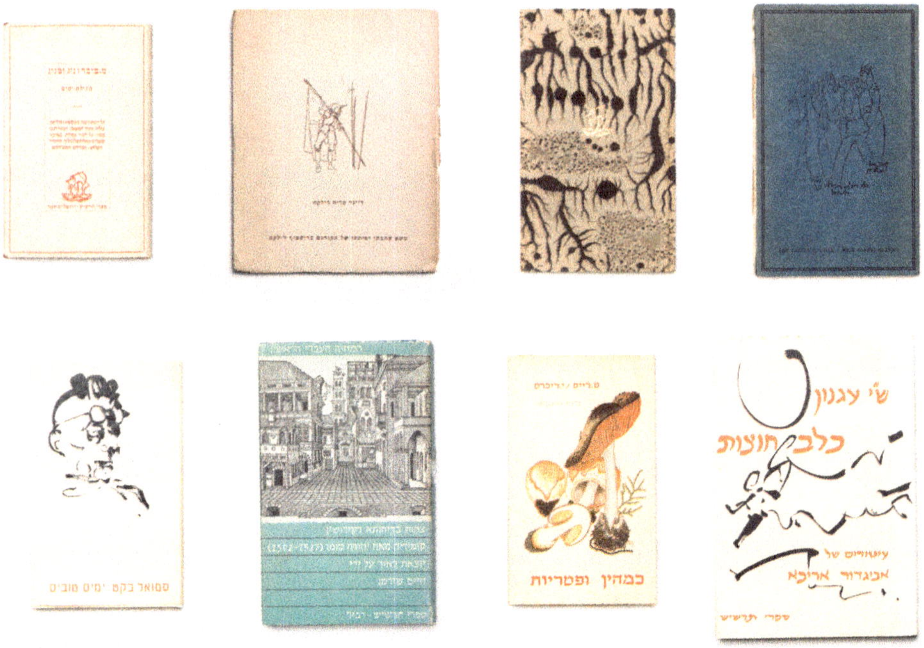

Fig. 4: Examples of Tarshish books (top to bottom, left to right): *Gog and Magog* by Martin Buber, printed in Frank Ruhl by Haaretz Press, Tel Aviv 1944; *The Love and Death of Cornet Christopher Rilke* by Rainer Maria Rilke, ²1952, Schocken typeface designed by Franziska Baruch; *Between Man and His Creator* by Immanuel Olsvanger, Drugulin typefaces, printed by Jerusalem Press, Jerusalem 1946; *My Blue Piano* by Else Lasker-Schüler, Jerusalem 1943, Bodoni Light typeface; *Happy Days* by Samuel Beckett, 1967, transl. by Mati Meged, cover illustration by Avigdor Arikha, cover: Aharoni Light typeface, text: David Upright and Italic typefaces; *The First Hebrew Play. The Comedy of Betrothal* by Yehuda Sommo (Leone Sommo de Portaleone), notes and appendices by J. Schirmann, Schelter-Giesecke typefaces, printed in 500 copies by Hebrew Press, Jerusalem 1946; *Fungi and Mushrooms* by T. Rayss and I. Reichert, 1952, illus. by Ruth Koppel, cover illustration and lettering by Franziska Baruch, Frank Ruhl and Miriam typefaces; *A Stray Dog* by S.Y. Agnon, 1960, illus. by Avigdor Arikha, David Upright and Italic typefaces.

Tarshish issued over a hundred titles from the 1940s to the 1970s (Fig. 4). Among the classics it published, one finds poems by Goethe, Hölderlin, and Lasker-Schüler; Balzac's stories; and Brecht's *Mr. Pontilla*—most of these translated into Hebrew for the first time, as were the three parts of Dante's *Divine Comedy*, chapters from Virgi's *Aeneid*, and a selection of Indian poetry. Further volumes included Shakespeare's *A Midsummer Night's Dream*, Beckett's *Happy Days*, Arthur Schnitzler's *The Green Cockatoo*, Rilke's *Cornet* prose poem, and *Michael Kohlhaas* by Heinrich von Kleist.

The story of Michael Kohlhaas, the sixteenth-century horse trader who fought for justice to the bitter end faced with the arbitrariness of the

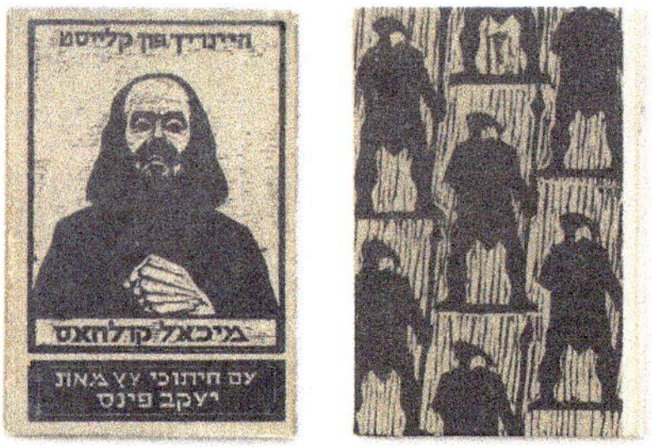

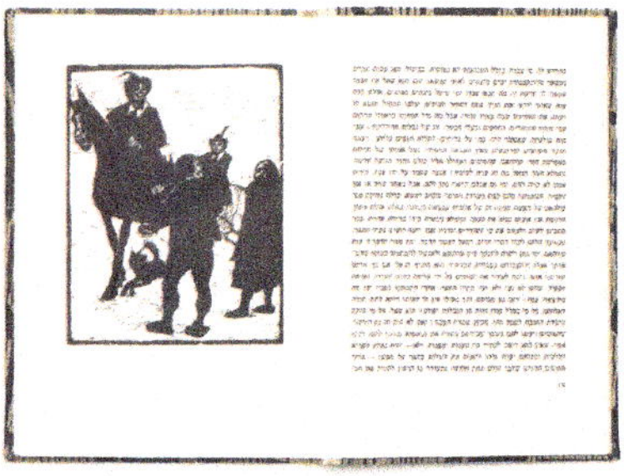

Fig. 5 and 6: Heinrich von Kleist, *Michael Kohlhaas*, with woodcuts by Jacob Pins, transl. into Hebrew by Meir Chartiner. Printed in a limited edition in Linotype Frank-Ruhl by Goldberg's Press, Jerusalem 1953.

ruler's officials, appeared in 1953 (figs. 5 and 6). By that time, Tarshish Publications was already well known in Israel as a quality and influential publishing house. A cursory glance at the book is sufficient to reveal the sensitive and refined manner in which Spitzer dressed up this German classic for the local Hebrew readership.

For the translation Spitzer recruited Meir Hartiner, who was praised by the critics for his work on this book, and the artist Jacob Pins, who produced illustrations in the form of woodcuts. Pins was born in Germany and belonged to a group of German artists who worked in Jerusalem during the 1940s; Jacob Steinhardt was one of his teachers.

Literary scholar Ariel Hirschfeld offers an instructive analysis of Pins's work on *Michael Kohlhaas* and explains why Spitzer chose these particular partners to translate and illustrate the book. He locates the style of Pins's woodcuts far beyond the sixteenth century, in which the plot is set, but also far from the beginning of the nineteenth century, when the book was written. The style belongs to this book, and to this book alone. Hirschfeld comments as follows:

> "Whoever is familiar with this story of Heinrich von Kleist knows that the immense power of the story lies in its tone rather than in its plot. The tone is judicial, pedantic, bureaucratic; it is the perfectly right tone to convey the terrible story of Michael Kohlhaas's all-destroying justice with such clarity, which [in its deepest, clearest sense] cuts the world as did Kohlhaas himself […]. Pins heard this voice, and honed it into a tool for sculpting the wood. I know of no other such book, neither here nor anywhere in the world; a book whose story gained so deserving an instrument, which holds it, treasures it, and expresses it as part of itself."[3]

3 Ariel Hirschfeld, Michael Kohlhaas, in: Ada Wardi / Ariel Wardi / Meron Eren (eds.), The Story of Moshe Spitzer and His Publishing House Tarshish, Jerusalem 2015, 204–208, here 206 (Heb.).

Hirschfeld admires the uniqueness of Meir Hartiner's Hebrew translation, which—like Pins's woodcuts—perfectly fits the tone of the book.

> "It is stylized, done with complete control of the literary Hebrew language of Bialik's generation with its frequent resorting to the language of *Hazal* [the Sages]. Hartiner created a dry and very practical language, and thus imparted to the Hebrew translation of *Michael Kohlhaas* the hard coherence of granite."[4]

Spitzer, the editor and designer of Tarshish, who chose Pins and Hartiner, then added a third layer that drew together all the components of the book. This was its coherent design, which ensured that each choice of visual material was meant to convey (not only illustratively) the essence of the story, namely Michael Kohlhaas's stubbornness and his insistence on gaining absolute justice. The entire book is built on dichotomous elements of black and white. The typography of the book produces a dark and somber layout that complements the weight of Pins's woodcuts. No attempt is made to lend it an appealing appearance; instead, Spitzer strove to give it a lean, simple, and dichotomous form; exactly like the story, which recounts a tale of truth and lies, justice and its miscarriage.

Spitzer chose a format that lies somewhere between a prose book and a small album. With two simple steps that exploit the format of the book as a three dimensional object, Spitzer summarizes its two principal themes. He places the austere figure of Kohlhaas on the dust jacket, and beneath it, a group of villagers. He thereby immediately registers the tension on which the story rests—the one against the other. The horse, the second protagonist that carries the plot forward, appears on the half-title page in all its splendor, facing left toward the next page. We meet up with the figure of the horse again on the final page—bony and stooping, facing right—toward the end of the story.

The figure of Michael Kohlhaas reappears on the title page, balanced—like the scales of justice against the sword at the center of the drawing. This is Kohlhaas's sword of vengeance, he who calls himself "the commissioner of the angel Michael who comes to punish with fire and sword."

In the year that *Michael Kohlhaas* was published, 1953, Spitzer issued ten of Pins's woodcuts in a separate folder, in an edition of twenty-five signed and numbered copies.

As previously mentioned, Spitzer was the first to issue *Michael Kohlhaas* in Hebrew in Israel. It is instructive to examine this edition alongside subsequent publications of the book, and observe how this German classic was assimilated into Hebrew culture, in a different format on each occasion.

4 Hirschfeld, Michael Kohlhaas, 206f.

A year later, in 1954, the Am Oved publishing house issued *Michael Kohlhaas* along with two other novels by Heinrich von Kleist, *The Marchioness of O*; and *Duel*, with an introduction by Max Brod. The cover of the book is decorated with woodcuts, reminiscent of Pins's work on the Tarshish book (the artist here is not identified). *Michael Kohlhaas* was translated here by Israel Zarhi. In an essay on the problems of translating the classics into Hebrew, which appeared in the daily *Al HaMishmar*, the critic lauds the translation of *Michael Kohlhaas* by Hartiner in the Tarshish edition as "an example of a faithful, meticulous, and responsible work of art." Hartiner's translation was subsequently used in an adaptation of *Michael Kohlhaas* into a radio play, broadcast on the Kol Yisrael station in 1962.

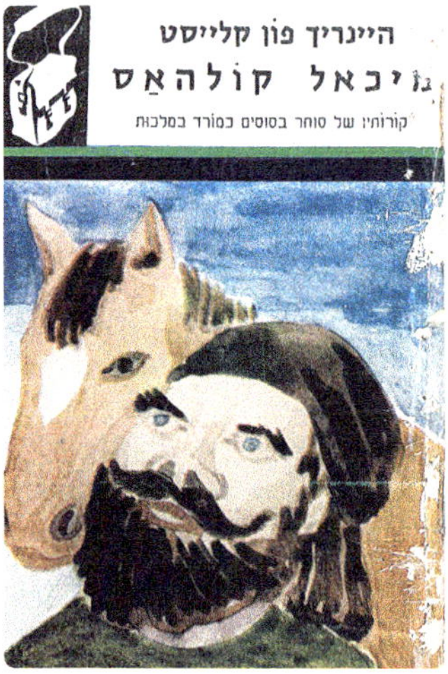

Fig. 7: Heinrich von Kleist, Michael Kohlhaas. The Events of a Horse Trader who Rebelled against a Kingdom, transl. into Hebrew by Meir Hartiner. Cover illustration: Audrey Bergner, Tarmil Books, publ. for IDF by Ministry of Defense, 1966.

In 1966, *Michael Kohlhaas* was reissued by Tarmil, a publishing house affiliated to the Israel Defense Forces and subsidized by it, to make classic and modern literature available to soldiers (fig. 7). Tarmil books are issued in a modest format, in paperback, priced inexpensively, and are sold to the general public as well as to members of the armed forces. The subtitle that Tarmil added in its edition, "Michael Kohlhaas and the events concerning a horse trader who rebelled against a kingdom," refers the reader to the book's central theme: the fight for justice. This edition used Hartiner's translation, but there was no room for Pins's illustrations in its modest pocketbook format.

That same year, an adaptation of the Kohlhaas tale appeared in the children's weekly magazine *Haaretz Shelanu* in the form of a comic strip. Titled *One against All*, it appeared for a number of weeks on the last page of the magazine. The text was adapted by Amatsiya Yariv (the pen name of the renowned poet and writer Pinhas Sade), and the dramatic drawings by Asher Edelstein accentuate the story of adventure. Despite the comic strip format of this adaptation for children, the story and illustrations preserve the spirit of the original.

In 1986, Pins's illustrations adorned the program of the play *Michael Kohlhaas* produced by the Chamber Theatre in Tel Aviv. The program gives "warm credit to the painter Jacob Pins, whose woodcuts for *Michael Kohlhaas* provided the inspiration and basis for the stage decor." The play was very well received and met with critical acclaim. It was included in the list of plays recommended by the Ministry of Education for high school pupils.

In 2002, two further editions of *Michael Kohlhaas* were issued, one by The New Library, and the other by Bavel. Like Tarshish in its time, Bavel is a small publishing house that issues selected translated and original texts. Like Tarshish, the name Bavel alludes to the publishers' vision, which is, most likely, to promote encounters between different cultures. This may explain the choice of illustration for the cover of the book, namely William Kentridge's horses, perhaps reflecting a desire to free *Michael Kohlhaas* from its strictly defined context, and place it within a timeless sphere. This brings us to a different phase of the story.

Michael Kohlhaas was indeed well received and welcomed into Hebrew literature, something that is not to be taken for granted. It is difficult—if not impossible—to understand in retrospect what kept this specific German classic alive in its Hebrew outfit, regularly reappearing in various forms. But it is worth noting that the book *Michael Kohlhaas* that Spitzer published in 1953 still stands out as a unique and exceptional volume on the Hebrew bookshelf.

Dror Burstein, poet and writer, compares Tarshish books to an object which is in fact a souvenir of our reading experience; indeed, the memories of Kohlhaas's story and of the book Spitzer published are intertwined. He writes as follows:

> "The Tarshish books are based on the assumption that the act of reading is—at its best—important and a one-off experience. A closed Tarshish book, even before one begins to read it, anticipates the future—a future when the reader has read it through, and the book that he has closed remains in his hand as a material memory of the reading experience, which has—in a small way or significantly—changed his life. The book as an object is, at its best, a singular memory of a special reading experience. It is the choice of the reader whether to turn the book—the material—into something of this kind. However, Tarshish books do seem to encourage the reader to read them in the way that they deserve."[5]

5 Dror Burstein, Comments on Tarshish Books (unpublished manuscript).

Literature

Emily D. Bilski, A Constellation of Bibliophiles. Moshe Spitzer and the Buber-Rosenzweig Bible Translation, in: Ada Wardi (ed.), New Types. Three Pioneers of Hebrew Graphic Design, Jerusalem 2016, 101–108.

Ariel Hirschfeld, Michael Kohlhaas, in: Ada Wardi / Ariel Wardi / Meron Eren (eds.), The Story of Moshe Spitzer and His Publication House Tarshish, Jerusalem 2015, 204–208 (Heb.).

Stefanie Mahrer, Tradition and Modernity. Salman Schocken and the Aestheticization of the Everyday, in: Ada Wardi (ed.), New Types. Three Pioneers of Hebrew Graphic Design, Jerusalem 2016, 69–86.

Halit Yeshurun, An Unfinished Conversation with Dr. Moshe Spitzer, in: Hadarim. Journal of Poetry, Winter (1982/83), 52–55 (Heb.).

Author

Ada Wardi, graphic designer and curator, researched the works of Moshe Spitzer and edited the book *The Story of Moshe Spitzer and His Publishing House Tarshish* (Jerusalem 2016; Heb.). She curated the exhibitions "New Types. Three Pioneers of Hebrew Graphic Design" at the Israel Museum, Jerusalem (2015–2016) and "Ad Acta. The Hebrew University, Jewish Scholars and the Exile from Europe" at the National Library of Israel, Jerusalem (2018–2019). Ada Wardi lives and works in Tel Aviv, Israel.

STEFANIE MAHRER

The Uncanny of the Schocken Villa: Interior Design and Objects of Exile

In his *The Poetics of Space*, the French philosopher Gaston Bachelard deals with the psychic function of space and focuses on the function of the house as a vessel of memory. "[T]he house is one of the greatest powers of integration for the thoughts, memories and dreams of mankind," he wrote. "Past, present and future give the house different dynamisms, which often interfere, at times opposing, at others, stimulating one another."[1] The space of the house, "our corner of the world,"[2] is a safe place where continuity is produced and contingencies thrust aside.[3]

According to Bachelard, the house (he is referring to the family home) is a safe haven, a place that evokes fond memories; a place that is a receptacle of memories for its (former) inhabitants. The bourgeois concept of the privacy of the home clearly resonates in this notion, but this does not detract from its function as a familiar and safe place for its inhabitants. "A house," writes Bachelard, "constitutes a body of images that give mankind proofs or illusions of stability."[4] Yet this stability is fragile. The experiences of the twentieth century with its horrors that have led to mass migrations and forced millions of people to relinquish their homes, have shown how flimsy this stability can be. German Jews were among the groups that lost their homes during the course of the first half of the previous century. Many of them fled in the early years of the Nazi regime and sought to carry on with their lives in exile. Among them was the Schocken family from Berlin.

Salman Schocken, a very wealthy and influential merchant as well as a cultural and economic Zionist and a publisher, left Germany late in 1933 together with his wife Lili and three of his four children, and settled in Jerusalem. Shortly after arriving in Mandatory Palestine, he hired the renowned architect Erich Mendelsohn, among the leading avant-garde proponents of modern architecture, to build his family home. The

1 Gaston Bachelard, The Poetics of Space, with a new foreword by John R. Stilgoe, transl. by Maria Jolas, New York 1994, 6 (1st edition 1956).
2 Bachelard, The Poetics of Space, 6.
3 Bachelard, The Poetics of Space, 8.
4 Bachelard, The Poetics of Space, 17.

Contested Heritage, 185–194 | doi.org/10.13109/9783666310836.185

family left behind their villa in Berlin Zehlendorf, a bourgeois neo-classical building, which, in the absence of the family, was maintained by loyal employees. Lili and Salman subsequently had all their belongings, which included precious paintings along with simple everyday objects, such as kitchen utensils and cutlery, shipped to Palestine to serve in their newly built house—a modern piece of architecture that sported the latest technology and finest materials.

In this essay I draw on the example of the Schockens to explore how the introduction of familiar objects to a new house can help build a home in exile. In other words, I seek to ascertain to what extent material culture can be used to fill an emotional void that results from (forced) migration. Research has shown that the "migration of things" should be perceived as an integral part of cultural transfer.[5] During the course of migration, however, these things may acquire a new meaning. The study of the migration of domestic possessions, ordinary mundane objects one might say, as part of the migratory household, helps to understand the negotiation of normality and the function of memory in a changing context.

Cold and Remote: The Schocken-Villa in Jerusalem

> "The house that I have seen functioning on this occasion for the first time made an excellent impression in its organization and its richness of detail; and the hulk [Edward Keith-Roach; British colonial administrator in the British Mandate of Palestine and governor of Jerusalem] was brought down by admiration. I smashed—obviously, you would say—one of the many Meißen knick-knacks and I was fairly fine with that."[6]

This is what Erich Mendelsohn had to say about the house in a letter to his wife Louise after visiting the Schocken Villa in Jerusalem in May 1938 (fig. 1).

5 Doerte Bischoff/Joachim Schlör, Dinge des Exils. Zur Einleitung, in: Exilforschung. Ein internationales Jahrbuch 31 (2013), 9–20.

6 "Das Haus, das ich dabei zum ersten Mal working sah, macht in der Organisation u. Reichhaltigkeit seiner Details einen ausgezeichneten Eindruck und der robuste Bulle [Edward Keith-Roach; British colonial administrator in the British Mandate of Palestine and governor of Jerusalem] wurde ganz klein vor Bewunderung. Ich zerbrach – natürlich wirst Du sagen – dabei eine der vielen Meißen Nippes u. fand das ganz in Ordnung." Staatliche Museen zu Berlin (henceforth SMB), Erich Mendelsohn Archiv, Letter 1222, Erich Mendelsohn to Louise Mendelsohn, 8 May 1938, <http://ema.smb.museum/1222> (1 August 2019).

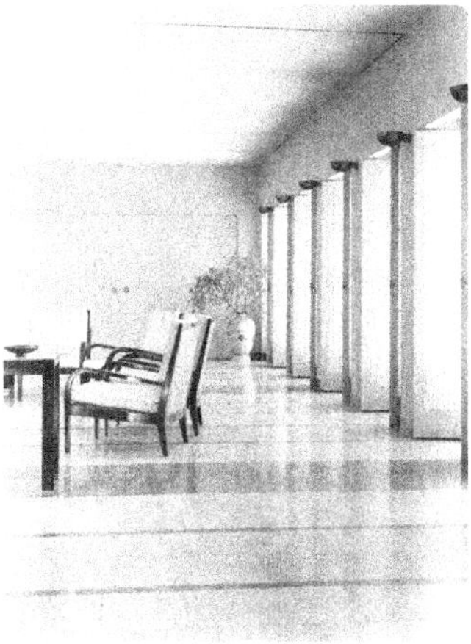

Fig. 1: Schocken Villa: Reception hall on the ground floor, with furniture designed by Erich Mendelsohn, c. 1937.

Lili Schocken worked valiantly to make her Jerusalem villa homelier. Having explicitly requested a modern house, and asked for a building that would resemble the architect's own former family home *Am Rupenhorn* in Berlin Charlottenburg, she was not at all happy with her new home. It felt cold and impersonal, and was too big and too formal to become an emotional safe haven in difficult times.[7]

Lili and Salman Schocken left Germany at the end of 1933 following the Nazis' seizure of power earlier that year. They settled in Jerusalem, where Salman Schocken hoped to make a name for himself. The family initially rented apartments on Rambam Street in the Rehavia neighborhood, in the midst of fellow German émigrés, and Schocken went about purchasing individual parcels of land on the boundary between the neighborhoods of Talbiyeh and Rehavia, until he had acquired a site large enough on which to build the house and garden.

Erich Mendelsohn, Schocken's personal architect in Germany, was hired to design the family home and to draw up plans for the Schocken library, which was to be housed in a separate building in close proximity. Lili Schocken, who was deeply impressed by Mendelsohn's former Berlin villa, requested that her new home be designed in a similar manner.

Lili was closely involved in the planning of the new house. Salman's business interests took him to Europe for several months each year, and Lili was left in charge in Jerusalem. She frequently met with Mendelsohn and corresponded not only with her husband but also with the architect's office regarding the details and progress of the construction. While Lili was a softer and warmer person than her notoriously domineering husband, she was very outspoken about her expectations and desires.

The house combined the finest quality German material and accessories with a lofty style of architecture that merged with its topographical setting. The architecture alluded to local traditions, such as the roof terrace and pergolas, and exploited natural light, while at the same time incorporating European luxuries such as central heating and air conditioning. The villa was set in a park-like garden, designed by the office of the famous British landscape architect Geoffrey Jellicoe, which perfectly complemented the house (fig. 2).

Yet Mendelsohn not only drew up the plans for the house. He also designed the interior. When sketching the building, he had the Schockens' impressive art collection in mind: two Cézannes, two Pissaros, three Renoirs, as well as a Van Gogh, a Manet, and a Chagall, among other

7 Interview with Dvorah Schocken conducted by the author, 13 November 2013.

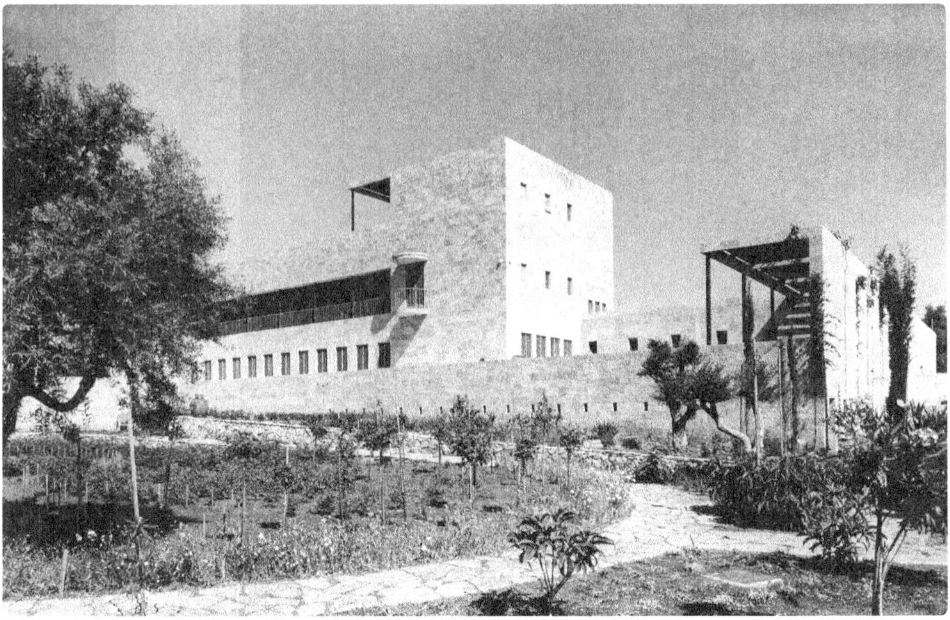

Fig. 2: The Schocken Villa and part of the garden, viewed from the south-west, c. 1937.

less precious but equally exquisite pieces of art. The art and the architecture were to complement each other. To achieve this, Mendelsohn not only designed the furniture for the public rooms, but also determined the arrangement of chairs, tables, and, of course, the art pieces. In a letter to his wife, the architect wrote in July 1936:

> "Schocken, who came back just now, visits with his wife and children [...] England for 2 months. But he is in a good mood—yesterday during the day I was at his construction sites and in the evening (Curfew-Pass) until after midnight at his place. He is very happy with the buildings and more or less accepted everything. The house's furnishing is partly old and partly new—but always with my permission. I comply with his requests as much as I can without dropping crucial things. [...] The planting follows my instructions."[8]

8 "Schocken, eben zurück, reist mit Frau u. Kinder [...] für 2 Monate nach England. Er ist aber guter Laune—war gestern Tag über auf seinen Bauten u. abends (Curfew-Pass) bis nach Mitternacht bei ihm. Ist von Bauten sehr befriedigt u. hat mehr oder weniger alles bestellt. Möblierung des Hauses teils alt teils neu—aber immer mit meiner Genehmigung. Komme ihm möglichst weit entgegen, ohne Grundsätzliches aufzugeben. [...] Bepflanzung nach meinen Angaben." SMB, Erich Mendelsohn Archiv, Letter 1155, Erich Mendelsohn to Louise Mendelsohn, 9 July 1936, <http://ema.smb.museum/1155> (1 August 2019).

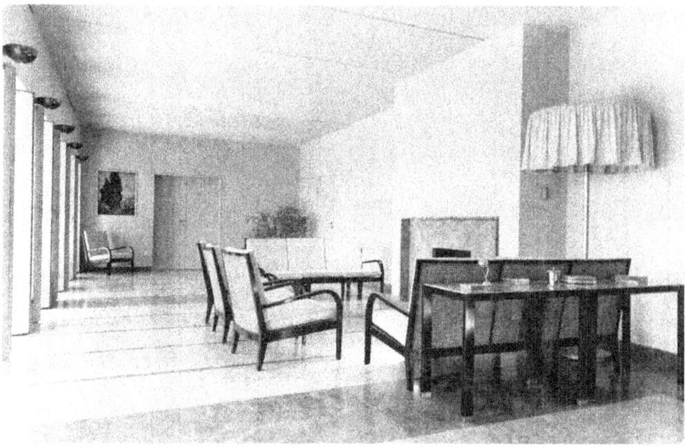

Fig. 3: Schocken Villa: Reception hall on the ground floor, with furniture designed by Erich Mendelsohn, c. 1937.

His instructions addressed the smallest details, as shown in the minutes of a meeting between Salman Schocken, Erich Mendelsohn, and Willy Heinze, the non-Jewish supervisor and manager of Schocken's construction sites in Jerusalem: Mendelsohn stipulated that highly colorful flowers should not be placed in the study, lest they detract from the delicate colors of the Cezanne. No red flowers were allowed on the mahogany dining table; only yellow or white ones were acceptable (figs. 3 and 4).[9]

Lili Schocken was not amused at these instructions on how to decorate and arrange her new house, nor did they impart to her a feeling of a secure and homely space; on the contrary, the perfectly designed house made her feel alienated and unhappy. It was the house she had dreamed of—a Middle Eastern adaptation of Mendelsohn's former family house in Berlin—but it failed to make her welcome. While Lili and Salman had approved Mendelsohn's external design, they took issue with his plans for the interior. Lili had her own ideas: She had in mind a combination of Mendelsohn's house *Am Rupenhorn* and her own bourgeois family home in Berlin.

By furnishing the Jerusalem villa with her German furniture and decorating it with her bric-a-brac; by placing lace doilies on Mendelsohn's carefully designed furniture; and by putting cyclamens in every room, she tried to make her new house homelier. She hoped to create a sense of *Gemütlichkeit*, a German term which can hardly be translated into any other language, in her new home.

Mendelsohn was an agent of modern architecture and therefore an advocate of clean lines free of the clutter of the past. "It was an attempt to free culture from [...] this overburdening 'sense of the past,'" writes Anthony Vidler in his *The Architectural Uncanny*, "that modernist architects, formed by futurism, attempted to erase its traces from their architecture."[10] This "housecleaning," as Vidler calls it, "produced its own ghosts,

9 The Schocken Institute for Jewish Research in Jerusalem, The Schocken Archive (henceforth SchA), Box 1, File 823, Besprechungsprotokoll der Herren Schocken, Mendelsohn, Heinze und Littmann, 30 May 1937.

10 All citations from Anthony Vidler, The Architectural Uncanny. Essays in the Modern Unhomely, Cambridge, Mass., 1992, 63.

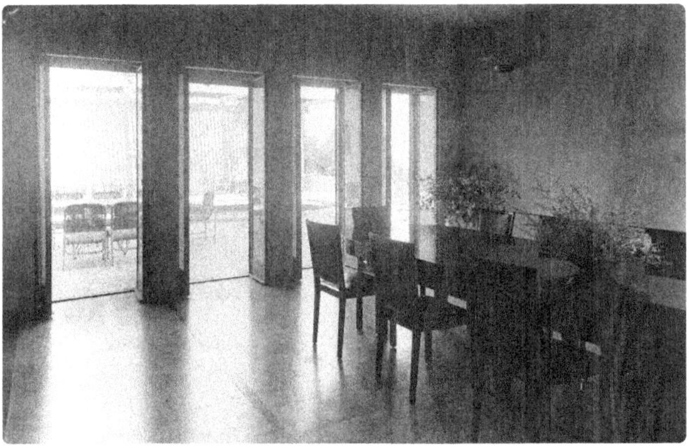

Fig. 4: Schocken Villa: Dining hall with view of the swimming pool, c. 1937.

the nostalgic shadows of all 'houses' now condemned to history."[11] The elimination of all historical elements turned the house into an instrument of nostalgia. Bachelard developed his concept of the house as a vessel for memories in the aftermath of World War II with modern architecture in view. The nostalgic house of the past, "our corner in the world," this "mental construct that included all houses yet inhabited" could not be found in modern architecture.[12] Bachelard's resistance to modern houses, which he termed "geometric cubes," should be understood in the context of the general skepticism toward modernity in the aftermath of the war. In 1944 Adorno wrote, "dwelling is now impossible," since houses are "manufactured by experts […] devoid of all relations to the occupant."[13]

Taking Sigmund Freud's essay on the uncanny as his point of departure for a study of the concept of the uncanny in modern architecture, Vidler regards the uncanny as a "powerful trope for imaging the 'lost' birthplace against the deracinated home of post-industrial society."[14] The German word "*unheimlich* (uncanny) is the opposite of *heimlich, heimisch, vertraut* (homely, local, feeling at home), and it seems obvious," according to Freud, "that something should be frightening precisely because it is unknown and unfamiliar."[15] Seeking to free itself from the remnants of the past, modern architecture estranges its inhabitants from their homes, which thus become "unhomely."[16]

Returning to the Schockens, one can understand Lili's efforts to decorate her new Jerusalem home as an attempt to restore the "precarious relationship between physical and psychological home." The sense of estrangement commonly experienced by people in exile was amplified

11 Vidler, The Architectural Uncanny, 63f.

12 Bachelard, The Poetics of Space, 65.

13 Theodor W. Adorno, Minima Moralia. Reflections from Damaged Life, transl. by E. F. N. Jephcott, London 1974, 38, here cit. in Vidler, The Architectural Uncanny, 65.

14 Vidler, The Architectural Uncanny, xi.

15 Sigmund Freud, The Uncanny, with an introduction by Hugh Haughton, transl. by David McLintock, London 2003, 124f. (1st edition 1919).

16 Vidler, The Architectural Uncanny, xi.

by the "unhomeliness" of the new family abode. Mendelsohn believed that architecture could not simply be transferred from Europe to the Middle East. On the contrary, he strove to integrate the new culture with his architectural language. He aimed to synthesize the Eastern and Western architectonic traditions into something new.[17] Ultimately, from an architectural point of view, the Schocken Villa represented a dual negation of the past. First, modernist architecture was aiming to free itself from the remnants of the past, and Mendelsohn envisaged creating something new, more suitable to the new surroundings. For Lili Schocken, who pined for her former house and for the known, this added to her sense of estrangement from her new home and homeland. Her house was unhomely. Mendelsohn, for his part, sought to create a new form of homeliness better suited to the new homeland. The architect's visions were, we must conclude, detached from the needs of his client.

Objects from Home

Unlike most Jewish emigrants from Germany and other European countries, Lili Schocken and her family did not lose everything upon leaving the homeland. They managed to salvage most of their assets, their furniture, books and works of art. Moreover, her husband's social circles remained largely intact. Thus, while German emigrants did not generally receive too warm a welcome in Palestine, the Schocken family, which moved among the elites, was hardly affected by this.

Yet although the Schockens were able not merely to salvage their possessions but also to maintain their social standing, they too suffered a sense of loss of home, *Verlust der Heimat*. Lili Schocken sought to fill the void created by her loss by placing familiar things, everyday objects, in her private space. Objects from home, or *Heimatobjekte*, as Hoba and Kotowski termed the things that emigrants took with them, replaced the actual home *(Heimat)*.[18]

Over the past decade, scholars of cultural studies have begun to include the study of material objects in their work. Inspired by fields such as art his-

17 See Ita Heinze-Greenberg, "Ich bin ein freier Bauer." Bauen in Palästina 1934 bis 1941, in: Regina Stephan (ed.), Erich Mendelsohn. Architekt 1887–1953. Gebaute Welten. Arbeiten für Europa, Palästina und Amerika, Ostfildern-Ruit 1998, 240–287, here 244.

18 See Katharina Hoba/Elke-Vera Kotowski, Ein geerbtes Stück Heimat. Der Umgang nachfolgender Generationen mit den Dingen des deutsch-jüdischen Exils, in: Elke-Vera Kotowski (ed.), Das Kulturerbe deutschsprachiger Juden. Eine Spurensuche in den Ursprungs-, Transit- und Emigrationsländen, Berlin/Munich/Boston, Mass., 2015, 473–488.

tory, anthropology, and archeology, historians have delved into the world of things. Daniel Miller, a British anthropologist who is also a trained archeologist, argued that human culture is first and foremost shaped by material culture. He takes issue with the subject-object duality and views culture as "the relationship through which objects are constituted as social forms." He therefore claims that material objects cannot be analyzed "in themselves," just as "society and social relations [… cannot be analyzed] in themselves."[19] His French colleague Bruno Latour offers a similar argument. By questioning the commonly accepted separation between subject and object, the two sociologists emphasize how closely things are connected with the social-cultural identity of human beings.[20]

When studying migration and migratory societies, the inclusion of the world of objects opens new perspectives in understanding socio-cultural behavioral patterns. When migrating, people take things with them. What happens to these things when they are taken out of their context? The migration of things in the context of the history of German-Jewish emigrants and refugees during the Nazi era has been studied before. It has been established that a great many emigrants managed to take at least some of their personal belongings with them. Packed and shipped in containers, the so-called *lifts*, beds, linen, porcelain, books, and sometimes complete libraries migrated together with their owners. These often bulky items were brought to the new place for both practical and sentimental reasons. In most cases, the migrants could not find the same quality of goods in their new place of residence; but more importantly, emigrants were generally unable to afford to buy new goods because the Nazis seized the fortunes of Jews who left Germany. Moreover, the transfer of things also had an important emotional dimension: The objects reminded the emigrants of home. In the uncertainty of the new environment, they turned into placeholders for the past and the lost home. Objects of migration embody the ambivalence of the emigrant's existence: memory of a lost home and the beginning of a new life.

These objects functioned in contrary ways: On the one hand, they served to fill the void created by forced migration, while at the same time they reminded their owners of what was lost. *Heimat* is a socio-cultural space that offers physical and emotional safety, protection, and intimacy. Yet home, *Heimat*, is a fragile construct. By transferring cultural behavior, social norms and also material objects, emigrants seek to establish a new home in the foreign land. The migration of things should thus be understood as part of cultural transfer.

19 Daniel Miller, Material Culture and Mass Consumption, Oxford 1987, 11.
20 Hoba/Kotowski, Ein geerbtes Stück Heimat, 478.

Conclusion

Lili Schocken had all her household goods shipped to Palestine. The lists to be found in the Schocken Archive bear witness to her attempt to recreate a German-bourgeois life in Jerusalem. The Schockens not only took their valuables and the famous library to Jerusalem; they also transferred furniture, linen, towels, kitchen-ware, and religious objects, as well as items that were used exclusively in bourgeois households, such as white caps for housemaids. Whereas in Germany these caps were an unremarkable part of every upper-middle class household, in Palestine they constituted an attempt to preserve social norms. The meaning of objects changes during the course of migration. A practical object turns into a vessel of memory or a remnant of the past. These objects may furthermore speak to their owners' effort to negotiate normality in their new surroundings.

Rather than a place for emigrants, the architect Mendelsohn sought to build a house for people who arrived in Jerusalem and embraced their new reality. Smashing one of Lili Schocken's many knick-knacks was, from his perspective, the right thing to do. It amused him to break at least one of the things that disturbed his perfect design. For Lili Schocken this was not even remotely funny. At least in her own home she wanted to establish a sense of homeliness. In this, however, she failed. Migration changed the meaning of the objects. Torn from their original surroundings, they stood for a lost past and turned into vessels of memory that reminded their owner of a world and a life that no longer existed.

Literature

Theodor W. Adorno, Minima Moralia. Reflections from Damaged Life, transl. by E. F. N. Jephcott, London 1974.

Gaston Bachelard, The Poetics of Space, with a new foreword by John R. Stilgoe, transl. by Maria Jolas, New York 1994 (1st edition 1956).

Doerte Bischoff/Joachim Schlör, Dinge des Exils. Zur Einleitung, in: Exilforschung. Ein internationales Jahrbuch 31 (2013), 9–20.

Sigmund Freud, The Uncanny, with an introduction by Hugh Haughton, transl. by David McLintock, London 2003 (1st edition 1919).

Katharina Hoba/Elke-Vera Kotowski, Ein geerbtes Stück Heimat. Der Umgang nachfolgender Generationen mit den Dingen des deutsch-jüdischen Exils, in: Elke-Vera Kotowski (ed.), Das Kulturerbe deutschsprachiger Juden. Eine Spurensuche in den Ursprungs-, Transit- und Emigrationsländen, Berlin 2015, 473–488.

Daniel Miller, Material Culture and Mass Consumption, Oxford 1987.

Anthony Vidler, The Architectural Uncanny. Essays in the Modern Unhomely, Cambridge, Mass., 1992.

Author

Stefanie Mahrer is a scholar of modern Jewish and general history at the University of Bern. Her area of research lies within the realms of 19th- and 20th-century Jewish history, focusing on questions of transnational migration, networks, and individual experience. She is currently funded by an excellence scholarship at Basel University and has just finished her second book *(Habilitationsschrift)*, titled *Salman Schocken. Topographien eines Lebens*. *Selected Publications*: Texts and Objects. The Books of the Schocken Publishing Houses in the Context of Their Time, in: Amir Eshel/Rachel Seelig (eds.), The German-Hebrew Dialogue. Studies of Encounter and Exchange, Berlin/Boston, Mass., 2017, 121–141; Transnationales Dasein zwischen Europa und Palästina. Salman Schockens Jerusalemer Jahre 1933 bis 1940, in: Antje Borrmann/Doreen Mölders/Sabine Wolfram (eds.), Konsum und Gestalt. Leben und Werk von Salman Schocken und Erich Mendelsohn vor 1933 und im Exil, Berlin 2016, 103–122; Handwerk der Moderne. Jüdische Uhrmacher und Uhrenunternehmer im Neuenburger Jura 1800–1914, Cologne/Weimar/Vienna 2012.

JOACHIM SCHLÖR

Reflections on the Loss: Objects in the Correspondence between Former Berliners and Their Hometown

Questions relating to the fate of German-Jewish cultural property after 1933—from the initial "loss" to eventual restitution—are generally addressed within the framework of state or other official institutions. Yet there is a further dimension to both the historical events and ongoing debates about them, namely that of the individual and personal experience. "Aryanization," theft, confiscation—these impacted individuals and families first of all. Those who were able to flee from Nazi persecution and emigrate to places all over the world were forced to leave property behind, to sell art collections or furniture for the lowest prices, or to hand over their firms and stores to whoever profited from their loss. In my current research on family letters and testimonies written during the process of emigration (and over many ensuing decades), I have come across numerous sources that have rarely been used in this context: Family members and relatives exchange information about the loss of material objects in documents that are, perforce, of a transnational character, while at the same time they refer to the former *Heimat*, their *home*—the place of departure. These documents afford us a valuable insight into the *meaning of things* for families and individuals.

A first source that demonstrates this importance of property to the emigrants and survivors is a letter written by Walter M. Danziger, 2907 Fallstaff Road, Apartment T5, in Baltimore, Maryland, on 29 April 1991. The letter is addressed to Dr. Klaus Sühl, Freie Universität Berlin, who had been commissioned by the Senate of Berlin to prepare the publication of the *Gedenkbuch der ermordeten Juden Berlins* (Memorial Book for the Murdered Jews of Berlin). Walter Danziger writes as follows:

> "Dear Dr. Suehl,
> With regard to your appeal in *Aktuell-Berlin*, I wish to inform you of what we went through in Berlin before we were finally permitted to emigrate to America. We also sadly lost many relatives in concentration camps, even entire families. My parents owned a department

Contested Heritage, 195–203 | doi.org/10.13109/9783666310836.195

> store in the Schlossstraße in Berlin-Koepenick, called Lichtenstein Nachf. D. Cohn. The building in which the store was based and where we lived belonged to my grandmother Emilie Cohn. Behind the building there was also a very beautiful garden, with a view over the Dahme, which also belonged to my grandmother Emilie Cohn. In 1938, my father was forced by a Nazi called Ahrendt to sell the store. This Nazi also bought all the other Jewish stores in Koepenick and took over our apartment. The City of Koepenick bought the building at a very low price. Life in Koepenick became very uncomfortable in 1939. Jewish families were taken out of their houses at night and led through the entire city accompanied by ugly taunts. Thus my parents decided to move to WestBerlin [sic], where we managed to get an apartment in Schaperstraße 8, near the Kaiserallee. Our friends were called Loewe. Our host owned a publishing house. His wife was descended from one Professor Abraham Geiger, who had founded Reform Judaism."[1]

This source forms part of a large body of correspondence that has not been accessible so far and which I was allowed to see in the archives of the Stiftung Neue Synagoge—Centrum Judaicum in Berlin's Oranienburger Straße. The task assigned to Klaus Sühl and his team, Ulrich Schulze-Marmeling and Rita Meyhöfer, was—as the correspondents frequently note—immense: to list all the Jews who had been deported from Berlin and murdered in the Holocaust, along with the dates of their deportation and the dates of their death, and any further information that could

1 "Sehr geehrter Herr Dr. Suehl, / In Bezug auf Ihren Aufruf im *Aktuell-Berlin* moechte ich Ihnen mitteilen, was wir in Berlin durchgemacht haben, bevor wir dann endlich in Amerika einwandern durften. Auch haben wir leider viele gute Verwandte in Konzentrationslagern verloren, sogar ganze Familien. Meine Eltern hatten ein Kaufhaus in Berlin-Koepenick in der Schlossstr. mit dem Namen Lichtenstein Nachf. D. Cohn. Das Haus, in dem das Geschaeft war und in dem wir wohnten, gehoerte meiner Grossmutter Emilie Cohn. Hinter dem Haus war noch ein sehr schoener Garten mit dem Ausblick auf die Dahme, welcher auch meiner Grossmutter Emilie Cohn gehoerte. / Im Jahre 1938 wurde mein Vater von einem Nazi mit dem Namen Ahrendt gezwungen, den Laden zu verkaufen. Der Nazi kaufte auch alle anderen juedischen Laeden in Koepenick und uebernahm unsere Wohnung. Die Stadt Koepenick kaufte das Haus fuer einen sehr geringen Preis. Das Leben in Koepenick wurde im Jahre 1939 sehr unangenehm. Man hat juedische Familien nachts aus ihren Haeusern geholt und sie durch die ganze Stadt mit haesslichen Beschimpfungen gefuehrt. So haben sich meine Eltern entschlossen, nach WestBerlin [sic] zu ziehen, wo wir eine Wohnung in der Schaperstr. 8 in der Naehe von der Kaiserallee bekamen. Die Freunde hiessen Loewe. Unser Wirt hatte einen Buecherverlag. Seine Frau stammte von einem Professor Abraham Geiger ab, der das Reformjudentum gegruendet hat." All the letters I refer to here are kept in the Stiftung Neue Synagoge Berlin—Centrum Judaicum—Archiv (henceforth CJA), 5C2, where they are alphabetically arranged.

possibly be found. What the researchers had not foreseen was that those who responded to the appeal titled "Aufruf an alle ehemaligen Berliner Juden" publicized in *Aufbau*, *Mitteilungsblatt*, *Semanario Israelita*, *AJR Information*, and many other newspapers and journals of German-Jewish émigrés worldwide, wished to tell—indeed *had* to tell—their own stories: stories of survival in concentration camps or living "illegally" on the streets of Berlin; tales of migration, of the many different ways in which their life in Berlin came to an end and how they began to build a new life elsewhere; and accounts of the material objects they were able to take along or were forced to leave behind.

This collection, originating in the idea to document the circumstances of death, has evolved into a reservoir of stories of survival. *Berlin-Aktuell* is the name of the journal—which appeared in print for many years, and today is mainly accessible online—founded by the so-called Emigrantenreferat of the Berlin Senate, whose main task has, since 1969, been to maintain the numerous forms of contact between the city and its former inhabitants, most importantly the regular visits of groups of "former Berliners." Letters addressed to and sent by *Berlin-Aktuell* and the Emigrantenreferat form a further body of sources, stored in the upper floor of Berlin's Rotes Rathaus. Together these two sets of sources, which comprise thousands of letters, provide insight into the multiple forms of relationship among the Berliners who now reside—or rather, as many have since passed away, resided at the time—in Baltimore, Maryland, and in so many other places around the globe. They furthermore give us an idea of the relationship between owners and their property as well as their sense of loss and hope for restoration.

What became of the house and the garden in Köpenick? Which parts of the family property were those who emigrated—Walter came to England with the *Kindertransport*—able to take along with them when they left? What role did the former property play in the subsequent lives of those who managed to escape? Did the emigrants try to retrieve it? Did they talk about it during family meetings? When we think of all the human lives destroyed by the Nazis, writing about material objects, from houses to children's toys, may seem trivial. Yet the letters show that this is not the case. Another former Berliner, Walter Lachman, wrote as follows from Longmeadow, Massachusetts, in the 1990s:

> "I am still suffering today from a terrible fear that I will again lose the tangible properties I have been able to amass in this world, and even more, that I will again lose my decent human instincts and cultural values."[2]

2 CJA, 5C2, Correspondence Lachmann.

The loss of property is an ever present event in the lives of those who remained and those who emigrated. These events mark the steps of persecution and marginalization. This emerges very clearly in another document I found among the collection in Centrum Judaicum. It is a report written by Hedwig Ems, Mommsenstraße 56 II re[chts], on 16 July 1947, to Lotte and Gerhard Ems, Calle Ejido 1129, Montevideo, Uruguay:

> "I have to go back a little and begin with the summer of 1939. I do not wish to report on the surrender of radios, electrical appliances, woolen goods, furs, jewelry, and silverware etc., because I know that your father already wrote to you about that. But whosoever has not seen this mountain of typewriters, irons, heating pads, etc., and above all the furs, cannot even begin to imagine what these actions were like."[3]

At that time Hedwig Ems still lived in a *Pension*, a boarding house, but in the following months she was obliged to move several times to ever smaller rooms, which meant that each time she had to leave behind some of her belongings. In February 1942 she found a room to let, at a time when what she calls the *Evakuierungen* (evacuations) had already begun. Every knock on the door could mean deportation. By 4 September 1942 she was prepared to take her own life, but others needed her help so she carried on.

> "The goodbyes began then, which were sadly to continue through all those years. First goodbye to the emigrants, and then to all the others. [...] The doorbell rang, and again there were two men from the Gestapo who had come to see me to look at the bedroom of Dr. Jungmanns. One of them commented: 'The bigwigs have probably already taken all the good things for themselves.' One of them told me that he wanted to get married and needed a nice bedroom."[4]

A month later she had to leave this flat and was picked up by a *Möbelwagen*, and two men, "who took me and my stuff in" ("die mich und meine Sachen

3 "Ich muß etwas zurückgreifen und mit dem Sommer 1939 beginnen. Über die Abgabe von Radios, elektrischen Apparaten, Wollsachen, Pelzen, Schmuck und Silbersachen etc. will ich nicht berichten, weil ich weiß, daß Euer Vater Euch das bereits geschrieben hat. Wer aber den Berg von Schreibmaschinen, Plätteisen, Heizkissen etc., Pelze vor allem nicht zu vergessen, nicht gesehen hat, der kann sich überhaupt keine Vorstellung von diesen Aktionen machen." CJA, 5C2, no. 6, Correspondence Ems.

4 "Damals hatte das Abschiednehmen begonnen, das sich dann dauernd leider durch all die Jahre fortsetzte. Zuerst durch die Auswandernden, dann durch all die anderen. [...] Es klingelte, als wieder zwei Herren von der Gestapo bei mir erschienen, um sich das Schlafzimmer von Dr. Jungmanns anzusehen. Der Eine meinte, ›die Bonzen haben sich wohl schon alles Gute weggeholt?‹ Der eine erzählte mir, dass er heiraten wolle und ein schönes Schlafzimmer brauche." CJA, 5C2, no. 6, Correspondence Ems.

abholten"), took her together with a group of others to the *Sammellager* (assembly point) on Große Hamburger Straße.

> "I put on 14 items of clothing, one on top of the other, all of my cardigans, my knitted dress, my jacket dress, a woolen dress, a winter coat, a rubber coat, blouses, and various undergarments. But this was to be my salvation, as I never received my suitcase with all my many nice things, linen, clothes, coats, and a ton of other beloved things, I would have had a very hard time during the cold winters. Our hand luggage was then inspected and all our money down to one mark [was taken] along with all the watches."[5]

The deportation to Theresienstadt began at Anhalter Bahnhof station. On the way to the station, Hedwig Ems set eyes on the Unter den Linden street for the first time in years and recorded that moment in her memory: *Abschied von Berlin* (Farewell to Berlin). And yet again, as her report documents, after arrival in Theresienstadt more "things" would be confiscated.

> "In the sluice we had to line up in single file and were led by the SS, who inspected our handbags and hand luggage and took everything that was valuable and irreplaceable to us. In my case, they took my flashlight, my medication, and all sorts of other little things."[6]

The report ends with Hedwig Ems' return to Berlin on 15 August 1945. Her experience illustrates Walter Danziger's assertion that the loss of property was no less significant than his memory of the loss of human dignity. This was equally true for those who managed to emigrate. Leo Eisenfeld writes as follows in his *Erinnerungen*, a report that he submitted to the *Gedenkbuch* team:

> "From January to July 1939, after I had to leave my mother alone in Berlin, she began wandering around Berlin in ever greater desperation, bullied terribly at the police precinct, to try nevertheless to obtain something in return for her apartment furnishings, to try

5 "Ich hatte 14 Sachen übereinander angezogen, meine sämtlichen Strickwesten, mein Strickkleid, mein Jackenkleid, ein Wollkleid, Wintermantel, Gummimantel, Blusen und mehrere Unterkleidung. Das war aber meine Rettung, denn da ich nie meinen Koffer mit all meinen vielen schönen Sachen, Wäsche, Kleider, Mäntel und noch eine Menge mir lieber Dinge erhalten habe, so wäre es mir in den kalten Wintern sehr schlimm ergangen. Dann fand eine Untersuchung unseres Handgepäcks statt, bei der einem alles Geld bis auf eine Mark [genommen wurde] und auch alle Uhren." CJA, 5C2, no. 6, Correspondence Ems.

6 "Also in der Schleuse mussten wir uns einzeln in einer Reihe anstellen und wurden vor die SS geführt, die unsere Handtaschen und unser Handgepäck durchsah und uns alles fortnahm, was für uns wertvoll und unersetzbar war. So mir meine Taschenlampe, Medikamente und noch allerhand Kleinigkeiten." CJA, 5C2, no. 6, Correspondence Ems.

> nevertheless to obtain certificates for Palestine or quotas for America. The little that she managed to get for her things she of course had to spend on her upkeep, to meet the emigration expenses, etc."[7]

The emigrants take stock of their belongings and their meanings—"Sitting cross-legged on the ground beside the empty overseas bag, I wonder what among the inventory of my previous life should go into this container and what should go onto the large pile of things that I have to leave behind"[8]—and the objects become travel companions whose presence is described in their memoirs: "I also recorded in the text descriptions of mementos among my items, of objects to which I was attached, because they remained with me on the entire journey described here."[9]

The many practical steps needed to prepare for emigration often led families to reassess their material possessions and to discuss their use and value. Exile research has recently begun to focus increasingly on the place of things, of material objects, in emigration. Objects are manufactured from particular materials, they are used during the course of everyday cultural practices in the context of work or home life; they are repaired (as part of a "makeshift economy"), inherited, rededicated, dug out again, forgotten, and then remembered once again. However, cultural anthropology has tended to focus on the objects that remained in place rather than on those that went "on a journey." But what happens when the "domestic environment," the home, is threatened, confiscated, destroyed? What happens to belongings and to their significance? Jewish families that decided to emigrate in the face of Nazi persecution were obliged to re-examine their belongings, assess whether they could be used in a different location, itemize them for the purpose of taxation, pack them and ship them. British legal theorist Jeremy Bentham highlighted the

7 "Von Januar bis Juli 1939, nachdem ich meine Mutter allein in Berlin lassen mußte, war sie in immer größer werdender Verzweiflung in Berlin herumgelaufen, vom Polizeirevier grausam gebulied, um vielleicht doch etwas für ihre Wohnungseinrichtung zu erhalten, um vielleicht doch noch Zertifikate für Palästina oder Quoten nach Amerika zu erhalten. Das Wenige, welches sie für ihre Sachen erhalten könnte, mußte sie doch für ihren Lebensunterhalt, für die Ausreisespesen u.s.w. ausgeben." CJA, 5C2, Correspondence Eisenfeld.

8 "Im Schneidersitz neben dem leeren Überseekoffer auf dem Boden sitzend, überlege ich, was von dem Inventar meines bisherigen Lebens in diesen Behälter wandern soll und was auf den großen Haufen der Dinge kommt, die ich zurücklassen muß." Vivian Jeanette Kaplan, Von Wien nach Shanghai. Die Flucht einer jüdischen Familie, transl. by Kurt Neff and Sibylle Hunzinger, Munich 2006, 93.

9 "Ich habe in den Text auch Beschreibungen von Erinnerungsstücken aus meinem Besitz aufgenommen, von Gegenständen, an denen mein Herz hängt, weil sie auf dem gesamten Wanderweg, der hier nachgezeichnet wurde, mit dabei waren." Kaplan, Von Wien nach Shanghai, 10.

importance of the relationship between an object and its owner as early as the end of the 18th century, observing that ownership is the basis of hope. Only the law can ensure that the relationship can endure into the future for the next generation, to provide "an assurance of future ownership." Should this security be attacked or threatened, more than the object itself is at stake: "Every attack upon this sentiment produces a distinct and special evil, which may be called a pain of disappointment."[10]

Objects make the world comfortable and homely by creating relationships between people who pass them on to one another and who leave personal traces on them, which later owners can come to know and love. Exile—the (violent) expulsion from one's familiar life environment—destroys this familiarity with objects and the communicative and mediatory function they perform within the close-knit world of owners of the same house—in both a literal and in a figurative sense.[11] As soon as the surviving family members and friends were able to get in touch with one another again, the topic of "things," of property once owned and then lost, resurfaces in the letters they write to one another. The correspondents do not simply bemoan the loss of some material object or another—they now use the objects as symbols of what they went through. The restitution they would claim was no doubt financially important but beyond this, restitution possesses a far broader dimension. Talking and writing about a lost house or stolen furniture becomes a means of re-assertion, enabling exiles to grapple with questions such as "Who are we now?" or "Who is still here to share the memories of things once owned and then lost?" When the city of Berlin (like many other cities in Germany), with the best intentions began to contact those who emigrated, the lost houses and the lost possessions became topics of discussion and means of negotiation: about money, about status, but also—to return to Walter Danziger's phrasing—about "cultural value" and human dignity.

Could they return? In an article about restitution after 1945, Veronica Albrink quotes a dialogue between Julius Posener (who emigrated to Palestine and returned in April 1945 as a soldier in the British Army) and a German acquaintance. Invited to return to Germany to help build a new society, Posener employs the notion of property as a key argument:

> "Do you think your reception will be so positive? The Jews, as you say, have rights, at least the right to retrieve their former property. This property has by now passed from hand to hand. Only in a very

10 Jeremy Bentham, The Theory of Legislation, transl. from the French of Etienne Dumont by Richard Hildreth, London ²1871, 111.

11 Joachim Schlör/Doerte Bischoff, Dinge des Exils. Zur Einleitung, in: Jahrbuch für Exilforschung 31 (2013), 9–20.

> few cases is the Nazi today still the beneficiary: a nation may readily repent; but people do not readily allow themselves to be thrown out of houses to which they have grown accustomed and which they regard as their own."[12]

The Berlin archives I consulted comprise 31 folders that contain thousands of letters. And even this constitutes only a tiny part of the immense project of retrieval of personal memories undertaken by these German-Jewish families. Most of this imagined collection has been lost. What remains should be considered a telling and significant element of German-Jewish cultural property. I find it so important because these sources possess a narrative dimension that is sometimes lacking in better-known cases of looted art or book collections. As Rom Harré has argued, "[w]hat turns a piece of stuff into a social object is its embedment in a narrative construction. The attribution of an active or a passive role to things in relation to persons is thus essentially story-relative: nothing happens or exists in the social world unless it is framed by human performative activity."[13]

This view corresponds with the concept of culture as process and practice that has evolved in the fields of European ethnology and cultural anthropology. Harré's insistence on the importance of the narrative helps us appreciate the significance of the letters stored in Centrum Judaicum and in Berlin's Rotes Rathaus: There are still so many stories waiting to be told. In the case of the *Gedenkbuch* correspondence, the emigrants felt that they had finally found someone to whom to tell them and who supported their endeavor to re-inscribe if not their ownership then at least their loss into the streets and houses of Berlin.

12 "Bist du sicher, die Aufnahme würde so günstig sein? Diese Juden haben, wie du sagst, Rechte, zumindest das, ihren vorigen Besitz wiederzuerhalten. Dieser Besitz ist inzwischen von Hand zu Hand gegangen. Es ist in den seltensten Fällen der Nazi heute noch der Nutznießer: Ein Volk bereut ganz gern; aber Leute lassen sich ungern aus Häusern hinauswerfen, die sie sich gewöhnt haben als ihre Häuser anzusehen." Veronica Albrink, Restitution nach 1945. Ein Schrecken ohne Ende?, März 2004, <https://www.topographie.de/aggb/treffen/bisherige-treffen/2004-maerz/vortrag-albrink/> (1 August 2019).

13 Rom Harré, Material Objects in Social Worlds, in: Theory, Culture & Society 19 (2002), no. 5–6, 23–33 (abstract).

Literature

Gedenkbuch Berlins der jüdischen Opfer des Nationalsozialismus, "Ihre Namen mögen nie vergessen werden!", Freie Universität Berlin. Zentralinstitut für Sozialwissenschaftliche Forschung, im Auftrag des Senators für Kulturelle Angelegenheiten, Berlin 1995.

Lina Nikou, Zwischen Imagepflege, moralischer Verpflichtung und Erinnerungen. Das Besuchsprogramm für jüdische ehemalige Hamburger Bürgerinnen und Bürger, Munich / Hamburg 2011.

Joachim Schlör, "Take down Mezuzahs, Remove Name-Plates." The Emigration of Material Objects from Germany to Palestine, in: Simon J. Bronner (ed.), Jewish Cultural Studies, 4 vols., Oxford 2008–2014, here vol. 1: Jewishness. Expression, Identity, and Representation, Oxford 2008, 133–150.

Joachim Schlör, "Irgendwo auf der Welt." The Emigration of Jews from Nazi Germany as a Transnational Experience, in: Jay Howard Geller / Leslie Morris (eds.), Three-Way Street. Jews, Germans, and the Transnational, Ann Arbor, Mich., 2016, 220–238.

Author

Joachim Schlör is a cultural historian with a research interest in urban history and the history of German-Jewish migration. He received his PhD from Tübingen University in 1990 and his Habilitation from Potsdam University in 2003. Since 2006 he has been professor for Modern Jewish / non-Jewish Relations at the University of Southampton. He is the editor of the journal *Jewish Culture and History* and co-editor, with Johanna Rolshoven, of the online journal *Mobile Culture Studies. Selected Publications*: "Liesel, it's time for you to leave." Von Heilbronn nach England. Die Flucht der Familie Rosenthal vor nationalsozialistischer Verfolgung, Heilbronn 2016; Werner Richard Heymann in Hollywood. A Case Study of German-Jewish Emigration after 1933 as a Transnational Experience, in: Jewish Culture and History 17 (2016), no. 1–2, 115–132; "Heimat im Koffer."—"Oder über das Emigrantendasein. (Falls nicht zu traurig)." Deutsch-österreichisch-jüdisches Kabarett im amerikanischen Exil, in: Aschkenas. Zeitschrift für Geschichte und Kultur der Juden 24 (2014), no. 2, 325–348.

LINA BAROUCH

"What Remains?" Jewish Cultural Practices of Writing and Walking in Barbara Honigmann and Gershom Scholem

Issues of cultural property are closely entwined with questions of cultural practice. In this essay I address the arguably Jewish practices of writing and walking, as aesthetically and thematically developed in selected and closely related texts by Barbara Honigmann and Gershom Scholem. The emphasis on practice rather than property helps demonstrate the ways in which the writing practices and narrative choices of Honigmann and Scholem link up with existing Jewish traditions of writing and walking, despite or perhaps because of the ruptures caused by World War II and the ensuing challenges of Jewish cultural reconstruction. In other words, the cry "What remains?" concerns not only Jewish material culture in the form of books, libraries, religious artefacts, and art collections; rather, the question is directed equally at transformed Jewish traditions and practices of dispersion and reconvening in the face of catastrophe.

Gershom Scholem naturally reflected on the question of cultural remnants in his still unpublished diaries from the years 1946 and 1949, in which he describes his travels in Europe after the War. The last page of the notebook quotes a conversation between Martin Buber and Rudolf Kassner held in Jerusalem (fig. 1):

> "Who will remain?
> Buber and R. Kassner descended the stairs of the house
> after a long conversation and asked each other:
> After two thousand years, or if suddenly
> all our *Western* civilization [*tarbut*] will be destroyed
> What is worth remaining? And both answered
> simultaneously, each without knowing
> the answer of the other: *Kierkegaard* and *Dostoevsky*."[1]

1 National Library of Israel, Archives Department (henceforth NLI), ARC. 4 1599/02/265.24, Gershom Scholem, Mi-nesi'otai be-shlihut be-Eiropa [From my Travels as Emissary in Europe], 84. All translations from German and Hebrew in this essay are my own, unless specified otherwise.

Contested Heritage, 205–217 | doi.org/10.13109/9783666310836.205

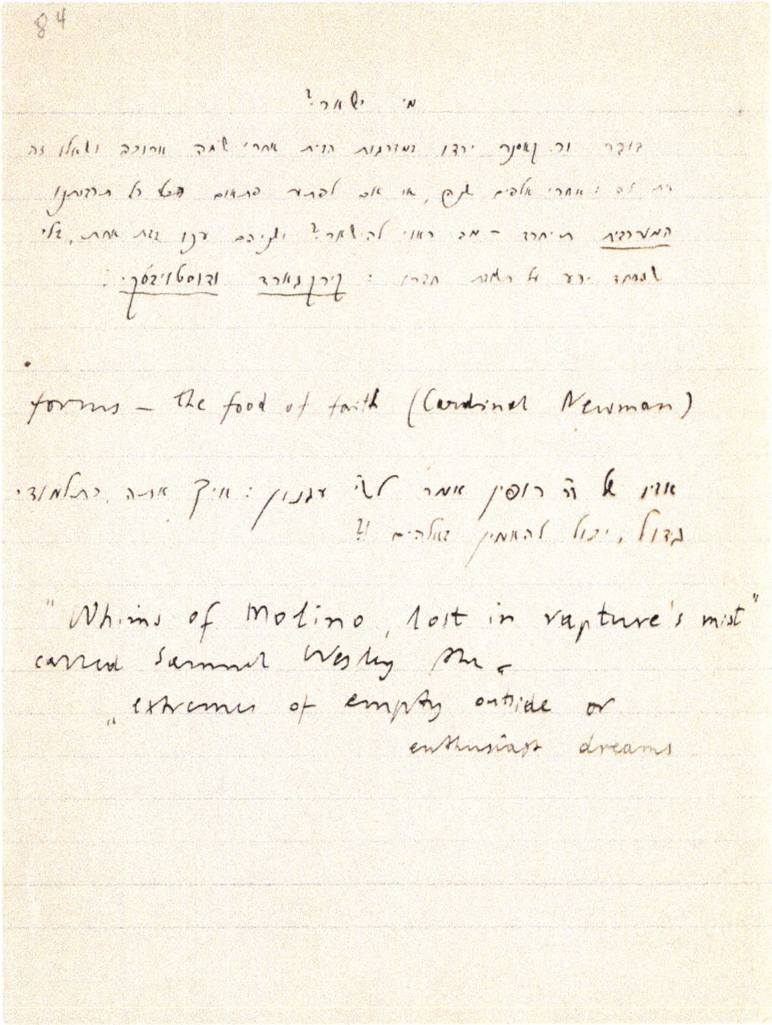
84

forms – the food of faith (Cardinal Newman)

"Whims of Molino, lost in rapture's mist"
called Samuel Wesley the
"extremes of empty outside or
enthusiast dreams"

Fig. 1: Gershom Scholem's diary *From my Travels as Emissary in Europe.*

Like many of Scholem's diary entries, this anecdote invites a wealth of speculation and leads. Let us begin by understanding the context of the notebook in which this conversation was recorded. Gershom Scholem was dispatched to Europe in 1946 as an emissary of the Hebrew University's Committee for the Salvaging of Diaspora Treasures. Apart from a wealth of official reports, updates, and letters that Scholem wrote during the months of his travels in Europe, in 1946 he also kept a diary, written mostly in Hebrew, with some sections in German. Still unpublished, excerpts from this diary have been quoted in secondary literature, such as in Elisabeth Gallas' book *A Mortuary of Books. The Rescue of Jewish Culture after the Holo-*

caust, and in Noam Zadoff's study *From Berlin to Jerusalem and Back*. Alongside these highly instructive studies of Scholem's role in the historical events and the shaping of underlying historical thought, the current paper offers an essentially literary perspective of Scholem's immediate, first-hand account of the challenging quest and journeys he undertook during the spring and summer of 1946 (fig. 2).

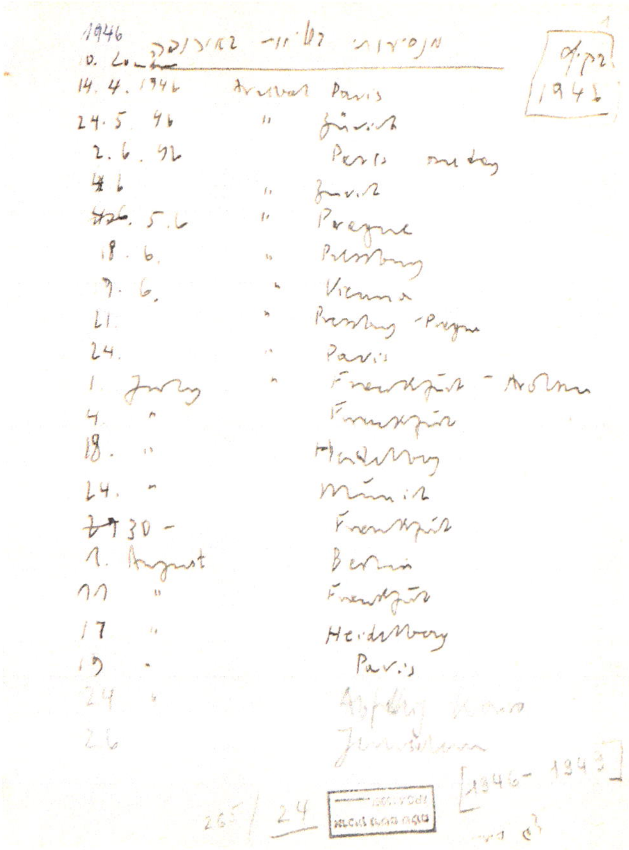

Fig. 2: Gershom Scholem's diary *From my Travels as Emissary in Europe*.

If Scholem's diary is a first-hand account of events (however complex the term "first-hand" may be), then Barbara Honigmann's *Nacherzählen* of Scholem's quest in her short story *Doppeltes Grab* (Double Grave) is a retelling, in indirect speech, of what Scholem told her about his 1946 journeys. Honigmann's literary re-narration accentuates key aspects of Scholem's postwar experiences in Europe by projecting them onto her account of his visit to East Berlin in 1981. Barbara Honigmann was born in East Berlin in 1949 to German-Jewish parents who spent the war years in Great Britain and returned to the Soviet-occupied zone of Berlin in 1947. Since the late 1970s Honigmann has published novels, short stories, and poetry and has won international literary prizes. She is also an accomplished painter, and has lived with her family in Strasbourg since 1984. Her prose includes biographical and autobiographical works such as *Ein Kapitel aus meinem Leben*, in which she depicts her mother's private life and political activism during the war years, as well as her own childhood in East Berlin. Her other autobiographical writings, including the essays *Gräber in London* and *Der Untergang von Wien* from the collection titled *Damals, danach und dann*, deal with the graves of Honigmann's mother in Vienna and her maternal grandparents' graves in London. *Gräber in London* recounts Honigmann's painful realization of the fact that her mother failed to respect her parents' written request and left their graves bare—without tombstones or the engraving of their names. Honigmann's depiction of her visit to her grandparents' graves and the way she grappled with their written request merits a separate study on the topics of legacy, genealogy, and (family) memory in her work, via the concrete and symbolic object of the grave. Indeed, *Doppeltes Grab* has an autobiographical dimension as well, and engages in part with the search for a Jewish family grave, which reconvenes the members and names of the dispersed Scholem family. The current essay, however, limits itself to a parallel reading of Honigmann's *Doppeltes Grab* alongside Scholem's diaries in order to flesh out their shared understanding and realization of Jewish practices of walking and writing in relation to questions of cultural reconstruction.

In *Doppeltes Grab* Honigmann depicts the visit of Gershom and Fania Scholem to East Berlin in 1981, where they were hosted by Barbara Honigmann and her husband Peter. During this stay, they visited the Scholem family grave together, as well as a local store and restaurant. They also spent an afternoon at the Honigmanns, where Gershom Scholem told them about his research and about his official trip to Europe in 1946. Both Scholem's journals and Honigmann's biographical prose deal with the topic of Jewish cultural reconstruction after the Holocaust, and depict the very same quest that Scholem undertook in 1946. Yet, beyond this thematic commonality, the texts also share the recurring motifs of movement and its impediment. On one level, movement and its curtailment appear in these texts as altogether concrete events: The texts depict travel by air, train, bus, automobile, taxi, and on foot; from Jerusalem to Europe, within postwar Central Europe, and in East Berlin in 1981; one encounters road blocks, transitional borders, visa issues, and other political and military obstacles. On another level—and this is my central argument—the authors bestow symbolic meaning upon the movement of persons and books, thereby subscribing to an existing Jewish tradition that intertwines walking and narrating. Thus, when contemplating the issue of Jewish cultural reconstruction, the selected texts demonstrate that "what remains" are not merely "salvaged" and "reconvened" Jewish books, libraries, and collections, but a centuries-long Jewish legacy of walking and writing, of dispersion and reconvening.

Jewish Walking and Writing in Postwar and Cold-War Europe

What is this legacy and how do Scholem and Honigmann continue to reenact and transform it? I argue that Scholem, as an agent and first-hand

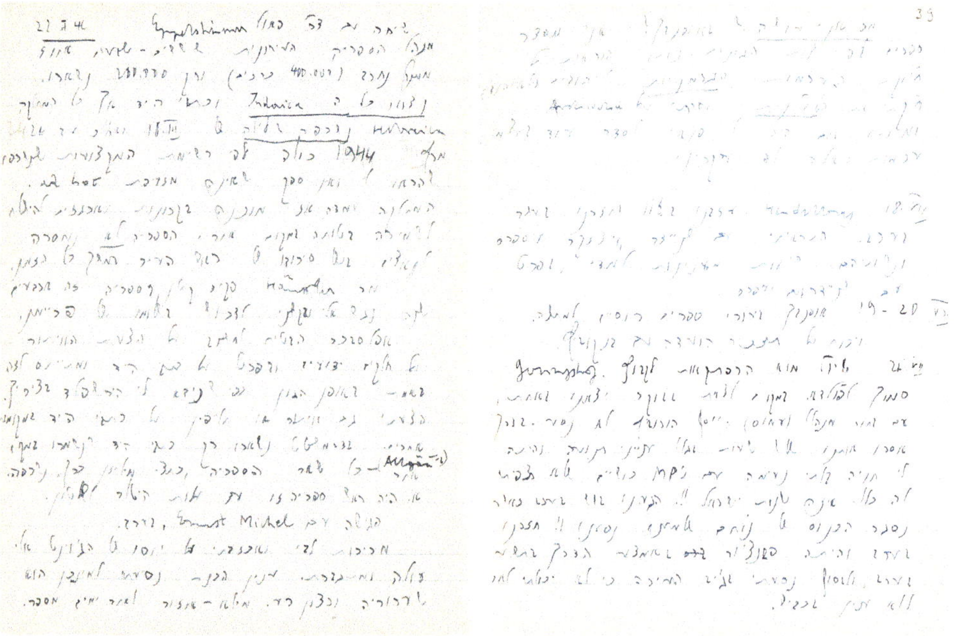

Fig. 3: Gershom Scholem's diary *From my Travels as Emissary in Europe*.

witness of the collection of books in postwar Europe, and Honigmann, as Scholem's hostess and second-hand re-collector in the early 1980s, narrate forms of "walking beyond trauma" *(halikha me-ever la-trauma)*. The latter is a term coined by Haviva Pedaya in her 2011 book *Walking through Trauma. Rituals of Movement in Jewish Myth, Mysticism and History*.[2] Pedaya's conceptualization of Jewish practices of walking or wandering (in or into exile), which correlate with practices of dispersion *(pizur)* and reconvening *(isuf)*, invites us to read Scholem's travels and journal-writing in Europe during 1946 as part of this Jewish heritage. Moreover, and as I show toward the end of the essay, this Jewish heritage is echoed also in Barbara Honigmann's short story.

Although recorded mainly in Hebrew, Scholem's 1946 diary begins on the left-hand side of the notebook, and is titled *Mi-nesi'otai be-shlihut be-Eiropa 1946* (From my Travels as Emissary in Europe in 1946). Below the title, Scholem listed the towns he visited in chronological order (Fig. 2). At first glance this strikes one as an extremely tight and efficient schedule. A closer reading of the diaries (alongside official documents and letters) reveals how very challenging it was to travel in Central Europe in the immediate aftermath of the war. The interlinear version of this dense list

2 Haviva Pedaya, Walking through Trauma. Rituals of Movement in Jewish Myth, Mysticism and History, Tel Aviv 2011 (Heb.).

relates prolonged waiting for visas and other transit permits (mainly from the American military authorities), and frustrating delays due, among other things, to the tense relations between the various Jewish organizations "competing" over the looted cultural artifacts and collections. At times Scholem sinks into despair, wondering if he should not return to Jerusalem, and questioning the viability of his quest in the face of concrete physical, bureaucratic, and political obstacles. On 21 July 1946, for example, Scholem planned to visit camps housing displaced persons in the Frankfurt area, such as the so-called "Buchenwald-Kibbutz" in Geringshof near Fulda, but his car was held up. In the diary Scholem describes the scene as follows (fig. 3):

> "An excursion filled with adventures to kibbutz Geringshof near Fulda. On the way we were jailed for three hours because of traffic problems and I had an unpleasant experience with Black MPs, which I didn't expect. What anti-semitism [*sin'at israel*]! We arrived at six in the evening by when the meeting for which we came was over!! We returned at night with a puncture in the middle of the road at around nine o'clock, and in the end I traveled by Jeep into town because I couldn't just wait by the road."[3]

In a letter to Judah Magnes, president of the Hebrew University, he reported just a week earlier (14 July 1946) that he wept every day at the thought of the work he could have done had he but managed to arrive at the book collection points earlier:

> "The main job that should have been done, and that I cannot do, is, in my opinion: *searching* for the vast buried and hidden material. That work would have required two conditions, which were not clear to us in Jerusalem: (1) *a very long time,* because this is a matter of 'espionage,' to find what the Americans and the English *didn't* find. (2) *total freedom of movement*, which was completely denied to me for reasons of the occupation authorities and of the conditions under which the JDC obtained my entry into Germany."[4]

After the visit to the book depot in Offenbach, Scholem bemoaned the late date of his arrival:

> "First Visit in Offenbach: I went around the building for two hours with Pinson and saw all the arrangements. Tons of books and neat

3 NLI, ARC. 4°1599/02/265.24, Gershom Scholem, Mi-nesi'otai be-shlihut be-Eiropa [From My Travels as Emissary in Europe], 39.

4 Cit. in Noam Zadoff, Gershom Scholem. From Berlin to Jerusalem and Back. An Intellectual Biography, Waltham, Mass., 2018, 118 (emphasis in the original).

> piles, instructions that allow everything! But we are absolutely too late. We could have done something months ago if we had found suitable people."[5]

While these diaries and letters can be read as a factual depiction of events, Scholem's early diaries of the 1910s and 1920s depict him as a highly self-reflective writer. By the mid-1940s Scholem had become a world-renowned scholar of Jewish mysticism, and his contemporary diaries, like the earlier ones, surely suggest an aspect of self-construction and self-styling that is not unrelated to his scholarly research and writings. Upon reading the accounts of his travels in Europe in 1946, as he moved between large book depots, displaced persons camps, and occupation zones, would it be fanciful to liken Gershom Scholem to the historical figures that he studied during these years, some of whom, according to Haviva Pedaya, "constructed a self in relation to the transcendental via rituals of diaspora"?[6] In other words, are we entitled to claim that in his diaries Scholem constructed a self through a return to postwar Europe—a temporary return that echoed Jewish rituals of dispersion and collection at the practical and symbolic levels? Scholem's movements of dispersion and reconvening were marked by concrete hindrances, impasses, and obstacles to travel between locations such as Paris, Offenbach, Prague, Berlin, Heidelberg, Zurich, etc. It follows that Scholem's "walking beyond trauma" combined these acutely material hardships[7] with a self-constructive, self-narrating aspect expressed in his journal writings of the period.

How, then, does Scholem inscribe his own person and position as delegate into the Jewish tradition of "walking beyond trauma," based on the dialectical practices of dispersion and collection *(pizur ve-isuf)*? Pedaya's study analyzes different practices of walking or wandering throughout Jewish mythology and Jewish history, mainly from the Middle Ages up to the Early Modern period. She conceives the myth of the prophet Ezekiel's "performance walk" as a form of paradigmatic, prophetic walking that represents the future of the people while also containing its past. This is the journey of an individual, which embodies a message for the entire community. As such, the biblical text also mirrors the sense of exile among its editors.[8] Jewish walking practices emerged and evolved in medieval Spain before and after the Jewish expulsion of 1492. In the thirteenth

5 NLI, ARC. 4°1599/02/265.24, Gershom Scholem, Mi-nesi'otai be-shlihut be-Eiropa [From My Travels as Emissary in Europe], 33.

6 Pedaya, Walking through Trauma, 79.

7 As we know from Fania Scholem's later account, after Scholem's return to Jerusalem this experience resulted in months of depression and an uncharacteristic lack of activity. See Zadoff, Gershom Scholem, 276.

8 Pedaya, Walking through Trauma, 18.

to fourteenth centuries, prior to the expulsion, a tradition of combined walking and writing emerged. This was a practice engaged in by wandering spiritualist preachers to whom it became a symbolic, even a messianic act, and this type of walking re-emerged in the Hasidic tradition of eighteenth-century Europe, especially in Galicia, Poland, and Podolya. Following the expulsion of the Jews from Spain in the fifteenth century, two main typologies of walking or wandering emerged: First, the immediate descendants of the Spanish refugees (such as Rabbi Moses Cordovero) developed a dialectical approach to dispersion and return. Second, later descendants of the expelled Spanish Jews and especially Rabbi Isaac Luria of the sixteenth century—the Ari—initiated a ritual of walking that was linked to his very own Kabbala. In other words, the Ari's practice of walking and its textual embodiment were related to the mystical ideas of contraction *(zimzum)*, breakage *(shvira)*, and restitution *(tikun)*.[9] In his studies on Jewish mysticism Scholem understood the concept of divine contraction in the Kabbala of the Ari as a form of divine exile (through which the Divinity withdraws from the world by way of contraction). Scholem furthermore interpreted the ideas of divine exile as expressions of the Jewish people's historical experiences of exile (a claim refuted by his students). The metaphor of breakage, which entails smashing and dispersion, in turn facilitates restitution in the form of the reconvening of divine sparks. Similarly, the fundamental myth of Jewish transcendental existence rests upon the idea of dispersion or exile, whereas its goal or purpose is reconvention *(isuf)*.[10]

Can we place Scholem's travels in Europe and their textual rendering in the tradition of dialectical Jewish practices of walking and narration that had arguably arisen, directly and indirectly, from experiences of expulsion and exile, which were, in Scholem's interpretation, later embedded in mystical ideas? Can Scholem's role in the broader postwar quest for Jewish cultural reconstruction be linked to the centuries old ideas of *tikun* and *isuf*, of restitution and reconvening? Do the transcendental and historical planes meet in the Jewish tradition? To address these questions we may be advised to take a leap into the nineteenth century: Pedaya describes in her study how at this point in time the urge to wander, which during the era of Hasidism became a project of salvation, begins to manifest itself in the real world. This is no longer the deliberate reconvention of sparks to a symbolic space, but rather the reconvening of the Jews themselves to a real, national place. In other words, the theological and political imperatives of *isuf* meet to create a political body in the Land of Israel.[11] In his postwar quest as

9 Pedaya, Walking through Trauma, 20–24.
10 Pedaya, Walking through Trauma, 21.
11 Pedaya, Walking through Trauma, 26.

emissary of the Hebrew University, Scholem acts as an agent in the transformation of this tradition: On the one hand, the diary is a self-reflective and self-constructive narration of a doomed, prophetic walking-wandering mission (Scholem also delivered public lectures and met with the remnants of displaced and shattered European Jewish communities). On the other hand, Scholem acted as the official delegate of an academic body that presumed to represent the entire Jewish people, thereby helping to form a mythology of "empty" libraries in the Land of Israel alongside the myth of an empty country that ought to be filled with salvaged Jewish cultural treasures. In sum, Scholem participated in the Jewish heritage of dispersion and reconvening on the theological and political planes, and his diaries and correspondence of 1946 provide ample evidence of this.

Stumbling upon Double Graves

Barbara Honigmann's short story *Doppeltes Grab* displays a remarkable affinity with Scholem's 1946 diary by engaging with walking or wandering and its impediments on the concrete and metaphorical planes. It has been argued that Honigmann's autobiographical prose steps beyond her private experiences to grapple with larger patterns of Jewish existence and its inherent tensions.[12] The title of the short story, which refers to Scholem's alleged "double grave"—one in Jerusalem and the other in Berlin—implies movement that continues beyond death: the movement of the German Jew between Jerusalem and Berlin, between Zion and the Diaspora, as an existential practice that transcends the life of the individual and encompasses an entire generation and perhaps even an entire people. And as previously mentioned, this suggestion should also be read as a reification of Honigmann's wrestling with her own Jewish identity.

The body of the text provides numerous examples of the ways in which Gershom and Fania Scholem attempt to maneuver in East Berlin during their 1981 visit, when they met with Barbara Honigmann and her husband Peter. The story begins with the four of them standing at the grave of Scholem's family in the Jewish cemetery in Berlin-Weißensee. Honigmann relates how they "cleared the grave" *(räumten das Grab frei)*—removing withered foliage, branches, sticks and parts of trees, as well as overgrown ivy from the grave. Scholem commented that "one needs an axe when one wants to visit the grave of an ancestor, in order to strike a path through the

12 Amir Eshel/Yfaat Weiss, Vorwort der Herausgeber, in: idem (eds.), Kurz hinter der Wahrheit und dicht neben der Lüge. Zum Werk Barbara Honigmanns, Paderborn 2013, 7–16.

accumulating time" *(Da braucht man eine Axt, wenn man das Grab eines Vorfahren besuchen will, um sich einen Weg durch die angewachsense Zeit zu schlagen).*[13] What is notable here is not merely the fact of the overgrown graves and the removal of debris, but also the stark language in which Scholem apparently described the act of approaching and visiting the graves of his ancestors (figs. 4 and 5). The scene at the graveyard continues as the party encounters further obstacles. Honigmann writes:

> "Close to the entrance, on the way to the grave, there was a building site, and although one could not make out what was being built there, and everything looked the same as it always had, much of the path was nonetheless cordoned off with a rope and a sign saying *Achtung Baustelle* [*Caution construction site*]." (90)

Honigmann then recounts a slightly comical scene in which Fania, without hesitation, removed the sign and walked across the building site, her husband Gershom calling after her: "Can't you see that the path is blocked?" Whereupon Fania replied: "Surely a rope will not prevent me from walking my path!" Gershom then nodded and followed her on the "forbidden path along the invisible building site, taking care to replace the rope after he passed through." (90 f.) Another seemingly more banal episode concerns a visit to a local store where Gershom Scholem hopes to find a "pigskin briefcase": "Scholem and Fania, his wife, entered the shop through the wrong door and were sent out to re-enter through the correct door, marked by an 'Entrance' sign." (91) These anecdotal, partly humorous depictions of the Scholems' maneuvers through Berlin's graveyards and stores are surely not arbitrary. It would seem that Honigmann found in them metaphors for Jewish exile and return, for free movement and its curtailment, for visible no-entry signs and invisible building sites. The immediate relevance of these anecdotes to the topic of cultural reconstruction after 1945 emerges halfway throughout the story, when the excursion through East Berlin with the local Jewish hosts, Barbara and Peter Honigmann, comes to a brief halt. When sitting, albeit in a "rocking chair," in the Honigmann apartment, Scholem begins to speak about Jewish history from the Frankists up to Walter Benjamin. The historian goes on to speak about the "*Gesamtarchiv der Juden*," then kept in Merseburg in the GDR, and about the former library of the Jewish Community in Berlin at Oranienburger Straße 86. Honigmann informed Scholem that the library was now extremely small but was still kept in the same street and the same house. "There [Scholem]

13 Barbara Honigmann, Doppeltes Grab, in: idem, Roman von einem Kinde. Sechs Erzählungen, Darmstadt 1986, 87–98, here 89 (the information in brackets in the main text henceforth refer to this work's page numbers).

had borrowed his first books of Jewish learning," he told the Honigmanns, and they replied, "we too." "That is where it all started," Scholem added, and again the Honigmanns responded "for us as well." (92 f.) Scholem then proceeded to speak about the fate of this library and the fate of Jewish books and libraries in war-torn Europe in general. Honigmann re-tells Scholem's account in indirect speech: She recounts how Scholem had been sent by the Israeli state (actually the Hebrew University) to trace this library and if possible to transfer it to Israel. Jewish books were not destroyed but rather "collected and catalogued" by the Nazis and later "deported" or *ausgelagert*, transferred to Prague, a city the Nazis believed would not be bombed and where, after the war, the books would be collected, assembled or *zusammengetragen* to serve as a sign of their triumph over the Jews. Clearly, Honigmann's retelling of Scholem's account uses the recurring motifs of dispersion and collecting: There is a starting point, which is the library, a *Nachforschen* (tracing), *Herüberbringen* (transferring or returning), *Auslagern* (deporting or relocating), and *Zusammentragen* (collecting, convening). These themes continue to define the fate of the books after the war, for the Czech government, notes Honigmann in the wake of Scholem, viewed the books as its own property and offered them for sale worldwide.[14] Thus, these books were "*überall hin verstreut*"—"dispersed in all directions." (93) Scholem rediscovered *(wiedergefunden)* some of them and bought them back *(wiedergekauft)* during his journeys, and kept them in his home in Jerusalem. And Scholem concluded, as Honigmann tells us, with the words "*Es ist den Büchern nicht besser ergangen als den Menschen.*" ("The books fared no better than the people"). (94) In the same vein, during lunch at the Berolina Hotel Scholem recited to the Honigmanns a saying from Pirkei Avot 4, 18: "Emigrate to a country where there is Torah-learning," and added that Jerusalem, New York, or London were appropriate places, but that Germany was no longer good for the Jews. One can no longer learn anything there, so there was no point in staying, it was too difficult. "How that should work out that you move there, I don't know, but I will think about it," he told the Honigmanns.[15] They would eventually emigrate to France and settle on the French-German border, to be precise, in the city of Strasbourg. After the Scholems departed from East Berlin, Barbara and Peter Honigmann rushed to the library at Oranienburger Straße and borrowed all the books by Scholem, which were shelved near the works of the German-nationalist Schoeps, an arrangement that Scholem apparently disliked. Soon after the visit, Scholem sent them his book on the Frankists, which he asked them to donate to the Jewish Library after reading it.

14 Honigmann, Doppeltes Grab, 95.
15 Honigmann, Doppeltes Grab, 94.

Final Remarks

What and who will remain, asks Scholem, via the brief anecdote of the conversation between Martin Buber and Rudolf Kassner on the Jerusalem staircase (an entire separate essay could of course be written about the fact that in this anecdote both protagonists chose Dostoevsky and Kierkegaard as "worth remaining"). I have tried to demonstrate that what remains are not merely salvaged, tangible items such as book collections and entire libraries, or their gaping lacunae; rather, what remains is far more a legacy: one of walking and migrating, of preaching and recording the movements of dispersion and reconvening. What remains is Scholem's "double grave," which keeps him from resting in peace and invites repeated movements of exile and homecoming; movements that capture the life of one individual but even more so typify the existence of an entire people. *"Es ist den Büchern nicht besser ergangen als den Menschen,"* said Scholem during his East Berlin visit: both people and books continue to undergo forced dispersion and migration and attempts to reconvene. As such, cultural reconstruction is not confined to a well-defined, clear-cut, one-directional reconvening of books and libraries, or of Jewish communities, but rather acknowledges the ongoing interplay between centrifugal and centripetal trajectories that have defined Jewish heritage for centuries. These are partly forced upon the Jews and partly reworked by generations of Jewish scholars, preachers, mystics, prophets, and bibliophiles, and more recently by quasi-state institutions and Jewish organizations. This is, at the same time, not merely a "modern" or "modernist" account of things. Rather, as Haviva Pedaya has shown, transformations of "walk-

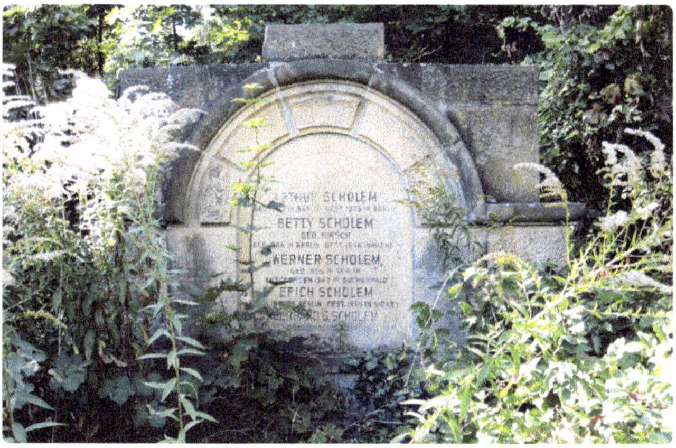

Fig. 4: Scholem family grave in Weissensee cemetery in Berlin.

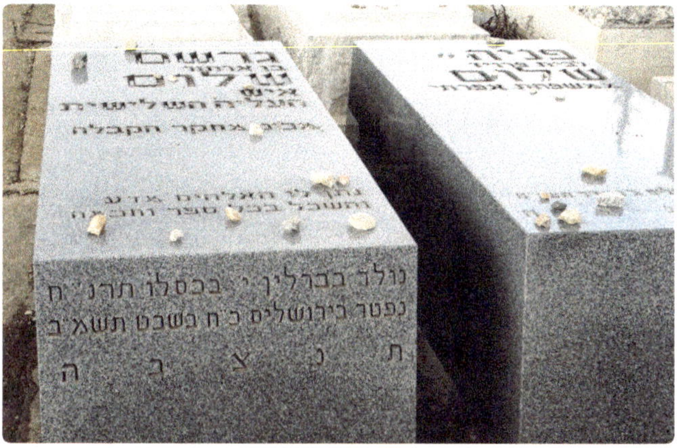

Fig. 5: Gershom and Fania Scholem's graves in Sanhedria cemetery in Jerusalem.

ing beyond trauma," practices of dispersion and ingathering, are traceable to the biblical texts, to medieval Jewish practices in Spain and Safed, and to the Hasidim of the eighteenth and nineteenth century. Last but not least, they find their very own unique textual expressions in the immediate postwar years in the 1946 diaries of Gershom Scholem and in the compact Berlin prose of Barbara Honigmann during the latter years of the German Democratic Republic.

Literature

Amir Eshel/Yfaat Weiss, Vorwort der Herausgeber, in: idem (eds.), Kurz hinter der Wahrheit und dicht neben der Lüge, Paderborn 2013, 7–16.

Elisabeth Gallas, A Mortuary of Books. The Rescue of Jewish Culture after the Holocaust, New York 2019 (Germ. 2013).

Barbara Honigmann, Damals, danach und dann, Munich 1999.

Barbara Honigmann, Doppeltes Grab, in: idem, Roman von einem Kinde. Sechs Erzählungen, Darmstadt 1986, 87–98.

Haviva Pedaya, Walking through Trauma. Rituals of Movement in Jewish Myth, Mysticism and History, Tel Aviv 2011 (Heb.).

Noam Zadoff, Gershom Scholem. From Berlin to Jerusalem and Back. An Intellectual Biography, Waltham, Mass., 2018.

Author

Lina Barouch obtained her PhD in German-Jewish literature at the University of Oxford. Until 2019, she was an associate researcher at the Franz Rosenzweig Minerva Research Center (FRMRC), the Hebrew University of Jerusalem, and academic coordinator of the international project "Traces of German-Jewish History. Preserving and Researching German-Jewish Archives in Israel," a collaboration between FRMRC and the Deutsches Literaturarchiv Marbach. *Selected Publications*: Between German and Hebrew. The Counterlanguages of Gershom Scholem, Werner Kraft and Ludwig Strauss, Berlin/Boston, Mass./Jerusalem 2016; Hölderlin in Jerusalem. Buber and Strauss on Poetry and the Limits of Dialogue, in: Naharaim. Zeitschrift für deutsch-jüdische Literatur und Kulturgeschichte/Journal of German-Jewish Literature and Cultural History 8 (2014), no. 2, 289–307; Anti-Purismus und Parodie. Die mehrsprachigen Gedichte von Ludwig Strauss in Palästina 1936–37, in: Jahrbuch für Exilforschung 32 (2014), 259–275; The Erasure and Endurance of Lament. Gershom Scholem's Early Critique of Zionism and Its Language, in: Jewish Studies Quarterly 21 (2014), no. 1, 13–26.

Picture Credits

Elisabeth Gallas, Capsules of Time, Tradition, and Memory:
Salvaging Jewish Books after 1945

Figs. 1, 5, 6: © Yad Vashem, Digital Collection.
Fig. 2: Courtesy of Yeshiva University Museum, copyright holder unknown.
Fig. 3: Courtesy of Ghetto Fighters House Archive, copyright holder unknown.
Fig. 4: © National Library of Israel, Archives Department.

Caroline Jessen, Affirming Ownership, Obscuring Provenance?
Émigré Collections in Israel and Germany after 1945

Figs. 1, 2: © Universitäts- und Landesbibliothek Darmstadt.
Fig. 3: © Deutsches Literaturarchiv Marbach / Chris Korner.
Fig. 4: © Deutsches Literaturarchiv Marbach / Jens Tremmel.
Fig. 5: © Bayerische Staatsbibliothek München.

Yonatan Shiloh-Dayan, *Bücherfreunde*:
German-Jewish Émigrés as Unintentional Guardians of German Books

Fig. 1: © Amitai Spitzer, Jerusalem / Deutsches Literaturarchiv Marbach.
Figs. 2, 3, 4, 5: © Deutsches Literaturarchiv Marbach.

Yechiel Weizman, Eliminating the Traces:
The Postwar Fate of the Synagogue in Olkusz, Poland

Figs. 1, 2, 4: © Yechiel Weizman.
Fig. 3: © Archive of the Regional Museum of the Polish Tourist and Sightseeing Society (Polskie Towarzystwo Turystyczno-Krajoznawcze, PTTK) in Olkusz.

Iris Lauterbach, Art Restitution in the Aftermath of World War II:
The Central Collecting Point in Munich

Figs. 1, 2, 4: © Zentralinstitut für Kunstgeschichte, Munich.
Fig. 3: © Bayerisches Nationalmuseum, Munich / Bastian Krack.
Fig. 5: Source: The Bavarian Economist, August 1947, 15.
Fig. 6: © Staatliche Graphische Sammlung, Munich; loan of the Ernst von Siemens Kunststiftung.

Bilha Shilo, When YIVO was Defined by Territory:
Two Perspectives on the Restitution of YIVO's Collections

Fig. 1: © YIVO Institute for Jewish Research, New York.
Fig. 2: © YIVO Institute for Jewish Research, New York / Alexander Archer.
Fig. 3: © American Jewish Historical Society.

Fig. 4: Source: Marie Rašková, Na našem městě nám záleží, 13 August 2014, <https://www.anobudelip.cz/cs/liberecky-kraj/makame/aktuality/novinky/marie-raskova-z-mimone-na-nasem-meste-nam-zalezi-17499.shtml> (1 August 2019).

Anna Holzer-Kawalko, The Dual Dynamics of Postwar Cultural Restoration: On the Salvage and Destruction of the Breslau Rabbinical Library

Figs. 1, 2, 4: © The Hebrew University of Jerusalem/Edgar Hirshbain.
Fig. 3: With courtesy of the National Library of Israel, Archives Department.

Enrico Lucca, A Safe Home for German Jewry: Hugo Bergman, *Oẓrot ha-Golah*, and His Return to Europe

Fig. 1: © Yad Vashem Archive, Digital Collection.
Fig. 2: © Lucy Dawidowicz Private Estate, courtesy of Laurie Sapakoff.
Fig. 3: © The Archives of the Hebrew University.
Fig. 4: © National Library of Israel, Archives Department.
Fig. 5: © The Archives of the Hebrew University/Yigal Pardo for Deutsches Literaturarchiv Marbach.

Amit Levy, A Discipline in a Suitcase: The Scientific *Nachlass* of Josef Horovitz

Fig. 1: © National Library of Israel, Archives Department.
Figs. 2, 3: From the collections of the National Library of Israel, Archives Department/Amit Levy.

Adi Livny, A History of Adversity: The Historical Archive of the Hebrew University of Jerusalem

Figs. 1, 2, 3, 4: The Historical Archive of the Hebrew University/Yigal Pardo for DLA Marbach.
Fig. 5: © The National Library of Israel, Archives Department/Strajmayster.

Yfaat Weiss, The Tricks of Memory: Salo W. Baron, Cecil Roth, and the Salvaging of Jewish Property in Europe

Fig. 1: © Stanford University Libraries, Department of Special Collections and University Archives, Salo W. Baron Papers, M0580, Box 695, Folder 23.
Fig. 2: © Stanford University Libraries, Department of Special Collections and University Archives, Salo W. Baron Papers, M0580, Box 695, Folder 22.
Fig. 3: © The Archives of the Hebrew University.
Fig. 4: © Ontario Jewish Archives.

Gil S. Rubin: Aftermath, Salo W. Baron in the Postwar Jewish World

Fig. 1: Courtesy of the Leo Baeck Institute, New York.
Fig. 2: Courtesy of Library of Congress, Prints and Photographs Division, G. Eric and Edith Matson Photograph Collection.
Fig. 3: Courtesy of Library of Congress, Prints and Photographs Division, New York World-Telegram and the Sun Newspaper Photograph Collection.

Ada Wardi, Reflections on Books as Vehicles of Cultural Transaction: The Design Work of Moshe Spitzer

Fig. 1: Private Collection / Ada Wardi.
Fig. 2: © Estate of Dr. Moshe Spitzer, Photo: The Israel Museum, Jerusalem / Elie Posner.
Fig. 3: © The Schocken Institute for Jewish Research in Jerusalem, Photo: The Israel Museum, Jerusalem / Elie Posner.
Figs. 4, 5, 6: © Meron Eren and Ada Wardi, Photo: The Israel Museum, Jerusalem / Elie Posner.
Fig. 7: Photo: The Israel Museum, Jerusalem / Elie Posner.

Stefanie Mahrer, The Uncanny of the Schocken Villa: Interior Design and Objects of Exile

Figs. 1, 3: © The Schocken Institute for Jewish Research, Jerusalem / Alfred Bernheim.
Fig. 2: © The Schocken Institute for Jewish Research, Jerusalem / Kalter.
Fig. 4: © The Schocken Institute for Jewish Research, Jerusalem.

Lina Barouch, "What Remains?" Jewish Cultural Practices of Writing and Walking in Barbara Honigmann and Gershom Scholem

Figs. 1, 2, 3: © The National Library of Israel, Archives Department.
Fig. 4: Photo: Gwendolin Engels.
Fig. 5: Photo: Bilha Shilo.